The Soul of China

THE SOUL OF CHINA

Richard Wilhelm

Translated by John Holroyd Reece
Poems by Arthur Waley

Maple Shade, NJ

This paperback edition released 2007 from Lethe Press

www.lethepressbooks.com
lethepress@aol.com

Originally published in 1928 in Great Britain by Butler & Tanner Ltd.

ISBN 1-59021-056-5

ISBN 978-1-59021-056-7

CONTENTS

PREFACE

"IN CHINA people count by centuries." Such was the verdict of the ancient colonists in the Far East, but this attitude has become false long ago. In China life proceeds today at a feverish speed. Each day brings new events and developments, and behind the daily turmoil and the struggle something immense is taking place: the advent of a new world. The process began slowly, but the wheel of action turned with ever-increasing speed, this wheel of reincarnation, which rolls what is old down into the lower world of oblivion and raises what is new up from nothingness. What seems new, however, is not created of its own accord. Its seeds lie in the past. The man who knows how to interpret the seeds of evolution can read the future from them.

I have enjoyed the good fortune of spending twenty-five years of my life in China. I learned to love the country and its people like everybody who has spent much time there. The last twenty-five years are particularly important because in this period the old and new elements met. I saw the old China which seemed destined to last for centuries upon centuries. I witnessed the collapse and saw new life budding from the ruins. In the old and in the new there was, nevertheless, a common element: the soul of China in the course of evolution; that soul which had not lost its gentleness nor its calm, and will, I hope, never lose them. If anything of this soul of China is revealed to the reader then the purpose of this book will have been fulfilled.

RICHARD WILHELM.

THE SOUL OF CHINA

MY ARRIVAL IN THE EAST

THE mists of Central Europe had disappeared beyond the horizon. The laughter and the song of Italy, the blue sky and silvery moonlit nights prepared me for the fair world of the East. I travelled to China in one of the old Lloyd steamers which were famous for their solid comfort. The sea voyage offered the usual variety: flying fishes, passing ships, phosphorescent lights, the distant twinkling of the Southern stars, the wide uniformity of the sea, brief visits to Southern ports and the luxuriant vegetation of the Tropics.

The noise of Shanghai was my first Chinese impression. Yet what I experienced there was not China. It was a compromise between those rigid habits of life which Englishmen bring with them wherever they set foot and the chaos of the deracinated Chinese population of a seaport; a compromise not unlike the language one used to hear in the streets in those days, namely pidgin-English, that dreadful abortion of bad slang and Chinese syntax, born of the mutual contempt of the trading populations of the East and the West. This pidgin-English has almost died out in China since then. The Chinese have learnt long ago the idiomatic expressions of the English and, shall we say, the American language, and they look down with compassion upon the backward European who should attempt to make himself understood in the old barbaric manner.

My journey took me northwards, out of the turmoil of the busy city on the banks of the Whang Poo, and I continued my sea voyage on board the *Knivsberg*, one of those small coasting steamers running between Shanghai and the northern outposts. The Laoshan mountains, swathed in hazy mists, rose from the sea, and a little later the steamer cast anchor at Tsingtao, where the passengers were lowered into sampans, small, flat, rowing boats, which swayed up and down in the waves until land could be reached.

It was the first period of the colony of the Yellow Sea,

destined to serve Germany as an entrance when the great melon of China was to be cut open and divided among the Europeans. The anxiety concerning the respective shares of the booty proved, later on, to have been superfluous since China showed itself capable of far greater resistance than people supposed after the victory of Japan. The locality had been occupied as the result of a *sanction* after a few members of the Steyler mission had fallen as martyrs at the hands of robbers in the interior of the province of Shantung. The occupation did not take place before the experts had declared the spot suitable for the construction of port works on a large scale.

Life in the new colony was full of adventure, and desire for action filled the air. The few Germans who had settled south of the Kiaochou Bay in the small fishing village of Tsingtao formed a large family which displayed all the quarrelsomeness usually associated with large families. No European house had yet been built. The hotel as well as a few other buildings were indeed in course of construction, but people lived in meagrely equipped Chinese fishermen's huts. As my house was not yet ready, I was taken to begin with to the Hotel Aegir. Here the colonists sat together at night helping themselves liberally to alcohol; they made plans and discussed the new arrivals who, black-coated and gloved, jumped through the mud of unfathomable roads. When it was fine they beat about them to cleanse themselves of dust and flies before making their first calls, occasions on which their hosts inquired if they had come by sea and whether they had had a good crossing.

The Hotel Aegir was insufficiently equipped for visitors who wished to sleep there. When I entered on the evening of my first day into my bedroom, whose tiled floor was covered sparsely with straw matting, the rats positively rattled under my bed and above the ceiling, which had merely been pasted together with paper. I went to sleep quite soon, none the less, although my room could not be locked. The shrill crowing of a cock awoke me. When I rubbed my eyes a Chinese cock sat on the lower edge of my bed and crowed, while the hens were busy scraping the floor. These companions were by no means the most disagreeable which one could meet in those days in Tsingtao.

The streets were being built. Broad and deep sand grooves ran down the hills, and it was not unusual for a returning colonist, whose head was full of plans, to slide down one of these ravines and to adopt the bottom of it, for the sake of simplicity, as his quarters for the night. This procedure on occasion involved the gentleman in question in finding his sleep disturbed by a subsequent arrival who had slipped down into the same hollow and who would refuse to listen to the strongest protest against his disturbance of the peace.

My duties consisted to begin with in providing for the care of the souls and the school work of the Germans of the colony. The religious services were held in the riding school of the naval barracks, in a manner which did not betray enthusiasm in the majority of the participants. The school consisted of three German boys each of whom formed a class, and there were also one German-speaking, one English-speaking and one Chinese-speaking girl, in addition to the small son of an American missionary, so that, at any rate, there was evidence of a certain variety. It did indeed take quite a while before the lessons could begin, because in the Chinese village of Upper Tsingtao there was an epidemic of typhoid and dysentery and the parents of the pupils were afraid of infection, for which they could not be blamed, especially as at that time a large percentage of the naval ratings had succumbed to these diseases.

Accordingly, I had enough time to prepare myself for the other part of my duties, which was to devote myself to the study of the Chinese language. I think I am entitled to say that I learnt Chinese in my sleep. At that time there were no proper teachers. People hired a Chinese village teacher or a scribe who had come down in the world somewhat, seated him in front of a textbook and let him read while one repeated after him what he said. The textbook of the day was the volume by the American missionary Mateer, entitled *Mandarin Lessons*. It began with sentences: I Ko Jen, Liang Ko Nan Jen, San Ko Nü Jen, Sï Ko Men, which means in English: a man, two men, three women, four doors. The profundity of these sentences was overwhelming, especially as the lessons were given in the early part of the afternoon at a temperature of 80 degrees. In the beginning the teacher and the students were kept lively owing to the flies, of which there were two kinds: a common grey sort which distinguished itself merely by its treacly stickiness; and the so-called green bean flies, greenly iridescent animals with enormous red eyes which revealed in their dull defiance the whole malignancy of inconsiderate bestiality. The only virtue of these animals was that they were not so large as tigers, but even so they have brought a sufficient number of people below the sod. On the walls there was an occasional *gecko* who caught sleeping mosquitoes which used to take the place of the flies in the evening. And thus the lesson proceeded · in a conversational rhythm. The teacher: "I Ko Jen; Liang Ko Nan Jen"; the pupil: "I Ko Jen; Liang Ko Nan Jen." Once I suddenly started, as one is startled in a mill when the wheels suddenly come to a standstill. I had ceased to talk and had gone to sleep. When I came to my senses, however, my teacher was dozing in his corner and only slowly there emanated snoring sounds from him: "I . . . Go . . . Jen . . ." This method of learning Chinese, which depends more upon an influence exercised upon the subconsciousness than upon intellectual activity, has, incidentally, been practised for thousands of years by the Chinese themselves. If you approached a Chinese school, it sounded from a distance like a hive of bees, and, close to, it resembled the noise of a village fair. The little lads said their lines severally for themselves without having the slightest conception of their meaning, while the teacher on duty was usually seated in his corner, lost in the profoundest contemplation of himself. Those were blissful times, and, after all, one learnt Chinese in this fashion. The main thing was that one had something to say and subsequently one hit upon the right expression. Chinese [1] is the easiest lan-

---

[1] That is to say, the spoken Chinese language which consists only of mono-syllabic and unchangeable words which acquire a definite meaning through their position in the sentence, their combination and intonation. There has

guage if it is learnt without self-consciousness, learnt by its meaning rather than by the examination of the individual expression. To the curious inquirer the language offers, however, a number of pitfalls for which the most modern method is useless.

At times there were interruptions in the business of learning Chinese. One fair summer evening as I sat behind my books a couple of horses went past my window. Chinese horses are, like everything Chinese, a little different from the corresponding European equivalents, and yet sufficiently similar for you to be aware that ultimately they are the same creatures. Chinese horses are, for instance, much smaller than European horses, less delicate and noble, incredibly long-suffering and tenacious. They exist only to serve man, for purposes of riding or drawing vehicles. Whatever the rider can endure they can endure. They do not even demand any great art to be ridden. You simply have to stay on top, determined to advance, and you must not be afraid. If they notice that the rider lacks one of these qualities they play with him, are lazy and stubborn, and sometimes they will throw him off. It was only later that I was able to understand the psychology of the Chinese horse. In those days I simply saw the animals pass pathetically into the uncertain country, deep into the golden sunshine of the evening. The desire for adventure took hold of me. I sent my Chinese servant to inquire if these horses could be hired, and he returned with the joyous news that everything was in order. We soon agreed about the goal of our journey. The Chinese servant proposed the town of Tsimo as our objective and I was quite agreeable. I believe his proposal was due to the fact that

been a great deal of talk about the intonation in the Chinese language, and it has been said that this peculiarity provides a special difficulty. In reality every language has its intonations, by means of which it acquires its full significance. Practical application is, for purposes of learning the language, far more important than these theoretical considerations. There have been many students of Chinese who carried about their meticulously painted Chinese words, each on a separate slip like a pack of cards, which they studied continuously—without success, whereas every child—even the European child—learns Chinese in China without the slightest effort and more easily than any other language. The reason is that children learn with their heart and not with their head.

he came from there and he wanted to use this opportunity to
take a holiday. It was not particularly wise to choose, for my
first ride, an objective which was ninety Chinese li—about
thirty miles—away, especially as the sun was already low.
Every European, however, considers his boy—this is the name
given in the East to every servant, irrespective of his age—in
certain matters as a higher kind of being who not only knows
whether it will be fine or whether it will rain tomorrow, but
who is also consulted when you buy Chinese works of art, and
who, in fact, is full of good counsel in every difficult situation.
As my boy had said that we could very well ride to Tsimo it had
to be possible. The biting reply of a friend whom I had asked
pro forma, to the effect that I would experience wonders, did
not weigh against the advice of my boy because, after all, that
was just what I wanted to see. And I did. I learnt to ride curiously quickly. We had well-trained, powerful animals which in
no way flirted with wild habits, but proceeded at a measured
trot with whatever burdens were imposed upon them. They
knew everything exactly. Weak attempts to induce a walk or
gallop were of no avail against the superior determination of
my horse, which reacted as little to its new rider as it did to
the swaying of the packs of goods which it was accustomed to
carry. I therefore resigned myself to the inevitable and enjoyed
my ride into the unknown to the full. Before long we had
passed the highest ridges of rock and the rich plain extended as
far as the peaks of the Laoshan, which began to glow in the
purple and golden radiance of the setting sun. The fields were
full of millet and kaoliang. This kaoliang grows in good
summers to such a height that even a horseman can hardly
look over the top of it. I also saw various kinds of soy beans,
peanuts, batatas, and other useful plants. Among them were
fruit trees in great numbers, and of these the sweet Shantung
pears and the red and glistening Kaki figs (persimona Kaki)
which in distinction from the tomatoes really taste as good as
they look. They grow plentifully in the district. On the horizon
there was a series of villages, surrounded by high, closely set
trees. The houses in the region of Tsingtao are usually built of

granite, which is the main substance of the neighbouring mountains. It is a fairly soft kind of granite which shows the
traces of exposure and is easily washed away by the rain,
with the result that ravines with peculiarly steep walls are
formed whose slopes are often covered in long stretches by the
green tendrils of the Pueraria plant. This stone is so easily
workable that it is a light task to build walls in a cyclopic manner. The floor consists of beaten clay. The doors have wooden
bolts and the grill-work of the windows is covered with paper
which tears gradually in the summer and allows the air to penetrate, whereas before the coming winter the windows are covered afresh. The front of the house is usually covered with
reeds and clay, and it consists of three intercommunicating
rooms. There is also a courtyard surrounded by walls which
forms a threshing floor. Here the corn is threshed with flails
and winnowed with a kind of woven spade-shaped basket.
On one side of the courtyard there are the stables for the small
reddish-coloured animals, which are never milked or killed for
eating purposes, but serve merely to aid man in his work in the
fields. Alongside, there are a few small donkeys which, though
they can be stubborn, are not considered to be stupid. The
women and the daughters of the house in question were occupied with grinding corn. The donkeys, blindfolded, trotted in
a circle to pull the mechanism of the mill. In another corner
there was a pigsty full of wrinkled, black-haired pigs thronging
round a trough in which all the remains are collected. A mon-
grel dog with a curly tail barked at the wanderers, and, if
you are polite, some member of the family will always persuade
him to shut up by heaving a stone at him. Hens cackled and
scratched on the floor everywhere. The village pond boasted
a few geese, so-called singing geese, with curious lumps on
their yellow beaks. There were cats, but they were not numerous and are considered as almost sacred: so much so that it would
be difficult, for instance, to find some one ready to kill them.
The children played beneath the entrance to the courtyard,
and the small boys are usually quite naked in the summer,
while the girls wear their little red trousers. Women, of course,

wear trousers in the country, and it is only in the cities that they put on skirts over them. The cloth they use is made of cotton and generally dyed indigo blue, that even blue of the sky, which together with the yellow of the earth and the green of the plants forms the fundamental chords of the Chinese landscape. The men usually wear similarly dyed materials, but either of a lighter or darker blue, whereas the women and the girls are re-splendent in all kinds of colours. Only where a family is in mourning do they wear colourless undyed sacking and let their hair grow without combing it.

The girls and the women sit in the evening in the gateways of their courtyards and chat and laugh and tell each other stories, while the older men gather together at the small temple of their protective genius, Kuanti, or else they for-gather beneath the great Sophora-tree where they smoke their thin straight little pipes and discuss the events of the village and the world concerning which they have to form an opinion.

The ride in the course of the evening was thus most agree-able, but the road stretched out farther and farther. The sun was setting behind the pointed spikes of the Pearl mountains beyond the bay of Kiaochou. Twilight had set in. The blue smoke rose up from the villages and a white fog settled upon the fields. Our goal, however, was not yet appreciably nearer. The horses trotted on, on paths which became more and more quiet. Finally the night set in and I felt a certain tiredness as a result of my unaccustomed position in the saddle. I was begin-ning to think of the adventures which my friend in Tsingtao had promised me. A broad strip in the landscape was set off luminously against the night. It was one of those north Chinese rivers which dry up more or less in the summer and whose broad beds are only filled with water during the rainy season. The horses threaded their way along narrow paths which had formed themselves out of sand and rubble and we proceeded farther into the night. The rocks on the horizon looked more and more strange and dusky and the branches assumed weird shapes. Boundary stones appeared at the side of the path. They were monuments in honour of faithful widows and pious

ˉdaughters. The dragons in interlaced attitudes which crowned these stones presented a fantastic silhouette in the last moments of brightness set against the rapidly darkening sky. Eventually even my servant began to be uncertain, but the horses trotted on quietly beneath the mellow radiance of the stars. The noises of the day had vanished and only the crickets chirped through the stillness. The night in China is not merely an absence of light. It is something substantial of a special kind. Everything alive had hidden itself behind walls and gateways. The stars shimmered strangely. Curious shadows flitted through the air and also whizzing bats and inaudible owls. The many funeral mounds on the fields began to throng each other in strange confusion, foxes and fitchets passed uncannily through the grass in pursuit of some ghostly project. It was the hour when the will-o'-the-wisp appears and ghostly fires hover above the ground and flit about the hillocks of the graves. It is an hour one prefers to spend at home. Many a gruesome ghost wanders about to draw its magic circle. My servant spoke in a lowered voice of myths and legends, of nightmares and of robbers. In the end he became almost a little frightened himself.

And then everything happened as in a fairy tale. At last a little light glimmered through the trees. We spurred on our tired horses and rode straight towards it. We were in luck. It was the K'out'apu Customs on the boundary of the German protectorate, a station of the Chinese Maritime Customs, but occupied by officials of German nationality, as indeed the entire Chinese Maritime Customs were staffed by Europeans in Chinese pay. The Customs officials gave us a kindly welcome. One of them even put his bed and mosquito-netting at my disposal while he spent the night in the open. I spent a dreamless night and slept well into the morning. When I woke up it took me a long time to remember where I was and why I was here. The whole adventure suddenly seemed to me so stupid. The idea of mounting a horse again seemed altogether absurd. I got up, walked about with my legs apart and could move only with difficulty. The Customs officers prepared an ample breakfast, and inquired sympathetically after my condition. They concealed their amusement and showed me every kindness and suggested the return journey. It was too late to turn back now. I thanked them for their hospitality, set my teeth and mounted my horse and spurred it on to depart as rapidly as possible. After a painful hour, I began to feel more comfortable in the saddle and, without noticing it, I had thus learnt how to ride.

In the cool of the morning the outrunners of the Laoshan came nearer to the road. The traffic of carts and donkeys began again, and we soon saw the stone battlements of the town of Tsimo. Walls, gateways and moats are the characteristic ensigns of all provincial towns in China. They are by no means superfluous up to this very day: on the contrary, they often serve a useful purpose in times when thieves and robbers alarm the district. The sandy bed of the river is seen in front of Tsimo. On this side of it, there is a suburb in which there are inns for travellers. We halted at one of them. The horses were unsaddled and were fed in the courtyard. I was taken to the central room and was offered a cup of tea on entering. One must not entertain the remotest thought of an hotel in connection with these Chinese inns. The rooms are smoked pitch black; primitive tables and chairs, and, in the interior room, a wooden erection of planks, on which you may spread your blankets if you have brought any, constitute the entire furniture. A smoking oil lamp reminiscent of Pompeian forms stands in a niche in the wall. The walls are covered with writing and illustrations left by earlier guests. Frequently there is an old picture of a Chinese saint in a corner, in front of which the pious stranger may say his prayers. My servant had disappeared. Soon, however, a cheerful fire crackled in the corner of the courtyard, and he returned proudly bearing a stewed chicken, three boiled eggs and a little cabbage. We thus partook of a frugal meal—with Chinese chopsticks, as I had not brought any knives and forks with me.

In the afternoon I looked at the town. A street ran through the dark archway into the city and along it there was a great number of so-called honorary arches. The houses of the distinguished citizens displayed two high, red flagmasts in front of the entrances, and courtyard upon courtyard stretched away mysteriously towards the back, though one saw flowers and blossoming trees peering over the walls. It happened to be market-day, which recurs every five days. A throng of people in the streets, laden donkeys, squeaking wheelbarrows, men with carrying poles, a drove of pigs—everything pushed peacefully forward. Then, again, a two-wheeled travelling cart would appear in the midst, but everything proceeded without the assistance of police, quietly, with mutual patience and occasional jests. This smooth procedure of the traffic in the midst of the greatest chaos is one of the marks of the level of Chinese culture which strike the new-comer. Practically nothing is forbidden. Here you may do almost anything and yet everything proceeds quietly and in orderly fashion.

My presence as a stranger of course caused some sensation, because a stranger was a rarity in these parts, which are visited only by an old missionary who complained of the violation of his privileges when another missionary wanted to settle down one hundred and fifty miles away from his residence. In spite of the general curiosity and notwithstanding the by no means friendly attitude to foreigners subsequent upon the occupation of Tsingtao, I was not molested in the slightest. One can say that in those times a European could move about in the interior of China less disturbed than a Chinaman could in a European town.

I fortunately refrained from the attempt to call upon the local mandarin when I was informed that he was indisposed. The same mandarin, later on, when a military expedition from Tsingtao came to negotiate with him concerning various points of controversy, not only shut the door of his Yamen (his official residence), but he even closed the gates of the town in front of their nose, and only gave way eventually to superior force, so that I had nothing to complain of.

I spent the evening in my inn, where a number of children gathered about me, with whom I played, and I also cut out figures from paper for them. The parents sat and squatted behind the children. They smoked their little pipes peacefully and inquired about the conditions in the far-off country from which I had come. There are few countries in which children are allowed to develop so naturally and free from restraint and where they are treated with so much consideration and kindness as in China. It says a good deal in favour of this free and easy method of education that these uncontrolled children develop into very useful and decent creatures. Through the children I soon established contact with the older generation and we had pleasant intercourse in spite of my insufficient knowledge of the language.

The night was restless. I was disturbed by countless mosquitoes which filled the air like a shrill trumpet call. When they had been smoked out through the windows and doors there still remained a sufficient number of insects of a more disagreeable kind which did not react to smoke. The horses fretted uneasily in the courtyard, and the sentimental donkeys gave vent to their amorous feelings by means of long howls which seemed to contain the entire misery of the world. And whenever one of them began, the rest of the company joined in the plaint. Eventually stones were attached to their tails, for donkeys always lift their tails when they start to wail. As the result of this manoeuvre it became a little more peaceful, but then it was the turn of the dogs, which barked at each other from all the streets, and finally the cocks greeted the morning with their crowing. Even these noises of the night in a Chinese inn have something romantic and impressive until eventually the chains begin to rattle and the water is drawn in buckets from the round orifice which serves for a well. The day began to dawn and the travellers arranged to depart after they had prepared a light breakfast for themselves.

The return journey passed quickly and without incident, and only my elderly friend was surprised that nothing serious had happened.

Shortly afterwards I made my first profound discovery, which was of such surprising simplicity that it seems strange that so few Europeans are aware of it: In the large European market-places in China one sees crowds of coolies going to work. They are considered to be quite a special race. They are regarded as lazy, impertinent and deceitful, and it is considered that the only way of dealing with them is to push and to beat them. This pearl of wisdom is inculcated into every newcomer at an early opportunity by all the experienced connoisseurs. This is why in Canton and Shanghai Europeans and Chinamen could live for years upon years side by side without understanding each other, impelled merely by the desire for gain and mutual contempt. What I now discovered was nothing but the fact that there simply were no coolies: they were all human beings, men with their joys and sufferings, men who had to fight the battle of life, who had to make their way by cunning and patience and who had to travel their road by straight or crooked paths. They had adopted certain forms of life consequent upon the European method of treatment of them; they had become cold and rigid and evasive wherever they met with violence. They opposed a dull smile to the outbursts of anger of their oppressors, and for the rest they kept their feelings to themselves. Now I noticed, however, that they were fathers, brothers and sons who were attached to their relations, who frequently earned and saved money in the face of the greatest self-sacrifice in order to nourish their aged parents, and they did it all cheerfully and innocently when they were among themselves and showed much patience and long-suffering in the presence of their enemies. This discovery opened for me the road to the heart of the Chinese people, for there is no people which is more friendly, faithful and kindly if one meets them on human ground, without wanting to derive for oneself anything in particular, neither money nor the exploitation of labour, nor, what is even more painful to them, the desire to convert them or to persuade them to join some alien institution for purposes of their eternal salvation. It was of course not very easy to defend this discovery in the presence of Europeans, because in those days quite a different attitude was predominant. For a long time I met merely with heated annoyance when I tried to defend my point of view. People were convinced of the superior culture of Europe which had to be protected against the yellow peril, while the people concerned did not notice that they themselves took the offensive and did everything to poison the seeds of the great culture of the Far East as thoroughly as possible. Even a culture can be poisoned by means of circumstances and suggestions which are deadly to it.

It must be said, however, that gradually a kind of understanding for the Chinese population and an interest in them began to develop in Tsingtao. A certain mutual friendliness made itself felt which acted as an antidote to the previous poison of the mutual relation. This change can be traced partially to the fact that a number of the officials and merchants learned Chinese, because, if one can talk with some one in his mother tongue, many of those misunderstandings which divide the nations resolve themselves of their own accord.

THE BIRTH OF A NEW ERA

IN the interior of Shantung there is the holy mountain called the T'aishan. This mountain stands out again and again in Chinese history. It symbolizes revelation as well as mystery, and it is considered to be the origin of life and death. Near by there is a small hill covered with cypresses and crowned by a pagoda. This was the place where ancient rulers brought sacrifices to the spirit of the holy mountain. There is a small temple dedicated to mysterious gods. In this temple a movement began round about the turn of the century which was destined to shake China to its very foundations; it was the beginning of a new era which, of course, developed along quite different lines from those which the men who had met in this temple of dusky spirits had intended.

What was the reason for their secret activity? In China there existed in all periods when circumstances became insupportable, when the machinery of government went wrong, when the crops failed and high prices weighted down the land, when pestilence and inundations threatened life, and robbers made the country unsafe, secret societies who attempted to destroy the old by the aid of the gods and to bring a new order to the light of day. Accordingly, the book of the history of the three kingdoms, which is the classical story for all kinds of knightly deeds in China, begins with the revolution of the Yellow Turbans, whose leader had mysteriously acquired magical power so that he could cause the storm and the rain, and distribute miraculous waters which healed men of the plague. The story is also told of him that he had the power of cutting soldiers out of paper who on such occasions acquired an artificial life. There are of course all kinds of special blessings for arms which protect men against the stroke of the sword and against shock and other magical prescriptions.

At the turn of the century conditions were once more ripe for such events. The T'aip'ing revolution had collapsed half a century before, but conditions had not improved. The foreigners had multiplied everywhere in the country. They had penetrated by means of violence and injustice. They had burnt down the fairy-like beauty of the summer palace, the Yuan Ming Yuan near Peking, in order to prove the superiority of their culture. They had published strange teachings which had been adopted by criminals and all kinds of ruffians. When quarrels occurred gunboats appeared and extortion was practised, so that the people were more and more oppressed by the strangers and their supporters. Had not the bay of Kiaochou recently been taken away from them, ostensibly because a few missionaries had been murdered by robbers? And, subsequently, did not the other European Powers, instead of preventing the activity of the robbers, follow their example? Was there not continual talk of the intention of dividing China like a melon? And the Manchurian Dynasty was not able to prevent any of these events. Indeed the Emperor himself was in the hands of the reformers, who wanted to make China into a state modelled after a foreign pattern. Therefore away with the alien rulers! Down with the Manchus, protection for the Chinaman!

The movement did not continue for long in this direction. The old Empress-Dowager had taken the reins of office out of the hands of her nephew and a reactionary spirit inimical to the foreigners made itself felt again at Court. Thus the motto was altered to: "Down with the foreigners, long live the Imperial Dynasty!"

In the provinces there were in many places societies for self-protection against the activities of the robbers who made the countryside unsafe. These institutions called themselves I Ho T'uan (Union for the Protection of the Public Peace). This title was later changed to I Ho Ch'üan (The Fist for the Protection of the Public Peace). This expression was subsequently wrongly translated by the word *Boxer*, although there was no question of boxing in the whole affair.

A superstitious atmosphere took possession of the movement and incited it to open fanaticism. People met in temples and secret places at night-time under the sign of the mysterious god of all magic, Chen Wu. This god, who is enthroned upon the North Pole, wearing long dishevelled hair and a magical sword, rules over demons and spirits who lie at his feet in the shape of serpents and tortoises. Apart from him the companions of the protective god Kuanti came with their arms in order to help. Mediums spoke in the name of the gods. The young men were initiated with mysterious magical ritual. They lost consciousness and fell to the ground as if dead, then got up again inspired by a savage courage and were henceforth members of the Union of the Great Knife, invulnerable against bullets or blows of the sword. This mass psychology spread like an epidemic. Everywhere in the towns and villages meetings were held and the spirits raged. Since the original objective of the movement had been diverted and was now directed against the aliens and no longer against the throne, the government allowed events to take their course. They were afraid to put their hand into the fire.

The movement attained its greatest magnitude first in Shantung. Definite aims began to take steps. People still remembered the days when China was free from the oppression of the strangers. China, the great empire, was to suffer humiliation at the hands of distant island inhabitants, whether they came from the east or the west! These islands were, after all, far away and without any importance. It would suffice to take the strangers who had established themselves and to kill them or throw them into the sea, and the remnant of those who had remained at home would certainly not dare to come again. Such were the ideas in the minds of the people. A strong manifestation of the dissatisfaction of the people was to be enough to put everything in order.

It cannot be denied that in those days even some of the Chinese officials did not see very far beyond the extent of these views. Reports from Chinese ambassadors in foreign parts which were couched in a different tenor were, not so very long ago, received even at Court in an unfriendly mood. Nevertheless, there were a number of more far-sighted men. Among them happened to be the Governor of Shantung, Yuan Shih

K'ai. He summoned the chief representatives of those who had
become invulnerable against wounds, and they say that, after
he had inquired exhaustively concerning their supernatural
capacities, he had them shot by his soldiers who were at hand.
At any rate he would stand no nonsense, and forced all those
who were in support of the movement to go beyond the frontiers of his province. They thereupon turned towards the capital, where they found protection and leadership under the old
fighter Tung Fu Hsiang and the prince Tuan. Apart from
Yuan Shih K'ai, the two generals of the Yangtse, Liu K'un Yi
and Chang Chih Tung, kept law and order, and Canton was
also quiet.

The movement was confined therefore, on the whole, to the
north and the north-west of China. Foreigners, especially missionaries from Shensi, and Christians were killed sometimes
in the most cruel manner, and a cry of protest rang through
the world. The Chinese at that time were brandmarked as
the objects of abhorrence of the entire human race just as the
Germans were during the Great War. In reality, we may say
that the movement was based upon an honest national enthusiasm. Cruelties always occur where the bestial impulses
of man are released through hatred. The methods differ perhaps according to the imagination of the individuals, but cruelty
and horror can only be avoided by self-controlled and not by
uncontrolled men. In view of the World War, the image of
the Boxer period pales into harmless insignificance.

What has been said above does not, however, preclude the
fact that people were mightily afraid in those days. The
foreign embassies in Peking were besieged. The badly organized efforts at relief made by Admiral Seymour failed and
very nearly ended in the complete annihilation of the relief
expedition.

At that time, the greatest excitement was rife in the German
colony at Tsingtao, especially as the larger portion of the naval
battalion had been moved to Tientsin. The small remnant of
soldiers who were left paraded the streets from time to time
in order to show themselves. The population armed itself to

the teeth. I believe our house was the only one which did not contain any arms. It was in the nature of things that in such circumstances all kinds of misunderstandings occurred. In this way, early one morning, a crowd of people fired on the signalling station for a prolonged period; the attackers in question had spent the greater part of the night drinking wine and courage and on returning home they were no longer in a condition to take account of the enemy who was to be destroyed.

Military training was organized even for the most sedate citizens, and the rustling of every leaf at night caused the blackest fears. Nothing very dreadful, however, occurred. Tsingtao, which at that time was wholly unfortified, survived the entire Boxer rising without being attacked. Peking, in the meantime, passed through weeks of dramatic excitement. If the Chinese Government had been wholeheartedly in sympathy with the Boxer movement all the embassies would have been destroyed. The Chinese Government was divided into several factions. Accordingly there was no systematic attack and the embassies were able to hold out until succour arrived, even if a few lives were sacrificed. A great deal of what people regarded as low cunning, as, for instance, the gift of melons to the embassies from the widow of the Emperor, was really meant kindly. The Empress-Dowager, when individual Boxers penetrated even into her palace, had indeed recognized the danger of the movement and assumed an energetic attitude towards it.

The relief expedition arrived at last. Japanese troops were the first to set foot in Peking and others followed in their wake. If the Boxer rising was regarded as evidence that China was behind the times, it must be said that the victorious troops which arrived put themselves to considerable trouble to show that the brutality and cruelty of the so-called civilized nations was in no way secondary to what was condemned in China with such abhorrence.

When people began to collect their senses after the victorious entry into Peking it was noticed that the Empress-Dowager had disappeared. While the foreign troops were marching through the streets she left the town dressed up as a Chinese peasant in a travelling cart. Her companion, Sheng Yun, who was subsequently Governor-General, told me later of the difficulties and trials of this escape to Hsianfu.

This escape placed the victorious Powers in an awkward position. They had indeed made a great pretence of equipping punitive expeditions. The German Kaiser, who attended to the matter with much vigour, had in fact nominated Count Waldersee "World Marshal." Circumstances, however, became more and more difficult. The various expeditionary forces did indeed move victoriously about the country, especially as there was no serious opposition anywhere since the Boxers had disappeared, after their collapse, among the mass of the population. The internal friction among the occupying armies, however, became greater and greater. The French commander in particular began to disregard the orders of the Count with assiduous frankness. All kinds of accidents, such as the burning down of the non-inflammable asbestos house of Count Waldersee, made the atmosphere still more uncomfortable, and eventually everybody was delighted when the aged Li Hung Chang sacrificed himself by seating himself in the name of the Chinese Government at the Peace Conference table.

To begin with, there was the question of fixing the blame. Although during the whole period of the expedition the fiction had been maintained, that it was not China but only the robbers who were being attacked, because the war would otherwise have assumed the most impossible dimensions, it was considered necessary to make the Government responsible for everything. Instead of consulting with the Chinese as to methods for the prevention of similar occurrences, instead of making an attempt to secure the unfathomable sources of assistance in China by a process of objective examination in the course of which everyone would have obtained satisfaction, there started an offensive bargaining for the heads of dignitaries and princes who were required as scapegoats. This led to the grotesque situation in which the wrong heads were demanded, the heads of men who had actually fought for moderation and the protection of the foreigners. This shows how badly people were informed. Enormous damages had to be paid, the amortization of which required incalculable periods of time and placed the great empire for an unlimited period under the financial control of the victorious Powers. An imperial prince had to visit Europe personally in order to apologize for the murder of the German ambassador. An arch of honour had to be erected in the Great Hatamen Street on which the misdeed perpetrated upon the German ambassador as well as its expiation had to be recorded in Chinese and Latin—as a lasting memory.

A piece of the wall of the British Embassy which had been damaged by bullets was left without being repaired and they wrote upon it: "Lest we forget!" These words, however, have faded long ago and the wall is covered with moss.

This period also brought minor disturbances in its wake in Shantung. The construction of the railway from Tsingtao to Tsinanfu had been started. Various circumstances contributed to making railway construction very unpopular among the Chinese population. Partially, superstition was still current which feared that the spirits of the ancestors might be disturbed, and partially, people feared—as was shown later— very justifiably that the railway dam would increase the danger of inundation for certain low-lying districts, and there were also misunderstandings between those employed by the railway and the people. In short, the construction of the railway was impeded, as a result of which a military expedition was equipped and sent into the back country of Tsingtao to Kaomi.

The result was a number of most regrettable conflicts between European and Asiatic methods of thought. When the German troops arrived the villages shut their gates and began to fire into the air with their prehistoric cannons, just as they used to do when robbers were in the district. How surprised they were when the German artillery was not in any way frightened, but fired in its turn, and with what devastating success! The women and children then tried to escape out of one of the side gateways. The Germans regarded these women in their red trousers as Boxers and covered them with machine-gun fire. In the meantime, some distant village would begin to fire off its mortars. The Germans immediately marched off to put fire to the village in question. When they returned the Boxers who had organized the effort of resistance in the first village had escaped, and the indigenous population had to suffer the miseries of war.

I heard of these events in Tsingtao. I was convinced that the cause was mutual misunderstanding. In spite of the advice of worried friends I determined to travel to the districts to attempt to save human lives by mediation.

There was a great deal to be done and to be discussed. As all negotiations had to be conducted in Chinese I acquired a mastery of the Chinese language in those weeks as a matter of course. Particular excitement was provided by the story of a distant village which had not dared to comply with the order to lay down arms. The punitive expedition was already planned. I obtained its delay until the next morning with the greatest difficulty. I went to the local official and explained the situation to him. His reply was: "There is nothing to be done for the stupid population which even now has failed to learn anything." I had to remind him most seriously of his responsibility. Mounted dispatches were sent off that very night. Next morning I counted the hours in great excitement. The punitive expedition was ready to march off. I received news that the arms were being brought and was able to delay the column a few minutes longer. The officer finally lost patience and was about to give marching orders when some people appeared over the crest of the nearest hill. They had brought their arms dutifully. They consisted of rusty swords, blunderbusses and a few old mortars out of which stone balls could be propelled a few hundred yards. The determination to carry out the disarmament thoroughly was very great at that time.

Eventually I succeeded in bringing the representatives of all the villages of the district together. They had surrendered their arms, and I was able to give them the assurance that in future they would not be molested. I was still busy for a long time with my assistants, bandaging and looking after the wounded, who consisted chiefly of women and children. The population subsequently displayed the most touching gratitude. I was handed a lot of honorary decorations made of silk by way of thanks for having saved them, and finally, at the instance of the provincial governor, I was presented with the button which confers the rank of mandarin by a representative of the Chinese Government.

The Boxer period was succeeded by a powerful reaction. If the Christians had previously been persecuted they now attempted to revenge themselves against their enemies. In fact many a man joined a church in order to obtain support by this means for a legal action which he happened to have against his neighbour. If he was successful in denouncing his neighbour as a former Boxer much was to be hoped for.

Such experiences made me give preference to quite a new missionary method for China. In a country like China a European will rarely succeed in recognizing and seeing through the moral level of a Christian whom he is to baptize. The church nevertheless assumes responsibility for its members, and nothing harms Christianity in China more than the dubious conduct of those who profess it. It is not the doctrine which makes men great, but it is man who makes the doctrine great. The Catholic Church, for whom the individual generation is nothing, counts upon these factors. It accepts without question doubtful elements in the firm assurance that the children and grandchildren of such converts will one day become good Christians. The individualism of the Protestants does not accept such long-dated bills.

Precisely for this reason it seemed to me to be better to confine myself to a simple life in accordance with Christian principles, to influence them through work in school and hospital, to live together with people and become intimate with them, while trusting to the Spirit as to what would become of it. A church in the midst of a cultured nation can only constitute itself; it cannot stand under the guidance of aliens without being itself condemned to inferiority. Accordingly, I never christened any one in China, and have therefore perhaps come closer into touch with the nature of the Chinese people. Moreover, I have never suffered from conflicts owing to the adhesion of undesirable converts.

Finally, a question should be answered which is frequently asked nowadays. Since a number of well-infomed people round about the turn of the century predicted an explosion which the leading personalities did not believe in, there are even today a number of people who think themselves particularly clever when they prophesy a new Boxer rising in the near future. The nightmare of the Yellow Peril belongs to the same realm. In reality, however, one can be fairly at ease. The Boxer rising was based, on the one hand, on national enthusiasm and religious fanaticism, but in order to assume the dimensions which it did then, the geographical ignorance of those days would be required. In China today people know something of the world. They know that the foreigners are not isolated inhabitants of distant islands, but real powers with whom one has to reckon and to come to an understanding. The process of arriving at an understanding may bring many surprises with it, but an outburst of the *Fist for the Protection of the Public Peace* will not occur again.

3
THE CHINESE REFORMS

THE Boxer period was the beginning of what is new in China. The Chinese reaction had collapsed in a feverish paroxysm. Secret blessings of arms were of no avail against European guns. This fact had been demonstrated to everybody. Now came the great change. The Empress-Dowager, Tsï Hsi, returned from her retreat in the far west to her capital, Peking. It was a triumphal march. The ladies of the embassies refused to miss the spectacle. Although recently hated as the most evil of all devils who wanted to exterminate the Europeans, she became the object of general curiosity. The ladies stood gathered together on top of the Ch'ien men, the great southern gateway of the inner imperial city of Peking, when the old lady in her yellow sedan was carried with imperial pomp along the endless dead-straight southern road of the outer Chinese town. She was not even cross at the offence against the ancient sacred laws which decree that all the people shall hide in the houses when the sedan chair of the ruler is borne through the streets. She performed her sacrifices in the two small red temples with yellow glazed roofs which flank the southern gate, of which the one is dedicated to Kuanyin, the mother of charity, and the other to the protective genius of the dynasty, Kuanti. In fact, she nodded kindly to the people above when she saw this strange gathering, and the ladies from the embassies waved their handkerchiefs at her with enthusiasm.

The old ruler had learned her lesson from these experiences. She, who had previously been the terror of the mightiest satraps, none of whom had ever knelt without trembling before her throne, was now pleased to appear in the rôle of the kindly matron. She was called the old Bodhisatva Kuanyin. On the occasion of a festival at Court she wore the robes of the goddess Kuanyin who was so near to her heart, and she even allowed herself to be photographed with her Court ladies and her favourite eunuch. Miss Carl, the American painter who graces the society of Peking to this day, was commanded to

make an oil painting of the new saint. For the whole of the
time required for this purpose she was housed in a palace in
the magnificent park and was provided with hundreds of servants, so that she lived close to the residence in which her
mistress spent her old age, the Summer Palace I Ho Yuan
(Park of Public Peace), whose name, owing to its unfortunate
echo of the Boxer period, was now changed to Wan Shou Shan
(Mountain of the Ten Thousand Years of Life). Tea parties
were arranged for the foreign ladies. The days were far off in
which battles were fought as to whether the alien barbarians,
in view of their stubborn ignorance, should be exempt from the
act of bowing the knee, by which every Chinaman honoured
his ruler, or whether the sacred ceremonies of antiquity should
be preserved from the aliens. Now they could all come, great
or small, old or young. The kindly mother overlooked with a
smile the insufficiencies of her foreign guests as far as habits
and manners were concerned, and they in turn were happy for
the rest of their lives after being allowed to kiss the golden
protective sheaths attached to the magnificent and lengthy
finger nails of her delicate feminine hand whose smallest sign
had cost hundreds of people their lives.

The Empress, however, did not confine herself to externals.
She now took the reforms which she had opposed so ardently
in hand herself.

The transition of China from the old to the new period took
place in several phases which extended over more than a half a
century. The old military aristocracy of the Manchus, which
had hitherto occupied the decisive offices of the Empire, had
lost its old power and vitality about the middle of the nineteenth century. They had been submerged in their enjoyment
of power and luxurious life as has always been the case at the
end of the history of the various dynasties in China. In the
south, in Canton, a youth who had failed in his examination
and who had consorted with the Christian missionaries had
appeared to found the *Empire of Peace*. It was his idea that in
changing the dynasty there should also be a change of religion;
Christianity was to rule henceforth in China. Divine revela-

tions had been vouchsafed to him and he knew that he was the younger brother of Jesus Christ. An uproar swept through the country as the wind blows through the decaying leaves. His triumphal progress was marked more and more by robbery and destruction. The southern capital, Nanking, fell into the hands of the rebels, who there inaugurated the capital of their new Empire T'aip'ing, the capital of the Great Peace. The Manchu aristocracy had lost its head altogether and was defenceless in the face of this storm. It seemed as if nature herself were ranged against the ruling dynasty, since China's chief anxiety, the Yellow River, overflowed its banks and once again flooded the wide plain which surrounds the peninsula of Shantung in the west. It took years before the waters had sickered away, and when this happened the bed of the great river was dry and it was possible to recognize it again only gradually in the considerably swollen Tatsing-Ho. Whereas the river had formerly flowed into the Yellow Sea south of the peninsula, it has now for seventy years flowed north of it into the gulf of Pechili. The ruling house seemed to be facing its end.

Suddenly a saviour appeared, drawn from a literary community: Tseng Kuo Fan. He tells the story of how they stripped off their long writers' robes and assumed warriors' clothing. "I gave orders through the intermediary of our young scholars to the peasants, in order to restore the peace of the Empire," he once said. He thus succeeded in gaining mastery over the rebellion and simultaneously in annihilating other dangerous movements which had made themselves felt in the north, the west, and the south. It is a well-known fact that a number of European and American leaders were in the Chinese service for purposes of repressing the rebellion, and above them towered, both in efficiency and character, the noble figure of General Gordon. The T'aip'ing rebels were driven back from position to position. Eventually they were shut up in Nanking, and there followed the spectacle of a famished religious fanaticism which displayed the most extraordinary similarity to the Anabaptists in Münster.

The problem now was to reorganize the ruins of the Empire on the one hand and, on the other, to find ways and means of adapting the Chinese world to the new era and its demands. The first problem was solved with admirable rapidity. When the Chinese literary group had stepped into the breach they had done so by no means from motives of slavish servility to the alien race of the Manchus. They had done so because the rulers of this race had identified themselves with the old Chinese culture. In Chinese history there are few rulers who stood in so large and pure-hearted a manner for the ideas of the Confucianism as, for instance, the Manchu ruler who controlled the Empire from 1662 to 1723 under the K'ang Hsi device. It was the fact that the Manchus had departed from the principles of a lofty and severe morality which had brought about their downfall. The problem now was to organize the Empire anew in accordance with the old principles. The result was that the chief influence was transferred from the aristocratic Manchu families into the hands of the Chinese scholars who revered in Tsêng Kuo Fan their spiritual leader. It was indicative of the greatness of the Empress-Dowager that she supported and assisted this movement. Tsêng Kuo Fan possessed in Tso Tsung T'ang, Li Hung Chang, and others, assistants who solved the difficult problem of the reorganization of the Empire with noteworthy ability. In this period achievements were attained which had in vain been striven for during the whole of the history of many thousand years. It was due to the work of these men that the danger of the Mohammedan rebellions which at various times threatened the very existence of the Empire was disposed of for ever. The wide and promising district of Chinese Turkestan, under the name of Sinkiang (the new district), came under the direct control of the central Government. The descendants of the original inhabitants in the south were finally brought to quiescence. A period of internal peace followed, during which the number of the population of the Chinese Empire rose to a hitherto undreamed of height, as shown by the best available authorities. The positive sides of these achievements must not be forgotten by any one who wishes to form an accurate picture of nineteenth-century China which failed again and again as far as Europe was concerned.

The other problem, of course, which the Chinese Government had set itself ended in failure. Tsêng Kuo Fan lived in the Confucian conceptions of the Chinese Middle Ages. For him and his followers the Western ideas which had shown such undesirable results in the T'aip'ing rebellion signified something which had to be avoided. Accordingly, he could find no contact and relationship with these problems. Li Hung Chang who, as the senior among the scholars, succeeded him, was more indulgent in his views. He had become acquainted with Europeans during the T'aip'ing rebellion, but he did not value them highly. The military hirelings had been coarse and greedy for money. The only one of them whose moral stature was altogether admirable, was Gordon, who, however, struck him as too doctrinaire since he had insisted categorically that it was absolutely essential to keep one's word even to the rebels. Li Hung Chang was in these matters rather a man of the Renaissance, and the captured rebels to whom Gordon had given his word of honour were beheaded by this gentleman without hesitation. He was of the opinion that, on the whole, it was quite easy to solve the problem of adaptation to the West. The European arms had shown their superiority in the wars of the Western Powers against China and during the T'aip'ing rebellion, and it was therefore necessary to introduce European weapons in order to meet the requirements of the Government. There came the period in which China acquired enormous quantities of arms and employed foreign military instructors. It was at this time that the naval school at Fuchou and the arsenal in Shanghai were founded. At the instigation of the arsenal the first books concerning Western sciences were translated into Chinese. These translations of course leave a great deal to be desired, much as the first translations of the missionaries, but they were at any rate a beginning of a transformation—even if at first no great attention was paid to it—of Chinese intellectual life.

Then came the Japanese war, which proved clearly that arms alone were not sufficient, but that the corresponding spirit behind the arms was necessary. Thus began the second period of the transformation of Chinese culture after the defeat of Li Hung Chang. This period displayed considerable fluctuations, and many of the leaders of the movement turned their steps later in different directions or became dispersed in the world.

One of the centres of reform during the second period was situated on the Yangtse in the old town of Wuch'ang which, together with Hank'ou and Hanyang, formed the habitation of millions in the centre of China. Here was the seat of the Governor-General Chang Chih Tung who, next to Li Hung Chang, was perhaps the most important of the old Chinese officials. While Li Hung Chang was rather a practical man who attached less value to fine feelings and motives than to what was directly useful, Chang Chih Tung was imbued with the spirit of mediaeval Confucianism with its demand for refinement and form.

For this reason the movement of reform emanating from Chang Chih Tung was of quite a different type. He first belonged to a reactionary movement, the so-called Ts'ing Liu Tang, which desired to defend the old Chinese spirit against the new epoch. Ku Hung Ming, who was the secretary of Chang Chih Tung for many years, distinguished himself in spite of his European training by a fanatical attachment to the ancient traditions and a fierce enmity to all that was alien. He has written about this movement, which he compares to the Oxford Movement.[1] He exaggerated its importance. A handful of literary idealists attempted to bring about a reaction without being equal to the situation. The whole movement failed hopelessly and barely represents an episode in the history of Chinese reform.

Chang Chih Tung turned away from these attempts in good time and devoted himself to the young aspiring Cantonese K'ang Yu We, Liang Ch'i Ch'ao, and others, who without having been to the West, or being able to talk any European

[1] Compare Ku Hung Ming, *A Chinese Oxford Movement*. Shanghai.

language, had realized nevertheless that a spirit of severe criticism had to be applied to their old culture, and that in any case the Europeanization of all the laws and the methods of state management was necessary. Through Chang Chih Tung's recommendation the youthful reformers gained the ear of the Emperor Kuanghsü, who held the reins of government since 1889, and was in the process of liberating himself from the moral influence of his aunt, the Empress-Dowager Tsï Hsi. At this point begins, after the collapse of the old system of Li Hung Chang, the reform era of 1898. Edict followed upon edict. The ancient examinations, which had for thousands of years been the sieve through which the officials had been sifted from the mass of the population, were abolished. Schools were to be founded everywhere according to the Western pattern, and the whole structure of the state was to be reformed upon a European model. The result was general consternation.

Chang Chih Tung found himself in a dilemma. He wrote his famous dissertation upon the necessity of learning. He attempted a compromise between the old and the new. The old and sacred teachings of Confucianism were to remain, as heretofore, the inviolable sanctuary of the soul. Here no spirit of criticism, or utilitarianism or positivism was to find a foothold, but, in a world of ugliness in which vileness was allied with power, it was necessary to appropriate the methods which supplied power in order to protect the position of the state upon earth. The solution which the aged scholar proposed in his difficulty was a system which was Confucian and moral at its centre and European and powerful at its periphery.

A reaction set in from a different side. The youthful monarch had wished to free himself from the burden of his aunt who weighed him down. He had chosen Yuan Shih K'ai, under cover of the greatest secrecy, for purposes of removing the Empress-Dowager and her supporters. He had not allowed for the fact that Yuan Shih K'ai was the intimate friend of Yung Lu, the confidential friend of the Empress-Dowager. Yuan Shih K'ai betrayed the whole plot. The old Empress was wild with rage. The reformers had to leave the capital in haste, and those who did not flee were killed—the foreign policy of the era of reform had not been fortunate. One by one from Kiaochou to Kuangchouwan, Port Arthur to Kowloong, a whole series of the most important harbours of China had been torn away from it and the end was not yet in sight. It was therefore not surprising that the Empress-Dowager enjoyed the sympathy of the population to the full when she turned the wheel backwards with her powerful hand. That was the atmosphere out of which the Boxer rising developed.

As has been mentioned before, the collapse of the second reactionary attempt coincided with the beginning of a new period of reform or, put more precisely, with a new phase in the second period which has already been indicated. In fact, there were no fundamentally new ideas to make themselves felt. The only principle was that the reforms were to be introduced at a slower pace. Periods were determined within which individual reforms were to be carried out so that, after a number of years, the ancient Chinese state should have become a modern constitutional monarchy.

In reality the movement took an essentially different turn. In order to understand the course of events, we must form a clear idea as to the distribution of political power in China. Chinese politics had grouped themselves round three centres for a considerable period. To begin with the north is of importance. There lies Peking on the edge of the great fruitful and mainly wheat-producing plain which forms the fluvial system of the Yellow River. Here is the seat of the oldest Chinese culture. A sober, severe and powerful spirit dominates the region. Confucianism in all its severe simplicity has set its mark upon the whole district. It was natural for this centre to gain in influence since the Manchus ruled China, because they too originated in the north and showed in certain traits a relationship to these characteristics. The most powerful man in the north at that time was Yuan Shih K'ai. He had saved the Empress-Dowager at the decisive moment. He had indeed remained neutral in Shantung during the Boxer period, but this attitude had been justified by subsequent events. Naturally enough he gained in influence in the new era even though the Empress-Dowager never trusted him altogether, as shown by many incidents in later years. His policy was based upon a simple point of view. The chief problem for him was, first of all, the concentration of a sufficient power. His reforms were therefore chiefly directed towards having at his disposal a well-trained and disciplined army. In order to create the necessary means for this purpose, he endeavoured to support commercial undertakings, industrial enterprises and mining operations. In northern China he undoubtedly achieved considerable results in this direction.

As far as the domain of culture and education was concerned, the general reforms, which had been planned, were carried out by him, although he did not betray any special interest in these methods. What made Yuan Shih K'ai powerful were the relations which he was able to establish on all sides. In view of his numerous descendants he had family connections with almost all the important and powerful people. His friendships were very far reaching also in other respects; it was always personal interest which enabled him to attach people to him. This well-chosen company of supporters made it possible for him to have his views expressed by others and enabled him to appear to be persuaded to act apparently in contradiction to his desires, but in reality he thus carried out his original intentions.

Another centre of political influence was situated on the Yangtse. Here sat Chang Chih Tung in Wuch'ang, who had been ordered there from Canton. In Nanking was Liu K'un Yi, who followed Chang Chih Tung's politics in decisive moments. Chang Chih Tung was a native of Tientsin, but in his politics he pursued a course of conduct essentially different from that of Yuan Shih K'ai, the practical politician. His main interest was directed towards the literary aspect of Confucianism. His was not a really well-balanced nature and could not claim to reach down to the depths of reality. Among scholars it was the common practice to describe him as the "Tiger's Head and Serpent's Tail." He too had called industrial undertakings into life on a large scale. He also formed a model regiment, but his main interest was devoted to questions of education. He was convinced that it was essential to modernize Chinese teaching methods. As an old man he was called to Peking. His reforms, however, were only a portion of his aims. What he attached importance to above all was that within the modern shell the old Confucian spirit should be preserved. Accordingly, he founded in Wuch'ang a great classical academy, which was his favourite institution and of which picturesque ruins have survived the revolution in the midst of a lake in Wuch'ang. The old glamour of course has passed away. The troops who lived in the academy after the revolution have left the traces of their lack of consideration in the buildings which were once upon a time so picturesque and beautiful.

Chang Chih Tung was a man of compromise. He was of course a creature of far stronger calibre than Ku Hung Ming, who had been his secretary for so many years and whom he suffered for a long time in spite of the younger man's fanatical hatred against the foreigners, but he never permitted him to exercise any influence in the conduct of affairs. Eventually, however, he failed, because he lacked profundity and originality. Nevertheless, the memory of his name and remnants of his work in Wuch'ang, which is now under the rule of a military governor, are still surprisingly alive.

Wuch'ang offers several instances of the extraordinary mixture of good taste in matters Chinese which can go hand in hand with an absolute lack of sense of proportion and direction in matters touching Europe. Wuch'ang is one of the places with a great historical past. The history of the three kingdoms has this district for one of its settings. In the neighbourhood there is the red wall, a wall of rock which descends abruptly to the stream and which according to the legend was burnt red by a fire in which a large fleet of one of the struggling kingdoms perished, and this catastrophe has thrown its shadow in Chinese poetry through several centuries. On a height in

Wuch'ang, overlooking the widening stream majestically, stood the Tower of the Yellow Cranes, a building which offered the finest view upstream and downstream and which, in itself, as the ensign of the town, owing to its architectural beauty, was one of the most famous places in China. As happened to many famous buildings it was burnt down a generation or so ago. In its place a modern European brick building in the style of a garrison church was erected, destined to receive foreign guests, and its grotesque ugliness is such as to spoil the entire district. The architect of this monstrosity was none the less a man possessed of a fine understanding of art as far as Chinese things were concerned. Here is the horrible element of these combinations of culture, namely, that European civilization reveals itself in its ugliest, its most vulgar manifestations, cheap and evil, and poisons local culture at its very root. When one contemplates these facts one can well understand the enmity precisely of the cultivated and educated Chinese scholars. This centre, in the middle of China, possessed incidentally, lower down on the Yangtse, in Nanking, a town which was likewise the seat of a governor-general. Nanking, the southern capital, which had once been the seat of government of the great Ch'in Ch'in Shih Huang Ti, contains within its walls an immense district both of hills and plains. As a result of the terrible destruction which descended upon the city in the wake of the T'aip'ing rebellion, it is now a deserted place. Its fate had really been sealed ever since Yunglo, the third ruler of the Ming Dynasty, transferred his capital for strategic reasons to Peking in the north. The district of Nanking, however, also contains Shanghai, the international town, in the vicinity of the mouth of the Yangtse, and this city has set its stamp upon the whole region. It goes without saying that here, where we find such enormous stock undertakings as the "Commercial Press," for instance, a print-works which belongs to the largest establishment of its kind in the world and where all the numerous, partly Chinese and partly European, trading, shipping and industrial enterprises are situated, the whole reform problem assumed a far more acute aspect from the very begin-

ning than in the case of the centres in the interior. Shanghai
is, as it were, the laboratory in which economic and industrial
matters of synthesis between Eastern and Western forms of
culture are experimented upon.

The third centre of the movement of reform is Canton. The
southern provinces are far removed from the ancient cradles of
Chinese culture. These districts have, as it were, been drawn
on the horizon of the Chinese mind at a comparatively late
period. There is a certain difference even racially. In spite of
the fact that most of the family names point to a Chinese origin,
and the dialect is even a more original and less polished form
of the Chinese language, the inhabitants of the districts are,
for all that, far more southern, more hot-blooded, more radical
and more superstitious than in the north. It is therefore not
an accident that the Chinese cultural complex is here of a
looser tissue and that it is from this region that the stream
of emigrants flows to the south and to the east—thus bringing
the island district of southern Asia more and more into economic subjection, no matter who the political rulers may be. The
economic influence of the Chinese settlers continues to expand in
the Dutch Indies as much as in the English Straits Settlements
and, since a large educational institution for non-local Chinamen has been founded in Shanghai, this section of the inhabitants is drawn together more and more in cultural matters.

The southern provinces are at the same time the seat of
radical movements. It was here that the T'aip'ing rebellion
began and the radical reformers K'ang Yu We and Liang Ch'i
Ch'ao had travelled north from these parts, and it was again
here that a set of non-local students came to be formed which
was to endanger, not merely the state of Chinese culture, but
even the dynasty itself.

The educational reforms introduced by the Empress-Dowager and her advisers suffered from lack of system. The
reformers in Japan, a handful of determined men, worked in
the full consciousness of their aims and in perfect secrecy in
pursuance of an almost mathematical plan. While the Japanese

witnessed the realization of their scheme step by step, conditions in China were far more chaotic. There was no one among
the great leaders of the nation in China who possessed the
necessary knowledge of detail required for the homogeneous
execution of such an enormous task. It must not be forgotten
that the problem in China was far more difficult than in Japan,
which is equivalent to one or two Chinese provinces at most.
Moreover, in China, unlike Japan, it was not a question of
changing the outer garment, but a genuine re-creation from the
very bottom. One would have supposed that China, even if it
did not as yet possess the men who had the positive knowledge
required for such reforms, would have adopted the Japanese
solution of employing foreign advisers on a sufficiently large
scale so that these employees would have been able to assume
responsibility for the correct execution of reforms. This device
was indeed adopted, but only to a certain degree. Here and
there advisers were consulted, but they were never given full
powers so that they were considerably hampered. There were
a number of reasons for this state of affairs. On the one hand,
contact between China and foreign countries had not yet been
established sufficiently to make the direct choice of the suitable
people possible. In addition, in the countries in question,
while there were, no doubt, technical experts, there were none
who were sufficiently acquainted with Chinese conditions to
secure them against making serious mistakes. It was therefore
necessary to choose advisers among the foreigners who were
present in China, with the result that the choice fell first and
foremost upon Customs officials and missionaries.

The Chinese Maritime Customs are the institution of Sir
Robert Hart, and for many years they were an administrative
body which operated in the most admirable manner. The postal
service and, later on, the salt monopoly were also managed
very creditably. It cannot be claimed either that these bodies,
considering their foreign staff, pursued a political course more
favourable to foreign nations than to China. The varied composition of the staff provided against such a contingency, all
the more so because the staff, if it was to exist at all, was com-

pelled to form a powerful unity irrespective of national limitations. The solidarity obtained was also satisfactory and it was
not until the World War that it went to pieces. The German
officials in these services were removed. This fact is deeply to
be regretted, even if it is certain that this Nemesis will run
its course: what happened to the Germans first will sooner or
later happen to the members of other countries. We may say
that in its previous form the Chinese Marine Customs were
dealt their death-blow during the Great War.

Even if the Maritime Customs functioned efficiently in
China as an administrative body, one cannot say, apart from a
few exceptions, that it could possibly serve as the cradle for the
other reforms which were to be instituted. As an economic and
comparatively well-defined institution, it could at a pinch survive the powerful independence of its foreign officials, who
acted in a pretty high-handed manner towards the Chinese
Government as far as the moneys were concerned which they
collected. In other departments such a state within the state
would have spelled death to Chinese independence. Sir Robert
Hart, moreover, did not use the opportunity which was given
to him by the founding of the high school T'ung Wen Kuan in
Peking in such a way as to make it a model of its kind. It is
only now, after lengthy and difficult labours under Chinese
direction, that its place has gradually been taken by the present
university of Peking.

Even the missionaries were unable, with the best will in the
world, to rid themselves on many occasions of their Christian
limitations. The universities under their direction always had
a tendency to give some kind of prerogative to the Christian members. In cases where some individual was more far-
sighted, he was attacked in the most hateful manner by the
others. The venerable old D. Martin, for instance, who dared
to say a good word for the worship of ancestors—which incidentally had provided no difficulty for the missionaries in Japan
—was outlawed and despised for many years. People had
somehow or other to feel their way in the dark.

On the other hand, students were sent into foreign countries in order to drink at the source what the new sciences had to offer. Even here there was no system. It was only when America refunded the excess payments of the Boxer indemnity to China and a number of Chinese students could be sent to American universities annually that a beginning was made to educate the youth of China scientifically. These events, however, took place later. The great stream of those who hungered for knowledge turned at first to Japan. It cannot be said that Japan was a match for the problem which was thus created for it, though, in justice to Japan, we must mention that the demand for admission to the higher Japanese schools was far in excess of their capacities. In consequence, private activities, often of a very dubious kind, interfered. At the same time the emissaries of the Chinese revolution were active among the younger students. A number of conflicts ensued, and eventually most of the students returned without having made appreciable progress in their knowledge, but they were ripe for the revolution.

4

THE REVOLUTION

WHILE events in China became more and more chaotic the Empress-Dowager Tsï Hsi died, and with her the only personality strong enough to control circumstances in accordance with a uniform plan and able to keep the ambition of individual satraps within such bounds as to avoid danger for the whole community. It had also been she who had defended the reforms against the Manchu circles and their supporters who resisted her in the capital. In view of the immense passive resistance of these people, who saw that the whole of their parasitical existence was in danger if the reforms could not be effectively frustrated, it was quite out of the question that any fundamental measure could be carried through without the presence of such a personality of outstanding strength.

The death of the Empress-Dowager occurred after a prolonged illness. Shortly before her weak nephew died upon the throne. There was much talk that, when she saw her own end approaching, she ordered him to be murdered. There are no proofs in support of this accusation. The Emperor had been in a bad state of health for a long time, and even if he was murdered it may have been done by his enemies among the eunuchs without their having had any instructions to do so. They treated him badly enough while he was alive and they let him kneel, on many occasions, for a long time in front of the gates when he wished to call upon his aunt. It would not be surprising if they did not wish to fall into his hands after the death of their mistress and they therefore resorted to a little artificial assistance to ensure the prevention of such an eventuality. At any rate, the old Empress-Dowager seemed on the whole to be relieved on hearing of his death. She proceeded immediately to have her two-year-old grand-nephew, the son of Prince Chun, proclaimed Emperor, although both the Princes P'u Lun and Kung were closer aspirants. She succeeded in realizing her determination in spite of everybody's opposition, and then she died.

No one can pretend that the task which fell to Prince Chun, who had to act as regent for his infant son, was by any means an easy one. Problems which had already been difficult for the dead Empress, with all her energy, were twice as difficult for him as he was not in so secure a position as she had occupied by virtue of long years of practice and experience. Quite on the contrary, he found himself in the midst of intrigue, which centred around Prince P'u Lun, who played the part of a kind of *citoyen Orléans*.[1]

Whatever circumstances are taken into consideration it must nevertheless be confessed that he also lacked the power which was required for so heroic a task. The mightiest man in China at that time, however, was Yuan Shih K'ai, but between him and the throne there lay the shadow of the dead Emperor. It is reported that the deceased left a manuscript behind him which is said to have been almost illegible, but it was supposed to begin: "I was the second son of Prince Chun,[2] when the Empress-Dowager chose me for the throne. She has always hated me, but the misery of the last ten years of my life is due to Yuan Shih K'ai. When the time comes I desire that he be beheaded without mercy." This document was disposed of later by the wife of the Emperor, but not before it had been

[1] The nomination of the little prince by the Empress-Dowager only confirmed the fact that she had transferred the succession from the older to the younger line of the dynasty in consideration of her own family, the Yehonola family, which had been connected with the younger line of the dynasty by a complete system of marriages. In view of the above it hardly counts that she tried to make good the old injustice she had perpetrated against her son by nominating no one who was able to make the ritual sacrifices to him, by the simple device of having the young Emperor adopted simultaneously by the two late Emperors. The successor had three fathers: a real one and two fathers by adoption. Altogether a singular case!

[2] Chun is a princely title rather like Kung which is handed on from generation to generation; thus it came about that the same title fell to the lot of the Prince-Regent, the father of the Imperial son.

[3] Compare J. O. P. Bland and E. Backhouse, *China under the Empress-Dowager*. London: W. Heinemann, 1912, p. 460. This book is an excellent piece of work, notably in that portion which is due to Backhouse, and based upon archive material.

seen by independent witnesses.[3] The Prince-Regent was therefore faced with a choice either of carrying out this last wish of
his dead brother and so making Yuan Shih K'ai harmless, or
else of disregarding the dead and offering his complete confidence to Yuan Shih K'ai. He did the only thing which was
impossible: he provoked the lion to the extreme without ren-
dering him harmless. He issued an edict by which the funeral
ceremonies for the dead Emperor were entrusted to Yuan Shih
K'ai. Some one was easily to be found who accused him of lack
of conscientiousness in the execution of his duty, with the result
that the Prince-Regent drove Yuan Shih K'ai from office and
honours much as he would have dismissed a valet. Yuan Shih
K'ai swallowed his resentment. He retired to his native province in Honan, where he lived quietly and had photographs
made of himself wearing a straw mantle in pastoral surroundings, devoted to the joys of fishing far from the great world
and its activities. He presented these photographs to his friends.
In secret, however, he held his threads in his own hands. He
had a good friend at Court in the senior of the Imperial household, Prince K'ing, with whom he had worked hand-in-glove
for a long time, and people whom he could rely upon occupied
almost all the important posts. He therefore waited until his
hour should come, and it came.

The Manchu aristocracy made use of the new chaotic conditions in order to feather their own nest. One reform crowded
out another. A great deal of money was spent and nothing
substantial was achieved. This state of affairs led to far-reaching
dissatisfaction throughout the Empire. The officials, who were
not given a clear and uniform lead by the authorities, were
placed in the most awkward positions as a result of having
to find money locally in accordance with the various edicts of
reform which followed rapidly one upon another. The bands
of authority began to loosen. It is not surprising that in these
circumstances, that is to say, in view of the failure of the machine of government, the representatives of the people wished
themselves to have the reshaping of the new conditions. They
were anxious to find the means necessary for the construction

of railways and for the sinking of mines in order to be independent of foreign capital and the oppressive conditions which were attached to financial control by a foreign Power.

In Peking an Imperial committee had been called which was to serve as a preparatory Parliament. This Imperial committee, under the presidency of Prince P'u Lun, had identified itself somewhat with the opposition. They demanded the urgent introduction of the constitution, a responsible ministerial Cabinet; the control of the treasury of the State through the representatives of the people—in fact, demands which caused the Government the greatest anxiety and which could be silenced for the present only by the adjournment of the Imperial committee.

If the adjournment of the Imperial committee seemed to bring about a retrogressive movement, the same thing happened as far as the financing of industrial undertakings by internal loans was concerned. The confidence in these ventures was lacking and consequently it was impossible to find the necessary money. The Government, on the other hand, did not wish to allow such important matters as the Great Central railway lines to be in the hands of private enterprises. Accordingly, an energetic individual was sought who should be able to put matters straight. Such a man was found in the railway king Sheng Hsüan Huai, a former member of the group round Li Hung Chang. When this gentleman celebrated his entry into Peking the old times seemed to have returned all of a sudden. He arranged large loans with the representatives of foreign banks. The Central Railway from Hankow to Canton, which was to traverse the whole Empire from north to south, and the railway from Hanchow to Szechuan, the diagonal link from this centre to the western districts, were about to be constructed with the money raised by these loans.

Unfortunately, there was a hitch. The amount of the national loan which had been subscribed for the construction of the railway was to be refunded. It became evident in the process that considerable sums had been misappropriated and that the lenders did not receive anything like the sums they had provided, and thus the fermentation continued.

Another circumstance also played its part. For years the revolutionary party had been at work, hoping to succeed in the efforts which had failed during the T'aip'ing rebellion, namely, the removal of the Manchu Dynasty. The party consisted for the most part of young students who had imbibed modern and republican ideas in Japan and America. Once more it was a Cantonese, Sun Wen (Sun Yat Sen), originally trained as a doctor in a missionary institution, who was the leader of the movement. Though he was battered about by fate in the strangest manner, he had gained large numbers of supporters, especially among the younger generation, through his idealism and the powerful personal influence which emanated from him, and he did not lose this influence over the hearts of the young men up to the time of his death in spite of all his failures and reverses. He was the only man among Chinese public men who, even if he did not always live up to his principles, nevertheless on the whole lived for one idea all his life. This idea was of a nationalist kind: China for the Chinese, not for an Emperor, least of all for one of foreign antecedents like the Manchu rulers; not for the exploitation of the foreigners, but China, free and independent. Within China itself one portion was not to rule over another—heretofore the north had, after all, always been predominant—but the various provinces were to meet with equal rights on level ground, with full powers for local self-government, merely united into a federal state somewhat upon the American pattern. Sun Yat Sen also combined social ideas with his political convictions. The industrialization of China on a large scale formed part of his programme, but this industrialization was to proceed in such a way that full justice would be done to the principles of Socialism.

Such revolutionary ideas were in themselves quite alien to the Chinese nature. The national idea had been overcome in China long ago in the course of its history. In the days of antiquity there had been national states upon Chinese soil which had developed from the great feudal structure of the

Holy Chinese Empire of the Chou Dynasty. During the centuries of "Contending States" which had preceded the formation of a monarchy of officials under Ts'in Shih Huang Ti (about 250 B.C.), there was no absence of national attitude and national struggles. All that was long ago. It was long ago that the *orbis terrarum*, the world, had assumed the pre-eminence of the nation as the highest entity. This state of affairs had not been changed at first when Europe entered into the horizon of China. One had always known that China was merely the middle kingdom which was surrounded by more or less troublesome barbaric regions and islands. Japan had been known for a long time as a nation of pirates, and now others came to be added. All this was unpleasant, but not extraordinary. It was only after the Boxer rising that these ideas disappeared. The young students had discovered that there was another and greater world outside and beyond the realm of ancient China. In that world China was one nation among many others, a nation large in territory and rich in population, possessed of fruitful soil and mineral wealth beyond that of any other country and yet ill-treated and tortured on all sides, despised and pushed aside and poorer in political influence than Switzerland. All these unsatisfactory conditions were ascribed to the Government, which was in the hands of an uneducated and foreign clan which devoured in its lazy luxury the very marrow of the Chinese people. Hence that enmity among the younger generation which was directed equally against the foreigners and their own Government. The Chinese Christians were decidedly sympathetic to the revolution. Many of the revolutionary leaders are themselves Christians. For the Christian, and notably the Evangelical Churches, which were and are strongly under American influence, showed marked inclinations toward democracy. The Christians had into the bargain been obliged to put up with so much under the oppression of the old Government that any upheaval meant liberation for them.

Revolutionary ideas had met at first with very little support from the mass of the population. The good citizens held aloof, since the revolutionaries undermined not only the authority of the state but also that of the family.

The revolutionaries were, however, very active. They occasionally instigated local disturbances. They found more and more support among young students, and many a dissatisfied official who considered himself treated unjustly was favourable to them in secret. The movement met with sympathy notably among the army. And yet the Government adopted a reticent attitude. Their outspoken hatred of the foreigners was perhaps not altogether disagreeable to many an official. Others again did not wish to burn their fingers, for the terrorism which they exercised did not fail to leave its mark. The hesitating attitude of the Government, on the other hand, of course fired the revolutionaries with courage.

There were two factors which eventually added to the influence of the revolutionaries to a degree which even the most optimistic among them could not have foreseen. The failure of the crops of the preceding years had brought dire distress to wide districts in China. Crops which fail are always something terrible. The mass of the population, which can only just exist when all goes well, invariably suffers want when the harvest is unsuccessful. Many succumb. Others attempt to eke out an existence as robbers. People begin to murmur against the emperor, who as the Son of Heaven is personally responsible for the provision of the wherewithal of life for the people.

All that has been mentioned above combined to exercise a cumulative effect. Rebellion broke out in Süchuan. The army mutinied in Wuch'ang. Li Yuan Hung was elected leader of the movement by his troops. The rebellion spread like wildfire,[1] the air was full of revolution and its opponents lost their

[1] The glorious revolution, as it was frequently called in the English Press, was nothing like as bloodless as was reported in many quarters. What occurred in the south and the great Yangtse centres in the Manchu garrisons can only be described as blood baths. Those parts in which Manchus lived were burnt down systematically and razed to the ground, while the entire population, men, women, children and the aged were massacred. In various places they jumped into the Yangtse by the score in order to escape from their pursuers

senses. A great portion of the Imperial officials, in so far as they did not openly go over to the revolutionary camp, fled from their posts. They went to Hong-Kong, Shanghai, Tientsin, and especially to Tsingtao, that is to say, to places where they were safe from the onslaught of the revolutionaries. The desertion practised by the high officials is an extraordinary phenomenon, usually interpreted as cowardice by Europeans. In reality the situation was different. The Chinese revolution, very much like the German revolution, was not only the victory of the revolutionary party, but also the collapse of the monarchy, as it were, of its own accord. When clear instructions from above are missing it is impossible for the officials to take up a strong line, because they do not know at any moment to what extent their actions will be supported by a central government which has, so to speak, lost its head. The Chinese officials retired during the revolution, and the more consistent among them are remaining in self-imposed exile to the very end. Not one of them, however, has published memoirs.

The cause of the dynasty was not lost at this time by any means. The northern troops had remained loyal on the whole, and began to advance victoriously all along the line. Such a course of events, however, was not to the advantage of the quiet fisherman Yuan Shih K'ai, whose hour was soon to strike. He had his connections, of course. When matters became dangerous the old Prince K'ing, his friend, appeared and said: "We need a strong man, and the only one we have is Yuan Shih K'ai."

This assertion did not remain unchallenged. The people were afraid of him. Finally he was recalled, nevertheless, and in co-operation with the generals whose arms had begun to be victorious, he was to take in hand what remained to be done.

---

through death. In the north they remained alive. The fate of these families, once so proud and distinguished but now reduced to such poverty that many of them live by selling their daughters, is hardly less severe. We see here a dying race. It happens again and again that an entire family seeks death together. There will only be a few who will save themselves out of the wreckage by work and adaptation to the new conditions. The only evidence that is left of their noble Manchu spirit is that they die without complaining.

He stayed at home. Thereupon the higher military command was offered to him in the rebellious area as well as the post of a governor-general. He promised to come. Simultaneously he quietly took contact with the leaders of the opposition. Then he was called to Peking and nominated the head of the Cabinet he was to form. At that moment he arrived.

A few energetic measures brought the north, where the revolution was beginning to spread, once more into his control. He constituted a Cabinet out of the most variegated elements, but it never sat. He called a constituent assembly after he had signed an armistice with the revolutionaries. This assembly never met because the popular government was sitting in Shanghai. He recalled the victorious troops and began to negotiate with the revolutionary government.

What follows now was an extraordinary intrigue in the course of which the dynasty of the Manchus was persuaded step by step to renounce the throne of its own accord in favour of Yuan Shih K'ai, whereas, on the other side, the newly elected president of the Republic of China, Sun Yat Sen, renounced the position of president, also in favour of Yuan Shih K'ai. In the course of these proceedings Yuan Shih K'ai could count upon foreign friends who were in his favour. The explanation for this attitude is to be found in the fact that, on the one hand, he was a particularly strong man, and on the other, he was ambitious and treacherous, so that he possessed all the qualities which appear to the European to constitute the greatness of a statesman. In China a really great statesman must possess not only superior diplomatic agility, but, above all, a clearly discernible moral personality on a large scale, and Yuan Shih K'ai was too ambiguous for that. As a Chinaman once said, he had thrown away the flag which the Manchu Dynasty had entrusted to him and which he had promised to uphold, giving as his reason that the act of throwing it away was, after all, the only way of preserving it.

Yuan Shih K'ai now had his pigtail [1] cut off, and hoisted the

---

[1] It is a well-known fact that the pigtail was a fashion introduced by the Manchus. The removal of the pigtail implied the departure from old traditions.

new five-coloured [1] flag of the republic outside his palace, and China was solemnly declared a republic. In all fairness it must be said in his favour that his treachery did not weigh in the balance as much as might appear. The ruling Prince-Regent had really not merited Yuan Shih K'ai's gratitude, and the fact that he sought him out as saviour at the last moment was not because he had faith in him, but because the regent had lost all counsel. Yuan Shih K'ai did after all "save the flag." He provided the ruling family with an *otium cum dignitate*, a quiet retreat, together with the necessary income which was paid as long as the means were available. The widow of the Emperor Kuanghsü, of course, who did not inherit the intelligence of her aunt by any means, had only noticed later what was really at stake when she renounced the throne. She then wept copious tears and for days at a time shut herself off from intercourse with the outer world. The princes all manifested their agreement with the exception of the Princess Su, who died later in Dalny, and the Prince Kung, who retired to Tsingtao.

In addition it must be avowed that Yuan was at that time really the only man who was able to restore order, and did so. He did indeed on the occasion of the second revolution in Shanghai, which broke out shortly afterwards, notably strengthen the loyalty of his faithful troops by paying them ten times the sum of the bribe offered to them by his opponents. He always knew all his life how to acquire friends by means of the unjust mammon. His skill consisted less in the fact that he used these sums judiciously, than in the fact that he always had the required amounts at his disposal. In this direction he was certainly not mean. Ku Hung Ming belonged to his bitterest enemies. He fought him publicly in Chinese and English and did not leave anything evil unsaid. Ku Hung Ming belonged more or less to the Bohemia of the scholars. Gifted with the capacity of spending a great deal of money, he nevertheless was

---

[1] The five colours of the Chinese flag signify the five races of which the Chinese republic is composed: red = Chinese, yellow = Manchus, blue = Mongols, white = Mohammedans, black = Thibetans; the former Imperial flag was a blue dragon on a yellow ground mostly of triangular shape.

above accepting bribes in a dirty manner. It thus came about that he lived in a continual state of want. Yuan Shih K'ai heard of this, and nominated him tutor to his son with a monthly salary of five hundred dollars. He was allowed to abuse him just as heretofore, and nothing was done to suggest that he should temper his speech. His complaints and accusations, however, ceased to have any influence since it was known that he was in the service of Yuan Shih K'ai.

Everything would no doubt have gone well, and Yuan Shih K'ai would probably have had the capacity of leading the old China into a state of well-organized modern republicanism, if he had contented himself with remaining president. While he did so, he stood on legal ground, no matter how one may judge his methods of action. Only he went one step too far and wanted to become Emperor. It remains an open question whether this was his own idea or whether other influences drove him to this step. Even in this matter he proceeded very cunningly in giving the initiative to his friends and appearing to give way reluctantly to their demands.

The time for his undertaking did not seem unsuitable. The World War had started and its echoes resounded also in the Far East. Yuan Shih K'ai did not allow himself to be persuaded to take an active part in it—he was too clever to give way to such incalculable possibilities—but on the other hand, he found a sympathetic ear among the foreign Powers. Step by step he proceeded to concentrate all possible power in his hands. A new coat of arms was created. The year 1915 was to be the first year of the Hung Hsie period. Yuan Shih K'ai performed the Imperial sacrifice on the Altar of Heaven in Peking himself according to a ceremony which had been specially created for the purpose, which was based upon a certain precedent of the Han period. The idea of sacrifice was indeed considerably changed in the positive sense. Whereas previously three red lanterns burnt on top of three high masts in the winter's night of the sacrifice in order to symbolize the divine element in heaven, upon earth and in man, the lamps for heaven and the earth were suppressed.

The cosmic relationship was left out of the divine service. God was merely a symbolical expression for the genius of mankind, to whom Yuan Shih K'ai did reverence. The extent to which the sacrifice had changed its significance may be deduced from the fact that Yuan Shih K'ai arrived immediately in front of the sacrificial altar in an armoured car—fearing assassination, and he disappeared in the same way, whereas previously the ruler proceeded in a sedan chair for a three days' fast to the Hall of Fasting.

The greatest difficulty arose from the relations with Japan. The fact that the Great Powers were occupied during the World War gave Japan a free hand in the Far East, and she did her best to exploit this opportunity. Under pretext of taking Tsingtao away from the Germans, the Japanese troops marched right through the Shantung peninsula, robbing and plundering the north, and directed their steps gradually to Tsingtao; proceeding in the meanwhile along the Shantung railway to the provincial capital of Shantung, Tsinanfu, before they thought of attacking Tsingtao seriously. They conducted the war against Germany in a lax manner and without any enthusiasm, never forgetting that they must not close the back door in case Germany should be victorious. It was therefore with all the less pretence that Japan attempted to bring China under its sway. Yuan Shih K'ai had never been a friend of Japan, and was therefore compelled to pay dearly in the form of the twenty-one conditions which Japan imposed upon the Chinese State in order to obtain her goodwill for his plans. By means of these conditions Japan wished not merely to take possession of the important coal mines in T'ing Hsiang, the immensely rich iron-ore mines of Hanyang, but China was to be handed over helplessly to the Japanese Government, also in other domains, notably as far as the army was concerned. These machinations were so bold that the Japanese thought fit to conceal the essential points even from the English, who were their allies. Down to the present, the day on which the twenty-one conditions came into force is regarded in China as the day of national humiliation.

And in spite of all these efforts Yuan Shih K'ai failed to achieve his aim. A rebellion broke out in Yunnan which spread very rapidly throughout the country. Province after province rebelled, and eventually nothing remained but to dispose of the "Hung Hsien" device after being in force for a few months and to take the retrogressive step from Emperor to President. Such occurrences, however, cannot take place unobserved. Just as everything became insecure for Wallenstein when he opposed his Emperor, so did success flee before the flags of Yuan Shih K'ai, who can be compared in more than one respect to Wallenstein. Eventually he died, so the story goes, alarmed and tortured by the spirit who refused to let him go: a man with a broken heart.

THE STRUGGLES OF THE DIADOCHI

YUAN SHIH K'AI had not always found it easy to control his various generals with a firm hand. He was, however, the unchallenged master in the North. He was always surrounded by intelligent men who were able to hold the military authorities in check. He brought them together in Peking as one invites one's friends, and in the course of these meetings there was a complete absence of the relation of subordinates to their chief, but rather that of friends advising their host. In intellectual significance, one man among them stood out among the rest. He was Hsü Shih Ch'ang, who had been given the title of teacher to the Emperor, and who left his retreat among the hills of Tsingtao near the sea rather unwillingly in order to be of service to his friend.

The antagonistic forces began to make themselves felt after the death of Yuan Shih K'ai. Li Yuan Hung sat upon the presidential chair. He was a man with a righteous outlook, who did not fail to call Parliament together and to entrust it with the elaborations of a permanent constitution. Tuan K'i Jui, the ablest of Yuan Shih K'ai's former generals, was Prime Minister. He had gathered a party, or rather a club of generals, statesmen and financiers about him. They were generally referred to as the Anfu club after the place in which they were accustomed to meet. Most of the members came from the Yangtse district. This group was opposed by another section of military leaders known as the Chihli party, which was led by two generals of the Northern army, Ts'ao K'un and Wu P'e Fu. Ts'ao K'un was an insignificant creature, who desired nothing but the enjoyment of the amenities which power bestows, but he was in the hands of vicious vulgar people. Wu P'e Fu was his superior by far in education and personal calibre. Wu P'e Fu's principle was the unification of China by a policy of blood and iron. He was faced by the constant difficulty of obtaining the necessary funds for the maintenance of his army, because Ts'ao K'un's family stole the public funds in the most shameless manner. This procedure indeed is al-

together typical of the times of the struggle of the Diadochi
in China, since the majority of the people who held power for a
longer or a shorter period enriched themselves on the most liberal scale by dipping into the public purse. In Europe people
have often spoken about the corruption which was practised by
the officials towards the end of the Imperial Dynasty, and, in
fact, it cannot be denied that this corruption was practised at any
rate by some—by no manner of means the majority—of the
higher officials, who in the course of a lifetime amassed one or
several millions. The sums involved, however, are negligible
compared to the moneys which were misappropriated in modern
China. Fortunes which had previously been set aside in decades
were now collected in a few years or months and in amounts
representing ten or more times as much as had been stolen
before.

Apart from these successors of Yuan Shih K'ai, there was
also a third group: the small handful of men who were faithful to the Imperial Dynasty. Among them General Chang
Hsün was the most outstanding personality. He was altogether
uneducated and a very simple nature. It is said that he began
as a stable boy and worked his way up gradually through the
personal assistance of the Empress-Dowager. He never forgot
his debt to the dynasty, nor did he lose his respect for the
conservative Confucian ideals. For many years he continued to
wear his pigtail, and his children also went about proudly with
their thick well-cared-for pigtails at a time when in Shanghai
and Peking pigtails were regarded as reactionary and were
cut off in the open streets by a service of policemen who were
specially appointed to fulfil this duty. He knew neither the
laws of tactics nor those of strategy, but he was an old fighter
with courage, and when it came to a struggle he fought with all
his might. For a certain period at any rate the governor and
commander of Manchuria, Chang Tso Lin, was on friendly
terms with him.

These were the chief representatives of the various opposing
parties. The first thing that happened was the outbreak of the
Great War. The American Ambassador, Paul Reinsch, a Ger-

man by birth, did what he could, first, to induce China to break off relations with Germany, and, subsequently, to make her enter into the war. To do so he was compelled to engender the most ambitious hopes for China without promising anything definite. The entire negotiations were based upon deceiving China on a large scale, since the faithfulness of Japan had been purchased long ago by means of secret treaties at the expense of China's integrity and sovereignty. England, France and Russia had all concluded secret treaties with Japan, and all of them were made at the expense of China, and some of them were so secret that the various partners of Japan and Japan itself concealed the contents of the agreement from the other partners. It was precisely for this reason that America had to come to the front, because she was not tied by any such agreement and was therefore in a more favourable position to raise hopes in China with a better conscience.

It therefore came about that Tuan K'i Jui, the Prime Minister, who was in favour of the war, purchased a majority in Parliament—Parliament became more and more a limited liability company which derived an excellent income by the sale of its votes without representing any one but itself—and in this manner it was decided to break off relations with Germany. Li Yuan Hung, who was opposed to this measure, was obliged, as President of the republic, to abide by the decision of Parliament.

The next step was the decision of Parliament to enter into the war against Germany. Sun Yat Sen and the South were opposed to this procedure. On this occasion no majority could be obtained in Parliament. Pressure was exerted upon the President to dissolve Parliament. The members of the assembly retired for the most part to the south, and Li Yuan Hung disappeared from the political firmament.

At this moment occurred the monarchist *coup d'état*, which had been organized by Chang Hsün. Chang Hsün was influenced from yet another side. In the end there was nothing for him to do but to place the young Emperor upon the throne. The new monarchy, however, only lasted for five days. The

preparatory organization was too bad. Above all, he had forgotten to come to an understanding with that mighty man
Tuan K'i Jui, who was not disposed by any means to recognize
the new state of affairs which had been created over night.
There was street fighting in Peking. Chang Hsün retired to
the protection of the diplomatic quarter. The Emperor—who
was after all in no way to blame—returned to his former
position, and Hsu Shih Ch'ang, the old friend of the late Yuan
Shih K'ai, became President of the republic. War was declared
against Germany under pressure from the Allies. Nevertheless, the general attitude in China remained very friendly towards Germany, and the German subjects who were interned
were treated exceedingly well. Even later on when, after the
armistice, the Germans were expelled violently from China on
English boats, with the intention of thus destroying German
trade entirely, the Chinese did what they could for the Germans and prevented many an inhuman harshness on the part
of Christian Europeans. Incidentally the result of sending the
German traders away was the precise opposite of what had
been intended. The traders happen to have been sent away at
the moment when the value of the Chinese silver dollar, which
was quoted at more than twice its par value during the war,
began to collapse. All the foreign firms who were doing business in China at this time suffered enormous losses and many
of them went bankrupt. The Germans were protected from
these circumstances by violent means, and when they returned
to China, which did not take long, they were able to take up
their business activities with fresh power.

The Government in Peking was, during the period 1919-
1920, in the hands of the party of Tuan K'i Jui, the so-called
Anfu party, which was in close touch with the Japanese. The
President attempted to compromise between the Anfu party
and the Chihli party in order to obtain a balance of forces which
should establish his authority. The attempt failed. Eventually
there were open battles between the Anfu and the Chihli
groups, whose military leader was Wu P'e Fu. Wu P'e Fu
was victorious, although Tuan K'i Jui had received consider-

able support from the Japanese. Tuan K'i Jui retreated to the foreign settlement of Tientsin into private life to bide his time. It is one of the greatest obstacles for the establishment of sound conditions in China that these foreign settlements, which are exempt from Chinese jurisdiction, exist. This method makes it almost impossible to bring about any final decision in political life. If an official or a member of Parliament acquires a certain sum of money and no longer feels sure of his ground, he flees with his money to Tientsin or to Shanghai and enjoys his life there in peace, without even the possibility of China being able to call him to account. In the same way when any fighting occurs the party which has been losing for the moment retires to the foreign settlement in order to reappear on the next suitable occasion.

After the victory of Wu P'e Fu the power of the Anfu party, which had hitherto been so great, waned considerably; the chief reason for this was their lack of popularity among the younger generation, who disapproved of the friendly attitude towards Japan entertained by the party. An opponent who was not to to be despised, however, remained. He believed in unification by a policy of blood and iron in Manchuria, and his name was Chang Tso Lin. He advanced into Chihli in the spring of 1922. There was a pitched battle near Peking. Chang Tso Lin was beaten. A large portion of his army was taken prisoner and later sent back to Manchuria at the expense of the State. Wu P'e Fu, however, underestimated the power of his opponent. He was content to push Chang Tso Lin back into Manchuria.

Wu P'e Fu, and through him Ts'ao K'un, were victorious, and his more or less unchallenged rule accordingly embraced the North from the Manchurian boundary down to the Yangtse. Further battles in Fukien and Szechuan were intended to expand the territory towards the south and the west, while the weak attempt on the part of Sun Yat Sen to send a punitive expedition to the North failed lamentably because he quarrelled in a very unpleasant manner with his general, Ch'en Ch'iung Ming.

Hsu Shih Ch'ang resigned the presidency, as he no longer saw any possibility of carrying out his ideas. Thereupon the presidential chair was filled by Li Yuan Hung, who had before been expelled, and he was allowed to remain there until the time seemed to be ripe for Ts'ao K'un, whereupon Li Yuan Hung was sent away once more.

From then on matters became more and more chaotic in the North. The battle raged backwards and forwards. A man who was a friend today became an opponent tomorrow, and vice versa. It is superfluous to attempt to follow the details of these struggles. The people, or, at any rate, the large majority of them, took no part in these affairs. It was, after all, nothing but the struggle for power of individual leaders, who spent the money and the strength of the country in a fight which was not in the interests of the public. Militarism, a European legacy to China, showed itself here from an angle which revealed the whole of its harmfulness for the country.

The only party in China which has a really constructive idea is the Kuo Min Tang, which is in the course of taking possession of the entire country, beginning from the South. Feng Yu Hsiang, the so-called Christian general, is closely associated with this Southern movement. On the whole this party, where it flourishes, is carrying into practice the ideas of Sun Yat Sen. It is a fact, the importance of which must not be under-estimated, that Sun Yat Sen, who had to struggle during his life with nothing but difficulties, has become, from the day of his death, the genius to whose flag every one is rallying, and who can be described as a Chinese Nationalist. Today there is only one government in China which is of more than local importance, and that is the government of the South.

The foreign Powers are faced by an entirely new situation in view of this fact, which can no longer be denied. So far they have been accustomed to addressing complaints and protests to whatever government was in power in Peking, although the success of this policy has never been very marked. This procedure has today become impossible. People have to get used to the idea that the Chinese Government is situated in the

South. It is no longer possible to maintain the fiction of Bolshevik influence in the revolutionary South. The facts have
to be looked in the face.

In this respect, England is in a difficult position. In the
nineteenth century she was the leader of the European Powers.
English influence was predominant in China and decisive in
every way. The appearance of the Kuo Min Tang [1] movement placed England in the centre of a struggle which caused
the greatest antagonism towards her on the part of the Chinese
without giving her anything positive in exchange. Even in
places which had been instigated by the Japanese, England
appeared finally as the only opponent of China. The practice
of boycotting in Canton and Hong-Kong has caused the greatest possible harm to British trade, without providing any opportunity for taking counter-measures. Whenever such measures were attempted, as, for instance, the firing upon the open
town of Wanpsi'en in the Yangtse in the year 1926, it has
only led to exciting anger against Great Britain more than
ever. But even here, a careful and calm investigation of China's
real difficulty will no doubt lead to improvement. British
policy has so far always shown the wisdom of modifying its
course at the right moment. America came very much to the
front for a time. America had never attempted to acquire
territory in China, and had frequently shown a generous and
helpful attitude, especially in financial matters. The United
States had, like China, refused to sign the treaty of Versailles,
by means of which China was condemned by way of reward
for its participation in the war against Germany to the loss of
the province of Shantung, which was to be handed over to
Japan. America had then called the Washington Conference
in order to make the peace of the world more secure. This
Conference *de facto* ended the Anglo-Japanese Alliance, when
America and France joined the union which developed quickly
into a combination of England and America against France and
Japan. In Washington negotiations also took place between

[1] Kuo Min Tang means the party of the people. It is the republican social
party of the South, whose influence is penetrating the whole of China today.

China and Japan, and with some assistance from England and America the Chinese succeeded in regaining Tsingtao, which had been occupied, the Shantung railway, and also the sovereignty in Shantung, from Japan to whom these privileges had been ceded. Today there are indeed a number of Japanese in Shantung, but their violent influence has been broken. Slowly but surely the reins of government are going back to the Chinese.

American influence was weakened none the less. The hopes which the United States had held out to China had not by any means all been realized. The removal of the extra-territorial rights which had been offered had not progressed one step nearer realization. The revision of the Customs contract was put off again and again. Even in Mongolian questions and the problem of the South Manchurian railway, the promised assistance of America was of no avail. The Chinese saw themselves delivered relentlessly to Japanese violence.

In addition, it must be remembered that after the adhesion of the Far Eastern republic to Soviet Russia, Russia practised at times a somewhat blatant but nevertheless skilful and accommodating policy. Karachan came to Peking with protestations that China was heavily oppressed on all sides, that Russia was its only good friend, and eventually after a certain amount of fuss, which was taken very quietly by the Chinese, a very favourable Russo-Chinese treaty was concluded. China will not become Bolshevik through Russia within a measurable distance of time, but it has gained a backbone of independence through the assistance of Russia.

Of late years a decided change of Japanese policy has taken place. Japan had exploited the War in the most open-handed manner in order to gag China and to subjugate it from a military point of view. There were, of course, sensible people even then in Japan who disapproved of such a policy, but they were unable to make themselves heard. The opportunity which had given Japan a free hand in the Far East seemed to offer too many advantages to those who were then in power. The situation of Japan, however, did not remain as advantageous as was expected. To its great misfortune that party, on whose side Japan had fought, won in the Great War in far too decisive a manner to suit Japanese desires. Japan would have been able to make a far more advantageous arrangement with a victorious but considerably weakened Germany. After all, it could not be denied, in spite of all alliances, that they had lost the confidence of the Allies. In addition the consequences of the war were felt too a much greater extent than had been anticipated. The Siberian adventure, which had been planned as an expedition against Bolshevism by the Allies, but had been carried out eventually only by Japan, had to be liquidated. Eventually there came the earthquake, which made a far more profound and depressing effect upon the Japanese mind than people in Europe have been able to understand. In the eyes of the Japanese, no less than in those of the Chinese, it was the manifestation of a divine judgment. The atmosphere accordingly changed in Japan, especially as the complications with America and Australia became more and more serious. Instead of planning the military subjugation of China, an attitude of peaceful concord was adopted.

In spite of occasional banquets, China received the Japanese overtures of culture and affection, but at first combined such tendencies with considerable coolness. The spectacle was too unexpected: the newly found brother, singing the song of peace. Nevertheless, new perspectives have opened up owing to recent events. Japan was also the first to attempt to extricate itself in good time from the conflict of 1925, which had arisen from the brutal treatment of Chinese workmen, and it left England in the lurch, isolated, with the result that Great Britain was in the position of being the only Power who was boycotted.

Germany occupies a special position in all these events. She is entirely disinterested. She is only interested in the development and promotion of economic and cultural relations. She has adopted, with determination, the demand for equal rights and the solution of the extra-territorial problem. It may safely be said that her experiences up to date are on the whole satisfactory. German science and efficiency are recognized in China and people are ready to make use of both in the process of building up the future. It cannot be expected, of course, that, as far as the Chinese are concerned, their interest in Germany goes beyond the points enumerated above. Such interest can only come about if the newly spun threads between Germany and China are woven far more firmly together. The German position is advantageous in so far as it implies progress along the road which the other Powers are bound to travel sooner or later; for there is no doubt whatsoever that, in spite of all appearances to the contrary, China will establish herself as an independent Power with equal rights.

Before we can deal with a new change in the political situation, we must cast a glance upon what was happening in the North of China and in Mongolia.

When the Bolshevist revolution broke out in Russia, there was some fighting in Eastern Siberia between the Red and the White Russians. The Allies interfered for purposes of supporting the White army, at the beginning Americans and Japanese together, but finally only the Japanese remained. The acts of violence in the Nikolajewsk, where the entire Japanese population had been killed by the Bolsheviks, had inflamed the Japanese in particular. Eventually the Japanese had to retire before the victorious and irresistible progress of the Russians, who founded the Far Eastern republic with its new capital Chita, which later united itself with Soviet Russia, largely because the danger of Bolshevism spreading to the Japanese troops was threatening, and the authorities in Japan were not certain as to what might result from such an influence. Nevertheless, the Japanese did everything they could in order to support such White Russians as Koltschak or Horwart, who were still fighting there.

Exactly the same thing happened in Mongolia. This State had made itself independent of China. The leaders were friendly to the Manchu Dynasty and would have been ready to join in a movement destined to reinstate the Manchus. In these districts there was among the White Russians the Cos-

sack chieftain, Seminoff, together with his "adviser," the Baron
Ungern-Sternberg. They attempted to exploit the Mongols
for their own purposes and manoeuvred for this reason with
the representatives of the Manchu Dynasty, through whom
they hoped to obtain authority over the Mongols—and all this
was done with the blessing of the Japanese. How little they
were concerned for the welfare of China is to be seen from the
fact that a Mongolian prince, who personally wished to make
contact with Manchu circles, was murdered in the most cruel
fashion. He and all his staff and the house they occupied were
simply riddled with bullets and the place was razed to the
ground, so that nothing remained but ruins. Later on they
excused themselves towards the Manchus by saying that the
whole incident was a mistake as he had been considered a
traitor and a revolutionary.

The Chinese troops belonging to the Anfu party, who were
to represent the Chinese interests in Mongolia, were entirely
cut to pieces at that time. Ungern-Sternberg, who was perhaps pathological rather than cruel, was more important than
Seminoff, whose assistant he had been at the beginning. It
was perhaps precisely as a result of what was pathological in
him that he would present a certain demoniac and powerful
quality which fascinated those who surrounded him. He
thought he was destined to be the ruler of Asia, like Genghis
Khan, whose horoscope was the same as his. He believed sin-
cerely in his destiny, which he pursued with a certain magnificent melancholy even when it led to his downfall. Among his
followers there were a few devils of special cruelty whom he
suffered either from superstition or indifference, though they
eventually caused his fall. Seminoff had a keen sense for his
own security, and when matters began to be dangerous he sent
first his wife, with chests of gold, over the frontier. He himself followed a little later, and awaited the development of
events.

In the end the Soviets succeeded, in spite of all these personalities, in getting a firm foothold in Mongolia, and then
something occurred which must be regarded as a huge joke in

the history of the world. The Mongols, whose actual evolution stands on the level, constituted themselves into a Soviet Republic. And the living Buddha became Prime Minister! Russian advisers were of course there to assist the various ministries. Since Russia has united herself with China, the independence of Mongolia is again to cease, just as that of the North Manchurian railway, because Russia is only concerned in making sure that neither district shall be used as the basis for attack by an enemy Power.

THE NEW CHINA

I F one really wishes to understand the new China which has come into being in the course of the last decades, it is not sufficient to follow the political circumstances as they manifested themselves outwardly and to understand the very complicated struggles of the military leaders. History in China is at present playing, as it were, a double part: the history of militarism imported from Europe which exhausts itself in mutual struggles, and the history of Chinese culture, which has been quickly growing, of which the Chinese are becoming more and more conscious. The leaders of this intellectual movement in young China have occasionally compared it to the period of the Renaissance in Europe. It is, at any rate, a period of rebirth in intellectual spheres.

At one time it had become customary in Europe to see in China a gigantic complex which had become rigid and immobile in the course of centuries and which was separated from all progress by a "Chinese Wall." This short-sighted judgment is due to the ignorance of internal Chinese conditions and to the superficiality of observation, which is always conscious of a uniform impression gained from the strange appearance of a nation, because the differentiating signs in the individual, as well as in entire epochs of history, are only discovered after the general traits have been noticed.

Nevertheless, Chinese culture has always been anything but monotonously uniform. The classical period of Chou culture was succeeded again and again by new epochs with new and independent cultural values, and even the last centuries have manifested a culture peculiar to themselves in the form of a strictly scientific and critical philology. It simply so happened that in Europe people knew nothing about it because nobody took the trouble to depart from the old, well-worn opinions and no one examined the more modern elements of intellectual life in China independently.

Among the representatives of the older scientific generation there is Chang T'ai Yen. He is not only a complete master of classical literature, but also a distinguished scholar of Mahayana Buddhism. Since he does not speak any European language, and has very few connections with foreigners, he is practically unknown in the West. He represents the central Chinese scientific traditions. He is considered in China today as the unchallenged leader in the field of literary science. His democratic attitude has brought him the veneration of the younger generation. Nevertheless, he exercises less influence upon practical life than upon science, with the result that he lives in a certain aristocratic isolation.

Among the scholars who have stood out in the course of the last century and who are active down to the present day in Southern China, two men must be named who have already been referred to as reformers, K'ang Yu We and Liang Chi Ch'ao. The older of the two, K'ang Yu We, was a friendly old man who has died only a few months ago. People spoke with a smile of him as "the new saint," and in so doing they referred to his connection with the new so-called Confucian Church. Nobody suspects, however, what a fiery spirit burned behind the kindly smile of this white-haired saint. When you wander about the Temple of Confucius in Peking, you find innumerable memorial tablets upon which the names of all those are cut in stone who have passed the highest examinations with the greatest distinction, and have therefore been permitted to enter the holy circle of sages, and who have been found worthy in the course of the centuries to spread the teachings of the Master, Confucius. One of the names on the tablet has been erased and condemned to oblivion. It is the name of the reformer K'ang Yu We. He himself had escaped the wrath of the old Empress, but, at any rate, his name was to die. From the point of view of the old lady, he no doubt deserved this fate, not only owing to his activity as a reformer, but even more so to what he wrote. He was a serious heretic, whose teachings do not deviate a great deal from those of Marx and Lenin, even though he protected his teachings as a secret from the rest of the world, which he did not consider ripe for it.

His first revolution was of a literary kind. In the course of
the last century attempts had been made to sort out the ancient
sacred writings and to bring a critical spirit to bear upon them.
Tradition declared that Confucius arranged and published
these writings, which belong to earliest antiquity, as a holy
inheritance for the future. In the course of the examinations
referred to above, a good deal of criticism was expressed.
Later additions and forgeries were found which were first
explained by saying that when Ts'in Shih Huang Ti burnt all
the books, the whole of Confucian literature had been destroyed, and that it was only with difficulty later put together
again and, in the circumstances, it was inevitable that the Imperial rewards which were offered for the discovery of old
writings should also bring to light manuscripts which had been
manufactured specially for this purpose, made old by artificial
means. The problem now was to discover and separate the
fraudulent documents. K'ang Yu We dared to make the stag-
gering assertion that the whole of the texts which were considered as the "old texts" because they appeared during the
Han period (round about the beginning of our era), were conscious forgeries, that the burning of the books by Ts'in Shih
Huang Ti had not destroyed the Confucian writings at all and
that the purpose of these forgeries had been to help Wang
Mang to usurp the throne. In the world of Chinese scholars
the excitement concerning this solution of the Gordian knot
had not yet calmed down when a new book appeared, which
was still more revolutionary: *The Reform of Confucius*. In this
work an attempt is made to prove that the old writings of
Confucius were not traditional, nor had they been edited by
him, but that he had written and invented them all himself in
order to lend an historical background for his teachings, which
were revolutionary for that period. He declared that it was
impossible for us to know whether the heroes of those ancient
times had ever lived or not. At any rate, what has come down
through Confucius was claimed to be pure inventions of the
Master. He was said to have invented his heroes Yao and
Shun exactly as Laotse invented Huang Ti, or Mo Ti the

great Yü, Hsü Hsing the famous Shen Nung, and just as all philosophers of that time projected their models into the past. The antiquarian scholar, for that is how many people used to regard Confucius, now suddenly became a bold innovator, who with creative genius had evolved a culture for centuries and centuries to come. His figure acquired a marvellous mystic profundity. Enigmatically he looks out upon the present generation from the secret which he had woven with an able hand about himself, and he no longer merited veneration merely as a wise man of bygone days, but deserved adoration as a divine saviour such as Jesus received from His disciples. K'ang Yu We determined from then onwards to found a Confucian Church after the manner of the Christian Church. This proceeding did not meet with any luck. The Confucian Church in Peking, of which we shall speak later, offers today a somewhat pathetic spectacle.

K'ang Yu We has, in spite of his veneration for Confucius, as it were, removed the saint from his unique position by virtue of this book, which caused more excitement than the first, of which the entire edition was destroyed by order of the Empress-Dowager. In a certain degree he has placed him in a parallel line with the other important men of his period, who also attempted somehow or other to arrange a part for themselves. His work made it possible to adopt a far more independent and objective attitude to ancient history than had been possible for thousands of years. K'ang Yu We was indeed himself far from being objective; his was a very obstinate nature. This fact is shown not only by his relation to old literature and its sources, but also in his behaviour to many people, notably to his pupils, many of whom he estranged from him. He could have been today the unchallenged leader of Young China if he had not been so stubborn about various peculiarities.

Most revolutionary of all is his third work, in which he proceeds to establish independent theories for the formation of human society. This work, *The Book of the Great Communion*, has been published in only a few copies printed as manuscript, because he is convinced that his time has not yet come. He goes back to a passage in the old book of rites in which a threefold period of humanity is contemplated: a period of disorder, a period of minor power, and the period of the great communion. He enunciates in his book the principles for the time of the great communion. The idea is not intended as a Utopia, but as a serious basis for the future regulation of human society. The main considerations of this work are:

1. The abolition of the State. The whole world has a common Government, subdivided into individual sections according to Nations.

2. The general Government and the Governments of the subsidiary sections are elected by the people.

3. Abolition of the family. Man and wife are to live together for only one year. At the expiration of this period a change takes place.

4. Pregnant women are sent to a maternity school: the new-born children are taken to a special institution for babies.

5. The children are brought, according to their age, into kindergartens and later to school.

6. The Government determines the professional activity of the grown-ups.

7. Hospitals exist for those who are ill, and special homes for the aged.

8. The maternity schools, infant welfare institutions, kindergartens, schools, hospitals, homes for the aged, are all carefully furnished so that their inmates can really feel at home there.

9. Grown-up men and women must serve a certain number of years in the above-named institutions in place of the present system of military service.

10. Dwellings and restaurants are public. Every individual has the free use of his earnings.

11. Laziness will be prevented by severe punishment.

12. Those who contribute to the progress of science, or who

have rendered noteworthy service in the official institutions will receive special distinction.

13. The dead will be burnt. Next to the crematoriums, the works for artificial manure are to be erected.

It must be pointed out here that these thoughts, which are surely as radical as any one might wish, were conceived quite independently. They were written down a generation ago, and were elaborated at a time when K'ang Yu We could not possibly have been in any kind of contact with the socialist and communist ideas of the West. The kernel of his system is to be found in the abolition of the family, which means that Buddhism, which desired to escape from the bitterness of life by fleeing from the family circle, becomes superfluous, just as all strife and struggle for property is rendered meaningless if the inheritance of property is no longer possible. The fact that the system contains a number of harsh and severe elements corresponds entirely to the fiery spirit of the man who invented it.

One point in the whole conception is very odd: he has conceived this new order for society in the greatest detail, but he always kept it secret. He only allowed chosen pupils access to these doctrines and, when in their enthusiasm they wanted to proceed to their realization, he prevented them. Even when he held the power in his hands, he never attempted to translate his ideas into reality, as he was convinced that at present people should not go beyond the methods of the present state of "Minor Powers." It thus came about that he remained a supporter of the Manchu Dynasty to the end. He has only quite recently permitted this heritage for the future to be printed. When I left China he presented me with a few copies of this book as well as of his other works. It belongs to the curious memories of my life, how the old man bade me farewell with visible emotion and gave me his blessing on my way beyond the seas.

I have dealt in somewhat greater detail with him because he offers proof how in China ideas which are destined to turn the world upside down can frequently be pronounced in secret and without anybody in Europe knowing anything about it. People continue to talk calmly of the stagnation of the intellectual life of the Chinese. Admittedly the case of K'ang Yu We is rather peculiar. He has drifted apart from what is new in the Chinese world through the curious duality in his life.

Among K'ang Yu We's pupils, by far the most distinguished is Liang Ch'i Ch'ao, who is probably today the most productive writer in China. The publications of this man, who is at the beginning of the fifties, go back quite a long way. Together with K'ang Yu We he fought for the adoption of Western education and Western methods and, together with him, he has created the new literary style, whose power influenced public opinion in China during the period of the great transition from the old to the new order. Liang Ch'i Ch'ao was far more radical in his attitude from the very beginning than K'ang Yu We. The ideas which his master had hidden almost shyly from the world were treated seriously by him. After the failure of his attempt, together with K'ang Yu We, to bring about a reform under the Emperor Kuanghsü, he had fled to Japan, where he continued to work actively to bring about the downfall of the old and to prepare for the new China. He returned to China after the revolution of 1911, and filled for a while various Government offices in the young republic. Subsequently he retired again from his official career, which compelled him to accept too many compromises, and he now leads the life of a scholar and a writer. His mind is extraordinarily mobile and quick at adapting itself, and he is, even today, one of the leaders to whom the young man listens most readily. In his religious views he is not far removed from Buddhism, which he considers the religion of China after a profound reform shall have removed the dross from it. Politically and economically his ideas are of a socialist kind, which is also the case in the whole course of the classic literature of the Chinese. The modern habit of talking about a Bolshevik danger in China is based upon the greatest error. China will not become Bolshevik by violent intrusion from the outside, because many vital thoughts which have given their motive power to Bolshevism have been at work in China for a long time and they have, to some extent, shaped events. This also explains why, in the new China, we find, in spite of all the struggles and party differences, an entirely homogeneous feeling among the people, which is expressing itself recently more and more in a definite public opinion. Liang Ch'i Ch'ao once summarized the substance of this public opinion in two fundamental sentences:

1. All those who are not Chinese have no right to interfere in Chinese affairs.
2. All those who are Chinese have the right to a voice in Chinese affairs.

He then elaborated these points in the following manner: The first statement expresses the opinion of the national state, the second the spirit of the republic. This double meaning was by no means altogether absent at an earlier time, but public opinion was asleep and dreamed dreams and did not find any clear expression. But in the course of the last fifty years, or to be more precise, in the last thirty years, it has found a very definite expression. I venture to assert that if, after the fall of the Manchus, an alien race attempts to follow the example of Wu Hu, Toba, Liao, Chin, Mongols or Manchus, and wishes to begin the old song of invasion and control of China once more, the sea will be dried up and the rocks will decay before such efforts are crowned with success. I dare to assert that the shield of the republic which now hangs above us cannot be torn down even in the course of many centuries. It does not matter whether a man be as holy as Yao and Shun, or as powerful as Ts'in Shih Huang Ti, or the ancestor of the Ming, or as cunning as Ts'ao or Tsü-Ma I: if he should attempt to become Emperor of China, there is no man who would suffer it. This fact must not be taken lightly and one may not say that we are here concerned only with words and not with reality. An old proverb rightly says: "The name is the test of reality." Everything which in society occupies the firm seat of a correct name, becomes secure, condensing itself into

CHAP. 6   THE NEW CHINA   83

reality in accordance with its name and becoming more secure in the consciousness of the people. In brief, what the Chinese have done in the last thirty years is, firstly, that they have put an end once and for ever to a state of affairs which has lasted for more than a thousand years, in which again and again foreign races have undertaken to control them from without; and, secondly, that they have removed for all eternity the arbitrary rule of absolutism which has weighed down upon them for two thousand years from the days of Ts'in Shih Huang Ti. Most of these things, moreover, are by no means the result of an unconscious action, but have been brought about owing to a profound awakening and by a great effort. Regarded from this point of view the results must be considered as a decidedly progressive step.

As far as the condition of the State during the decade of the republic is concerned, it must be admitted that it met with the general contempt of foreign nations. Nevertheless, I believe that there is no reason to despair, for these circumstances are determined by two extraordinary causes, both of which will shortly be removed. One cause is that during the revolution, while the power of the people was not yet sufficient, the assistance of external power had to be sought.[1] The old policy of power is a spectre of the past days. Since this spectre has a history of two thousand years behind it and is very clever in the application of its means, it was not possible to prevent it from continuing to exercise its effects for a few decades. The sand has nearly run out of its glass and will soon have come to the end. As soon as this period is over a new political atmosphere will manifest itself of its own accord. The second cause lies in the natural course of the expansion of any movement. The individual stages of the transition were achieved by a series of real heroes through the sacrifice of their entire strength. In the circumstances it is natural that in due course

---

[1] This statement refers to the military leaders who, indispensable at the beginning of the revolution as heirs of Yuan Shih K'ai are together with their hireling soldiers the cause of considerable embarrassment.

a momentary condition of fatigue becomes evident, and, incidentally and unfortunately, quite a number of the most determined fighters have fallen victims to time. The successors
did not succeed immediately in continuing at the level of their
predecessors, and thus an interval was created; but I believe
that this lapse also is now over. The old leaders have rested
a little and can rouse themselves anew to the enthusiasm of
the fight; and since the ranks of those who come to fight
swell from day to day, the situation is such that a new era
may be expected.

As has been said above, all these three leading personalities
have leanings toward Buddhism, and K'ang Yu We mentioned it occasionally in his writings. It is, of course, due to
historical circumstances that Buddhism, which succumbed for
a period and had sunk to the level of a low kind of superstition, raised its head again and is beginning to be fashionable
once more in China among cultivated people. It was a secretary of the well-known statesman Tsêng Kuo Fan, by the
name of Yang Wen Hui, who later went with the son of
Tsêng Kuo Fan, the well-known Marquis Tsêng, when he became Ambassador to London, who exercised great influence
upon the scholars of the new school in this connection. He
had enjoyed a particularly thorough and profound education,
and settled in later years in Nanking, where he devoted himself to the research of Buddhism and to the initiation of young
followers into the secrets of the Buddhistic world of thought.
He died on the day before the outbreak of the revolution. The
circle which he started exists in a certain form to this day in
Nanking.

Buddhism undoubtedly possessed certain dangers for many
of its more superficial adherents. Many people were, so to
speak, brought to its arms owing to dissatisfaction with the
world and a desire to escape from the hubbub of life. This pessimistic attitude, which is not necessarily based on Mahayana
Buddhism, implies, of course, a lowering of the standard just
as much as that period in Christianity in which people attempted
to flee from this earthly vale of woe by turning away from

the world. The very popular sect of the "Pure Country," which
in many ways is reminiscent of Protestantism in so far as it
hopes for the salvation, not through a man's work, but through
faith alone, has done even greater harm. This sect renounces
from the very start the possibility of finding perfection in this
life. They trust in Amida and call upon him, in Chinese
"Amit'ofo," and by this process they obtain the power by
which they enter after death into the "Pure Country," paradise, where they are born again in order to attain Nirvana;
and such a faith implies a considerable reduction of peoples'
difficulties. It is a faith which can be found among people of a
very dubious kind. They pray and meditate, then they go and
continue to sin cheerfully, for they know that the simple call
of "Amit'ofo" induces the return of all blessedness. It is part
and parcel of the same tendency that the representative of
Buddhism encouraged the activities of the various spiritualistic
and other occult secret societies which generally shunned the
light of day. In this connection a reform of Buddhism is at
work. It is hardly pleasing news, though it does not belong to
the essential nature of the affair, that in the process these forms
borrow from Christianity in so far as they celebrate jubilees
of a Christian type, publish papers, and found Young Men's
Buddhistic Association (Y.M.B.A.). Serious men among the
leaders of the younger generation are of the opinion that the
rebirth of Europe, by means of the revival of Greek culture
through the Renaissance and the revival of Christianity
through the Reformation, were brought about by means of
this kind of double route, and that the Chinese Rinascimento,
about which the young men of China talk so much today, will
also need this double foundation: in the domain of aesthetics
the rejuvenation of literature and art, and in the realm of philosophy, a revival of Buddhism. Christianity apparently is too
far removed from these circles. They do not fight against it:
it is regarded as a power which is in the process of drying out
in Europe; they are tired of the many quarrels connected with
it. They consider the Christian attitude towards the many
new questions which occupy their intellectual life as anti-

quated. The judgment which is passed after weighing the pros and cons is—"neither praise nor blame."[1]

Among the leaders of the new China we must also here refer to Sun Wen (Sun Yat Sen), who died recently, and who also came originally from the province of Canton, that is to say, from the extreme south of China. He has been referred to already in connection with the Chinese revolution. Here we can only say that he has left in a book magnificent plans for the economic development of China: a network of railways was to cover the country, great harbour works were to be constructed on the coast. Everything was conceived with imagination and on a large scale, expressed in figures which can find their parallel only in America. The suggestive power of Sun Yat Sen does not really lie in his literary work. The excitement of his life, full of danger and pursuit, did not leave him with time for literary profundities, but he was important as a kind of centre-point. He held high the banner of revolution until the republic had become the governmental form of China. After this political revolution he turned his thoughts towards social reconstruction, as he realized that the change in the form of government did not in itself achieve very much. The fact, however, that it was he who set out upon the new road resulted in the unification of those forces which strove towards the new. He aroused the social consciousness of citizenship and carried it along for the greater part into the channels of social reform. The great strength of the new China lies in the fact that today merchants, students and workpeople form a homogeneous mass and that even the soldiers join them at moments of crisis. This spirit is so powerful and homogeneous that it carries the certainty of victory with it. The name of Sun Yat Sen signifies to a wide circle of Chinese people a symbol of unification. His power will, perhaps, become even greater now that he is dead, because during his life, especially in Canton,

[1] This judgment, which reminds us suspiciously of the phrase, "I know thy work, but thou art neither cold nor warm," from Apoc. iii. 15, is, for instance, expressed without any hesitation by Liang Ch'i Ch'ao in his *History of Knowledge during the Ts'ing Dynasty*.

he had a number of opponents, and also because during the continual struggles, in the midst of which he stood, and which fluctuated between victory and defeat, he was sometimes compelled to resort to certain measures to provide himself with the money for his purposes, which did not always increase his popularity amongst the sections who were hit by them.

The president of the Peking National University, Ts'ai Yüan P'e, plays an important part, especially among the young students. Ts'ai Yüan P'e belonged to the old school. He was a member of the old Hanlin academy and is a perfect master of ancient Chinese scholarship and of the old style. He supported the new movement, however, from the very beginning with conviction, and he soon occupied a leading place in it. He is the only one of the literary leaders of the older generation who has spent any length of time in European universities. When he returned to China he was acting as minister of education, and finally he was entrusted with the presidency of the Peking National University. His work was the re-creation of the Chinese educational and cultural system. We have seen that the Chinese work of reform hesitated for a long time as to how much it was to accept of Western civilization without creating the necessity of limiting or discarding the old traditional culture. This attempt was, of course, predestined to failure. To master the old Chinese writings, the old style, the old philosophy, the old history, was a problem which had hitherto exacted the entire powers of the normal student. If foreign languages, economics and other studies were to be added, it was bound to be at the expense either of the "new" subject or of the "old," according to individual tendencies. The attempts which had been made hitherto were in reality a transition from the older to the newer subjects.

The first introduction of Western sciences by the Jesuits is left out of consideration here, in so far as the Western knowledge which they brought with them was not introduced as a part of the general education, which continued quietly in its old course and was merely adopted and worked upon by a portion of the scholars of those days. The influence upon Chinese knowledge could have been more fruitful if the Jesuits had imported from Europe what was then the most modern science. They were impeded, however—owing to religious causes— by sticking to the astronomy of Tycho Brahe, so that it was indeed easier for them to penetrate into Chinese philosophy —for the attitude which they adopted did not differ in prin- ciple from the ancient Chinese outlook—but they did not revolutionize Chinese science. The Chinese works which were written on the basis of what they had brought with them were necessarily predestined to be out of date as soon as they were published.

The adoption of modern European science was embarked upon, as has already been shown, with the greatest hesitancy. Western knowledge seemed to be suited only for practical application in which one saw mere technique rather than science. Even Chang Chih Tung, in his well-known mani- festo, represented the point of view that the reformation of edu- cation demanded that the kernel of education should remain old Chinese and only its practice should become European. This distinction was in the forefront of discussion for many years and it solved the difficulty with an elegant phrase. In reality people were, of course, compelled to allow the kernel to shrink more and more because the practical "shell" had expanded more and more, and as a result the students became, as it were, deracinated in a manner which was truly deplorable. You could see, especially in the missionary schools, that the pupils could express themselves passably in English, but they no longer knew their mother-tongue well enough to be able to write a simple letter. As a result, the value of their foreign training fell, in the domain of Chinese culture, to the signifi- cance of the language qualifications of a waiter. The pupils who left such Christian universities, therefore, frequently did not get any farther than obtaining positions as interpreters, scribes, or office clerks in foreign employ, which other people with a little wit managed to achieve in a far shorter time with- out a "university education."

On the other hand, there arose the unsatisfactory position

that it was precisely the representatives of new learning, the reformers like K'ang Yu We or Liang Ch'i Ch'ao, who did not understand any foreign languages and were for this reason dependent upon translations for their knowledge of the West. These translations were, for the most part, superficial and inexact like most of those made during the earlier period, or else they were written in very elegant Chinese like the famous translations by Yen Fu. But these works were translated so smoothly, or rather transcribed in such a manner that they read like old Chinese books, and what was new in their ideas was, so to speak, wrapped up and covered over by the old literary style. These translations were just as if we tried to translate Darwin's works by a series of quotations out of the Bible. Into the bargain it must be remembered that the works which had been translated were by no manner of means the most important, but books of secondary rank: such works as those of Huxley, Spencer, Stuart Mill, Montesquieu. These books formed the quintessence of modern knowledge for a certain period in China.

Nothing but a bold decision could put an end to these imported attempts of bringing the East and West together and of recapturing a homogeneous education for the people. It was necessary to remove the ballast of what was old, which was only an impediment and gave the pupils no benefit, in order to gain time for education in the Chinese written language and modern subjects. Hitherto the classical works of the old philosophers had served simultaneously in the lessons for reading and writing. A compendium of Confucian morals, philosophy and history served as the first primer; it was the so-called book of the three characters, a name which had been derived from the fact that it was written in verses consisting each of three characters. It began with the following profound words:

"The beginning of man
Is good in the root of its nature.
By nature they are close to one another.
By habit they grow apart from one another."

These writings were learnt by heart word for word—only according to their sound—so that the pupil at first did not understand that he was reading. It was not until he had committed to memory entire works that their sense was explained to him in a second course, and then, generally, very superficially. It can easily be imagined that the profound teachings of wisdom of the greatest thinkers of the old days were not exactly easily digestible fare for people who were beginning their A B C, and the doctrine did not—especially in view of the superficial teaching methods of recent times—contribute much to the vital moral education of the boys who had been overfed on this fare.

Ts'ai Yüan P'e, while he was Minister of Education, took the decisive step, which had been prepared in many ways by his predecessors, of removing the old classic writings from the elementary curriculum and giving them the place which was their due: the university. Here the old writings were to be studied philologically, historically and philosophically, and thus made fruitful for the present generation. In the schools reading-books were introduced, which were no longer written in the difficult language of hieroglyphics of bygone days, but, being based upon modern thought, were destined to acquaint the pupil with the written and spoken usages of their mother-tongue.

It is impossible to imagine the significance of this reform. The entire method of education was not only changed, but the method of learning was altered fundamentally according to pedagogic principles, and Confucianism ceased to be the religious basis of education. Literary education was attained in old China in the school community which was ultimately based upon the master of the ten thousand generations, Confucius. If this school community did not possess the severe organization of a church it constituted, nevertheless, the background of a firm philosophy. The "master" hovered invisibly over all the schools. Knowledge was simultaneously religion and morality. The written word was sacred. It was considered a crime to throw away paper containing writing. Special boxes had been fitted in the school in which papers were collected to be burnt solemnly from time to time. The process of learning frequently went hand in hand with practical domestic service in the house of the teacher. The pupil grew into the great cultural community which extended over centuries. The fact that the classic Confucian writings have become the object of university study, and that their principles—considerably modified in parts —are only taught in the school of ethics, has produced a new attitude of its own accord. Confucius is indeed referred to with respect and veneration, as the sage of antiquity, but his vital contact with the masses has been interrupted. The school has been, as it were, dechurched.

When Ts'ai Yüan P'e took over the direction of the governmental university of Peking, he transformed it into an extensive educational and research institution. He divided it into faculties and departments. The teaching department acquired an independent voice in the management of the whole institution, because it elected the officers of the university. Ts'ai Yüan P'e succeeded in gathering the most distinguished of the younger brains about him. A scientific activity of incredible vitality began. In spite of low pay, which is often months in arrears, owing to the hopeless financial conditions, there is an unequalled enthusiasm for work among the professors and a close contact between students and teachers. Ts'ai Yüan P'e made a principle of the unconditional expression of views, while highly conservative teachers can participate without interference. Even the reactionary Ku Hung Ming taught at the university for a certain time.

It can be said that the university of Peking stands at the head of all intellectual movements in China and represents a vital force in direct touch with the life of the people. All the professors consider it an honour to belong to this community. The students seek and obtain contact with the widest sections of the people. They voluntarily help in the evening classes given for the people. Any question of an aesthetic, scientific or social kind meets with interest, and there are a number of free unions in which teachers and students cope with new problems as they arise. In this way the university of Peking, as founded by Ts'ai Yüan P'e and his collaborators, occupies an exceedingly important place in the mental life of new China.

One of the most important acts of the group around the governmental university of Peking is the creation of a new colloquial Chinese language. The old Chinese written language goes back, on the whole, to the language of the last centuries before the Christian era. At that time the somewhat awkward pre-classical written language and writing had developed into an exceedingly elegant, pliable and yet clearly written form which is defined in the better known works of that period. This written language had been preserved, for the most part, throughout the centuries and was always imitated in new compositions, even at a time when the spoken language had deviated along paths of its own, so remote from the written language that the written word could no longer be understood when it was read aloud and the written image had to be seen to be intelligible. Even since the days of the divergent developments of the written and the spoken language, there existed side by side with the written language a literature in the language which was current from time to time. The famous scholar Chu Hsi of the Sung period published, for instance, his conversations with his disciples in the colloquial language. In addition there appeared a popular literature of dramas, stories and novels all of which approximated to the colloquial language. The whole of this literature was relegated to a secondary rank and was never given full appreciation.

The new era also brought new requirements with it. A literary revolution took place, which can be compared with the great movements of the Renaissance, in the course of which the national languages of Europe became written literary languages. People wanted a language which could really be adapted to the new ideas and which should be easily and generally intelligible. This literary revolution found its first expression in the journal of *The New Youth*, which was founded by the head of the literary faculty of the university of Peking, Chen Tu Hsiu. The journal represented politically and socially an exceedingly left-wing policy and adopted the principles of naturalism in literature. A highly talented young professor, Hu Shih, who had returned from a prolonged period of study in America, not only spoke and wrote English fluently, but had also imbibed the pragmatic philosophy of America. He outlined his new programme in the journal and made serious use of this new popular language in a whole series of publications. A row of other journals followed. At times there were more than four hundred journals and newspapers written in this popular language whose material was chiefly drawn from foreign texts in translations. So many papers could, of course, not maintain themselves in the long run, and a considerable proportion of them closed their doors. Hu Shih published a history of Chinese philosophy which caused the greatest sensation. The first part appeared in the new language and thus proved that it too was a pliable and useful means of making oneself understood for scientific purposes.

A storm of protest was raised against the revolution. The men in the camp of the ancients were offended by the ruthlessly popular element of the new language. Where was the delicacy, where the balanced rhythm, where the hidden lustre of the language of the past which had been so rich in quotations? It was all so clear, so direct, so open, so vulgar. The opposition was, of course, influenced by the fact that the literary revolution, very much like the literary revolution in Europe at the end of the last century, was connected with the great social and political tendencies of the day. Chen Tu Hsiu had to flee from Peking. He went to the foreigners' quarter of Shanghai, where he published a number of somewhat radical opposition papers.

The literary leader of the opponents of the new movement was, for a period, Lin Shu, who, by his activities as a translator, had acquired a good position which was called in question by the new language. In addition, he was also in political contact with the Anfu party, which he attempted to defend against the young radicals.

In the meantime, the new movement has modified itself and has become a well-established fact. Not only aspiring members

of the new movement like Hu Shih and Liang Shu Ming or
the modern poet Hsü Chih Mo, but also many others have
written valuable works in the new language. Liang Ch'i Ch'ao
and Ts'ai Yüan P'e have joined the movement also, thus
raising it to an unchallengeable level.

Great vitality in the whole mental life of China is connected
with this literary movement. The barriers against the foreign
countries have been rased. The open and unreserved examination and interchange of ideas with the West has begun.
There is no longer a special Chinese domain to which people
attempt to cling as Chang Chih Tung had still tried to do. A
philosophical society was founded under the presidency of
Liang Ch'i Ch'ao, Chiang Po Li, and the well-known Dr.
Carsun Chang, which invited foreign professors to China.
The call has so far been answered by Bertram Russell from
England, Dewey from America, Hans Driesch from Germany,
and Rabindranath Tagore from India, and others will follow.

It seemed for a time as if the cultural independence of China
would be irretrievably lost in the influx of new ideas. The war
effected a change here. The Western European and American
states showed during the war all too clearly the terrible dangerous side of their culture. China awoke from its dreams of
cosmic politics into which it had entered with enthusiasm, as
revealed in the writings of K'ang Yu We and other con-
temporaries, and acquired an awakened national consciousness.
In this connection the Russian influences which had lately been
revealed also exercised their special effect. The new Russia
which Europe often would wish to dispose of with a thoughtless stigma, "Bolshevism," is a far more complex phenomenon
than we realize over here. Apart from the principle of Communism, that Soviet idea, which signifies the free co-operation
of completely independent social and national formation, is
very powerful. This Soviet idea strengthens the national element everywhere in Asia and thus also in China. We are not
to suspect any "Yellow peril," the empty phantom of the bad
conscience of Europe, no bloody agrarian Communism, no Bolshevism in this sense, but we can expect the firm determination

of the Chinese to be master in their own house, to repudiate the age-long servility brought about by European arrogance, to be a nation with equal rights among the others, and to collaborate in common with them in the great problems of humanity. These are the aims of the new China. Germany and Russia have recognized this right of their own free will. The other nations, which are regarded as oppressors by the Chinese, find themselves faced by a powerful passive resistance which unifies the entire Chinese nation. These alien Powers fight with tanks and machine-guns to which China opposes only the new weapon of determination. In this way decisive struggles for a new formation of the world take place before our eyes.

7
A JOURNEY TO THE TOMB OF CONFUCIUS AND THE WEDDING OF HIS DESCENDANT

I HAD set out with a few Chinese pupils to experience something of the past of China. At that time the Shantung railway, which links Tsingtao with the capital of Shantung, Tsinanfu, had not yet been completed. In the provinces we were still in the old China. The inhabitants had at first opposed the construction of the railway. They feared that the spirits of the telegraph wires which hummed in the air and the snorting and rattling of the "fire chariots" might disturb the peace of the ancestral graves. Their fears were justified. The railway literally scared their ancestors from their graves. The earth opened her mouth and spat out what had rested in her bosom in holy secrecy for many centuries. Mysterious magic mirrors with a black and luminous patina came out of the graves. Heavy malachite green bronzes of severe old form appeared and their inscriptions told of the time and the place of their creation. The oldest oracular bones were dragged to the light which allowed men to gaze into the mysterious depths of Chinese antiquity. Old signs covered their smooth surfaces and much that sounds like old mythology is carried upon them in picture signs. All those countless tomb accessories were and continue to be brought out: women and servants, horses and camels and strangely silent gods of the dead, all those companions into the strange beyond which were given to the dead throughout long centuries and are now gathered together under the name of T'ang sculpture by the European collector. The disturbed spirits of the ancestors have brought many other things with them. The calm of well-established customs which lay over China for many centuries was interrupted and the chaos of new activity spread over the land. In those first years of the present century, little of this future was known in the provinces. The construction of the railway had presented difficulties, though they were not greater than once upon a time

96

in Europe. The donkey of the peasants ran away when the "steam horse" arrived puffing and snorting, and the peasants were antagonistic. Before long they came to make use of the new means of transport, and eventually they were surprised that the train did not travel much faster.

We took the train as far as Wehsien. This town lies approximately in the centre of the Shantung peninsula, and has for many generations been the residence of learned families. The town is surrounded by high walls with battlements and is situated on the banks of a wide river whose sandy bed is used for the food markets which are held at regular intervals and can take place there because the river is usually dry but for a small trickle of water. We found lodgings in an inn. The official had heard of my arrival [1] and sent a few servants out with refreshments. The room in the inn was also decorated festively for my benefit. The dust of centuries upon the clay floor flew about in the air as a result of vigorous sweeping with short hand brooms. Red cushions were put on the chairs and strips of red silk and curtains were attached to the doors.

I sent my Chinese visiting card into the Yamen (the governmental building) to announce my visit to the official. It had grown dark before I could set out on my way. I was carried in a sedan chair through the twilit streets. The official servants went in front at a rapid pace bearing paper lanterns to clear the way. The population which crowded the narrow streets made way respectfully. We passed through the high vault of the gateway of the city beneath which the steps of the bearers reverberated. The gigantic wings of the gateway with their

---

[1] Some time previously I had received one of the higher Chinese official ranks as I had refused a decoration. The various grades of rank are distinguished by different kinds of balls which are worn on the Chinese cap: ranks 9 to 7 were gilt balls of bronze, 6 a milk-white ball, 5 one of mountain crystal, 4 one of lapis lazuli, 3 one of sapphire, 2 one of coral, 1 of rose quartz. The members of the higher ranks are entitled to various travelling facilities through the assistance of the local official. Though this right is not obligatory in the case of foreigners, the officials nevertheless do everything they can out of courtesy to satisfy foreign visitors.

iron fittings were still open. The gates shut with a creak only when night has fallen and after the signal has been given in the form of a shrill call, on a horn, and by the rumbling of drums. These city gates with their defiant aspect, frequently surmounted by small temples, usually have a long history both of war and peace behind them: and these events have left an uncanny atmosphere about them. In their depths there may, for instance, be a little box behind a grill containing a pair of shoes. They are the shoes of a just and beloved official which have been taken from him as a souvenir on the occasion of his departure, by a grateful population which presented him with a new pair with the wish that they shall smooth the path of his ascent. Sometimes other things can be seen, for instance, the head of a notorious robber, which is often exhibited for weeks in a small cage as a warning. On the present occasion, in Wehsien, there was, as a matter of fact, no head in the gateway, and we proceeded quietly through the paved street past dimly illuminated shops, booths and workshops, until the bearers turned at last through a high tower building into the Yamen. The official received me in a small private room and was most courteous and arranged everything for the continuation of our journey which had been planned for the next day.

Next morning, at the grey of dawn, a travelling sedan chair was sent, with two teams of carriers for me and a travelling cart for the pupils and the luggage. The Chinese travelling carts are two-wheeled vehicles without springs and a barrel-like superstructure, which is as a rule covered with a blue cloth. The cart rests upon two shafts which are harnessed directly to the horse. In the plain one horse is enough, but if the road is difficult, a second horse is harnessed in front of it. These carts are exactly as they were thousands of years ago, built very sturdily so that even on the worst roads, which often tip them up at a dangerous angle, they can re-establish themselves, and it is rare that they upset. The Chinese fill the cart so full with luggage and rugs that they are securely entrenched between soft objects and they can therefore stand the shaking of the springless cart without concern. Later on I also learnt to appreciate the advantages of a Chinese travelling cart, but until one has got used to it one can only regard it as an instrument of torture. The riding horses which one gets along the journey are mostly bony animals which answer to continual beating with only few short trots, because the batman who accompanies the animal on foot twists the horse's tail round his hand and lets himself be pulled as well. Hence the sedan chair remains the only comfortable means of travelling. One soon gets used to its regular swaying. A teapot is placed on the crossbar in the front of the sedan chair and one can pour out tea at one's pleasure. In addition, one can crack melon seeds and regard the landscape and read. On that occasion, so long as we were going through flat country, I read the Chinese novel of the faithful wife, that story of two young people who were so virtuous that the emperor eventually united them after they had withstood the severest temptations.[1] In the history of Chinese literature this story plays quite an insignificant part because the style is dry and its action suggestive of puppets, but it was frequently translated in Europe in the eighteenth century because it suited the *chinoiserie* of that period so well.

Our next big halt after Wehsien was the town of Ch'ing-choufu. There are a number of earth pyramids there, the tombs of former kings. It used to be the capital of the old princes of Ch'i at whose court Confucius had once spent some time and had heard there the famous Shao music, which overwhelmed him to such an extent that he forgot the taste of meat for three months. Here was the snow palace in which Mengtzü had held that famous conversation with the king of Ch'i about the true joy of a ruler which consisted in his enjoying all the beauties of music and of his gardens and palaces together with his people. The place is still shown where the marble palace used to stand. A few lions of stone, from a much later period, stand on the barren plain, in the background of which there is somewhere a broken-down building which serves as a refuge for the beggars of the town. The remnants of a very ancient

[1] *Hao Ch'iu Chuna.*

city gateway stand up like a hill from the plain. In the local idiom this hill is called the mountain of ants.

Separated from the Chinese town by a special enclosure there was in Ch'ing-choufu a fortified Manchu camp, whose commander also received me. This was partly due to courtesy and partly to curiosity. Among the Manchu population the women are distinguished from the Chinese by the fact that their feet are not crimpled, that they wear thick-soled boots, long undivided garments, and also a curious structure for their head-dress. The men can be distinguished by a foreigner only with difficulty. The entire population lived in wretched circumstances as it was solely dependent upon the tribute money of the courts and never did any work of any kind itself.

There was also a strong Mohammedan element in the town. The Chinese Mohammedans are for the greater part descendants of Turks whose ancestors have come into the country as soldiers. The commonest family name amongst them is Ma—a Chinese form of the name of Mohammed. Here and there one still finds an Arabian Koran and some other Arabic works which even the Mollahs only know by heart without really being able to read them. In other respects they are distinguished by the fact that they do not eat any pork, but mainly mutton, which is sold in what are called Hui-Hui, which is the Mohammedan name for a slaughter-house. Neither do they drink wine. Only officials obtain a dispensation from this commandment so as not to be ill at ease in the execution of their official duties, which also include a certain amount of social intercourse. Mosques whose style is strongly reminiscent of Chinese buildings are to be found in most places where there is a Mohammedan population.

From Ch'ing-choufu our road took us for several days past the Iron Mountains near Ch'inlingchen to the provincial capital, Tsinanfu. Tsinanfu was in those days still an old Chinese town without the noisy dusty foreigners' quarter which has established itself in the meantime outside the wall. The town lies at the foot of the Thousand Buddha Mountain, which rises up in the south with its temples and monasteries. The town is exceedingly rich in springs, which flow from the ground in crystal clearness in all kinds of corners. The place is surrounded by temples and tea-houses. A market-place with its booths and human bustle enlivens the river bank. From the various springs rivulets run through all the streets, and for this reason Tsin-anfu is one of the cleanest towns in China. An old insignificant pavilion is situated at the bend of the watercourse. There the early market takes place. In the morning, long before the break of day, ancient objects and other valuables are taken there, gen-erally secretly, by the servants of impoverished noble families or by dealers, and sometimes also by thieves. These are there bought by merchants. The thronging and bargaining in the cool of the morning is exceedingly romantic. If one knows anything about it, one can occasionally buy good pieces, but one can also —and this is probably the rule for the innocent European—be thoroughly cheated. As soon as a European appears the people come out of the surrounding shops with their treasures and show them in a mysterious manner, as it were secretly, to arouse curiosity and a wish to purchase. Since moreover in Wehsien, for instance, an extensive manufacture of bronze antiques flour-ishes, it can readily be understood that the tremulous flickering of nocturnal lanterns sometimes shines upon objects which prove a disappointment in the light of day.

The rivulets of this town are gathered on the northern side in a lotus lake called Taming-Hu. This lake is the meeting-place of the idle youths who come from the fine houses. Broad boats, with superstructures built of glass walls in which tea and melon seeds are served on inlaid tables, glide through the open watercourses between the big lotus leaves, past the large fragrant pale pink flowers, to disappear among the greenery. Here and there gay laughter is heard or the bright garments of a singer shimmer through the thicket; or else some one is heard playing a lute in accompaniment of some aria from an opera. There are various stations on the lake which are sit-uated on islands where pavilions are hidden beneath high wil-lows. Memorial halls and ancestral temples, which have been built for famous men of an earlier age, rise up, and they contain gardens and rooms in which the visitor can talk and drink tea and dream into the landscape, and one can even see theatrical performances, which go much farther in keeping alive, in the minds of the people, the names of those in whose memory they were erected, than the European monuments which after a few years are examined at most by an occasional stranger. In the north the lake extends as far as the town wall where the temple of the North Pole is erected in a high terrace. From there one can overlook everything which takes place on the lake. On the horizon the Thousand Buddha Mountain shimmers against the blue sky in an atmosphere of delicate fragrance, and the crowded houses of the town are interspersed and shaded by the delicate green of the tall willow trees.

From Tsinanfu, the road turns towards the mountains. You notice that you are passing through an ancient civilization. The traffic along the roads of soft black soil has worn them down in the course of the centuries so that they lie far below the surface of the plain. When a road has cut its way too deeply, it is abandoned and lies there like a deep ravine, while a new road is begun next to it. In certain places three or four roads can be seen side by side. The form of the mountains is peculiar. They look as if steep walls stood on the top, and frequently there are caves at the foot of the rocks. It is a peculiar sensation when one is far below the summit and suddenly sees the sky shine through one of these caves.

I halted again in Ningyang, a town in a department near the home of Confucius. The local official was a friend of mine and was delighted to be able to put me up in the Yamen. The country roads were planted with acacias, which had somehow found their way from Tsingtao to the interior. Everything was clean and well kept.

When we arrived the official was still busy in the hall which serves as a law court. It is a large open room in which the civilian criminal proceedings are judged. The underlings stand about holding sticks with which people are beaten. The accused, the prosecutors and the witnesses kneel before a table on which stands a large official seal and behind which the official himself is seated. His presence spreads fear and terror about him. When any one says anything which does not seem right to the judge, he slams a board on the table, which causes every one to tremble as it is always possible that this threat may be followed by a bastinado with a view to arriving at the truth. The procedure is generally rather summary and conducted less in accordance with ingenious legal rules than in conformity with the sound common sense of the people. One can say that a lawsuit is always something terrible for those concerned on account of the underlings who take part in this affair and who always know how to keep themselves free from blame on such occasions. The Emperor K'ang Hsi himself had warned his subjects in a holy edict against the Imperial law court! Nevertheless, it must be recognized that a competent official usually arrives very fairly at the facts and his judgments are supported by popular opinion.[1] The legal proceedings conducted by my friend were soon over and he greeted us in the comfortably furnished private apartment in which we had awaited the termination of his business. We were offered friendly hospitality and talked of earlier times. It is quite incredible what a good memory Chinese officials have. They recall conversations of many years ago and remember all the attendant circumstances where a European would at most call to mind vague general impressions. My friend was not very happy in his present position. The place was rather out of the way, caused him a great deal of work and brought him few receipts. I knew, when I entered the Yamen, that he was not contented here, because I had seen a mirror on the door opposite the so-called wall of the spirits, which is placed in front of the entrance as a kind of protective wall. This is a magical practice which is to make the person living there succeed in his career.

[1] All this is changed today. Modern laws and modern legal procedure have been introduced into China. In practice it, of course, varies considerably. In the towns with a foreign population, Chinese legal procedure resembles the European system closely, but in the country, legal practice is still much more primitive.

He was of the greatest assistance to me with regard to the continuation of my journey. He was a personal friend of the Prince K'ung in K'üfou, the seventy-third descendant of Confucius. He told me that just then a great wedding was being celebrated, and he sent letters ahead which assured me an invitation to the ceremony.

When next morning, before daybreak, the bugle calls of the watchman resounded through the grey air, and the dull rumbling of the drums announced that the gates of the town were open, my journey continued through the fruitful fields of the ancient civilization.

We soon reached K'üfou. The town which today possesses a railway station and an hotel built in a foreign style was then still quite untouched by any alien element. The place was inhabited almost exclusively by the descendants of the master K'ung, who have now multiplied so as to form a large tribe. Here lives what is probably the oldest aristocracy of the whole world. The family can trace the family tree not only directly back to the master K'ung, who lived at the time of the sixth and fifth century B.C., but they can trace it beyond that date with considerable certainty to the year 1000 B.C. and with very fair probability back to the middle of the third millennium before Christ. Only one member of the family, however, bears, from generation to generation, the title of "Prince, who carries on the holy one." The other members of the family sink rank by rank to the level of the common people as is the case of all Chinese aristocrats. It should also be mentioned that the family, in the whole course of its history, can point to a considerable number of distinguished members.

In the midst of this population, whose very number is a visible embodiment of the blessing of the reverence for children which K'ungtse made the basis of his doctrine for the organization of humanity, there stands the temple in which the master is honoured. There is a temple to Confucius in every departmental town in the whole of the Chinese empire. These temples and the sacrifices which are offered on certain dates honour him as the representative of the Chinese social idea. Here, on the other hand, he is honoured as the ancestor of the family which has collected about him. Whereas accordingly the other Confucius temples quite correctly show no image in the place of veneration, but only an upright wooden tablet on which his titles of honour are recorded and round about the tablets of his faithful followers, here in the temple, upon the throne of the ruler, is seen a seated figure of the saint with his face turned towards the south. He is represented in a naturalistic way, in that form which is regarded by tradition as true to nature: a dusky face, a long white beard, the lips parted slightly, and a kindly expression in the eyes. He holds a sceptre in his hand, and on his head he wears a tiara from which a number of ropes of pearls fall over his face. The altar shows precious sacrificial vessels, the gifts of rulers of the past. According to Chinese tradition, it is customary for a man to be buried with the honours which correspond to his rank. The sacrifices which are offered to him by his successors are made in the form which corresponds to their rank. In order, therefore, to honour the master with increasingly magnificent ancestral sacrifices, his successors had to be given higher and higher ranks. The late Manchu Dynasty wanted in the end to cling, as it were, to the great master of the ages. They gave his successor the title of a royal prince and, for this reason, the ancestral sacrifices are offered up to K'ungtse in royal vessels made of jade, thus setting him on a level with God. This honour unfortunately did not help much, and with the passing of the dynasty the master honoured like a god has also lost much veneration.

The temple, with its magnificent dragon-encircled pillars of marble and its noble and severe atmosphere, stands in the midst of ancient cypress trees which have kept guard for long centuries. Some of these trees are merely dry stems crumbling and collapsing more and more. In other cases the roots have produced new shoots and strange manifestations of form and growth are to be found among these holy and gigantic trees. Here indeed is holy ground. Every spot is full of memories of the life of the master, and each holy tree bears a memorial stone which reveals its meaning in the signs graven upon them in the ancient days. The holy grove in which the family is buried is even more impressive. The way leads through a long row of cypresses into more and more mysterious rooms until, eventually, we stand before the grave of the master. It is quite simple: a mound of earth overgrown with grass and shaded by trees which spread above it and are full of the most ancient wisdom. Birds, old dusky birds with strange voices, dwell in their branches. It seems as if in their language they spoke of him who takes his rest beneath them. Even the herbs which grow upon his grave possess miraculous powers. They are the holy achillea which are gathered and then serve as oracular wands for the purpose of taking oracles from the old book of wisdom of transition. A simple stone stands before the grave and tells who rests there.

In this holy stillness, which is deepened by the shadow of the cypress trees and the strange voices of the birds, the human heart is touched by eternity. Time and the petty turmoil of men shrink together and the figures of those who have moulded men, who with their creative touch have made mankind into what it is today, loom up in their full stature like the distant summits of gigantic mountains. Among them the man who has pointed the way which leads to rest and peace for the greatest people of the earth for scores of centuries occupies a position, commanding veneration.

The mark of terror is upon our age. All that is venerable, all that was firmly established and has lasted for thousands of years, begins to sway and to fall. New questions and problems are raised, asking to be solved, and for which the resources of the past are insufficient. Thus the spiritual world which K'ungtse built up has had to give way before the onslaught of what is new. He built up his world upon a magnificent harmony with the natural conditions of his day. He conceived men rooted in the intuitive cohesion of the family. His order of the world is founded upon this cohesion: the attachment which is natural within the family, the love of the parents for their children: feelings which manifest themselves in natural men of their own accord without compulsion. These feelings were the material which K'ungtse used for his teaching. He strove to find the right form, the right expression for their emotion, because feelings are corrupted or wither if they do not find their true and natural expression. K'ungtse therefore strove to find the true expression for this central harmony of the emotions. He attempted to attain this end by the establishment of firm customs for external behaviour and by the influence of music upon man's inner attitude. With the family as the centre he extended the range of his action. What is nature within the family was to be culture in the cohesion of the state, which represents an enlargement of the family. He fixed, as the star above all natural states, the vision of humanity: "within the four seas all are brothers," and as the father of men he set up the Godhead which, full of eternal wisdom, wrought without sound or scent what is right for all living things, and it is also the only source for all that lives in man of the highest thoughts and the happiest destinies.

These ideas are laid down in documents of antiquity which he edited and filled with the profundity of their significance. He provided, in addition to the written texts which were as concise and clear as possible, a verbal tradition to explain their meaning. He then preserved, in a tumultuous period in which the structure of contemporary culture had begun to be shaken to its foundation, the plan according to which, subject to different circumstances and yet consistent with the spirit of his heritage, the culture of China was built up once more. There is probably not another great man among the creative spirits of humanity who succeeded as completely as K'ungtse in realizing his essential thoughts among the great public.

Today China is also faced by new problems. It is not only the feudal state that has collapsed. The collapse has overcome the Confucian system. It became dominating precisely at the moment in which China became a centralized bureaucratic state. Today the family, the real, natural basis of this system, is in course of dissolution, not, of course, among the millions of the provincial population of China, but amongst the most advanced members of the country. The constituent calls of the individual sever themselves more and more from their former cohesion. The family and the state are ceasing to be the vessels in which the essential life of humanity is stored. New formations and connections must appear out of the chaos if mankind is not to be split up into atoms, and the teaching of the Confucian system has thus come to an end. It is not an accident that the holy writings of Confucianism, which have hitherto been the mother's milk with which the growing boy imbibed education, knowledge and morality, have been banned from the elementary schools to become the object of scholarly studies in the universities.

Even if what is mortal in K'ungtse should be dissolved in this new world, what is eternal in him, the great truth of the harmony between nature and culture, will remain and will supply a powerful impetus for the new philosophy and for the new development of men. In this respect he is eternal.

In the course of the last years many attempts have been made to exalt the efficacy of the great saint, also in external matters. An effort was set on foot to found in K'üfou a great university for the study of the Chinese classics, but the means were not forthcoming. Even the temple shows traces of decay here and there. The family of the saint have suffered many misfortunes. From time to time outbreaks of fire have destroyed many important treasures, and the spirit of the sage hovers no longer over his representatives upon earth.[1]

[1] In Peking a Confucian church has been formed. It is a mixture of archaic rites—which are not taken seriously by the majority of those who perform them—and modern usages rather like those of the Y.M.C.A. The founder of this church, who is dependent upon its existence for his means of livelihood, has collected money and obtained quite a large sum. He intended to build a round tower in Peking, after the manner of an American skyscraper. It was to contain lecture rooms, halls dedicated to worship, libraries, club rooms, and baths. A roof of yellow glazed tiles was to dominate a great distance of the country-side. Unfortunately the money that was collected came to an end when the armed concrete foundation for this tower had been sunk into the ground. The founder has accordingly the satisfaction of having a very fine and strong concrete circle in his garden, which, of course, is flooded in the latter part of the summer and forms a pond. Instead of the proclamation of the doctrine, the croaking of frogs is heard in the pond.

When I returned from the grave of the master I found a messenger in the inn from the Prince K'ung, who wished me to attend the wedding. The prince was about to be married for the second time. Although he was fairly young, he had become a widower after a childless marriage.

A Chinese wedding is always a great feast. A suitable day is chosen in the calendar after the preparations and customs connected with the engagement, which take many months, have been performed. The bridegroom then sets out in a magnificent sedan chair to bring the bride into the house of his parents. Contrary to our customs in Europe, the wedding is celebrated, not in the family of the bride, but in that of the bridegroom, just as the dowry is presented by the bridegroom to the bride. Where purchase is customary, the parents of the bridegroom buy a suitable wife for him.

Festive joy reigned at the court of the prince. The bride had already arrived and had been led into the apartments, where she discarded her red veil after the performance of the wedding ceremony, and then she could be inspected by the visitors. This inspection is part of a Chinese wedding. When the bridegroom fetches the bride she wears a red silk head-dress of such a kind that she is completely unrecognizable by the bridegroom. She is led by female servants to the sedan chair and then she is carried off towards her new and unknown home. The actual marriage takes place with great ceremony in the presence of the representatives of both families. The bridal pair drink wine out of two cups connected by a silken thread. They kneel down to reverence the God of heaven and earth, and then they do honour to the parents of the bridegroom, to whom the young wife must henceforth be subject. The veil falls and the young man now beholds the wife for the first time [1] and can take his decision about their future communal life. The young wife now sits down to be looked at for the remainder of the day, and

[1] This at any rate is the story. In practice the bridegroom has usually, even according to the old customs, received an impression beforehand of the companion chosen for him by his parents.

whereas subsequently she is severely secluded from the gaze
of the outer world, on her wedding day she must expose herself
to the approval of all the guests, which is not always an easy
task. In the case of the prince, the proceedings were, of course,
far more respectable than is usual, and apart from near relatives, nobody saw her.

When I arrived, the prince appeared to greet me and to receive my congratulations. He spoke a few friendly words to me
about the interest I took in his ancestor and thereupon invited
me to be seated at one of the tables. Chinese delicacies of all
kinds were built up on countless tables. The walls of the rooms
and of the courtyards, which had been converted into halls
by the erection of partitions made of straw matting, were entirely covered with the red silk curtains of honour and with
writings hung upon them expressing good wishes. Presents and
congratulations were received from all parts. During the dinner the most famous actors played upon a stage which had
been specially built for the purpose. On such occasions it is
very rare that entire pieces are given, but only selected acts.
Since the subjects of the dramas are, of course, completely
familiar to every Chinese spectator, he can with ease follow the
action of even a fragment of a piece. The performance was
particularly distinguished by the fact that the costumes of the
historical pieces were exclusively real old silk dresses from the
chests of the K'ung family such as could otherwise only be seen
at the Imperial Court in Peking. Shortly after I had taken my
seat one of the actors came towards me with an ivory tablet on
which the names of the plays which formed the repertoire of
the actors were recorded. The guests of honour were allowed to
choose their favourite piece, which was then performed. It
was then up to the guest to find something suitable at a glance.
Naturally the eyes of every one are turned upon the stranger,
because they are curious to know what play he will choose.
After the performance of the piece it is the custom to give the
actors a tip, a few strands of the pierced coins which were still
current at that time. Fortunately I had instinctively given a
liberal tip, for who could describe my surprise when, after-

wards, the T'ien Kuan (the official of heaven) appeared and performed the pantomime of a magical dance. Thereupon four bearers came with a little table on which the strands of money had been placed, set it down in the middle of the stage and announced in a loud voice: "We thank the great man Wei for his reward." I became, of course, once more the object of general attention, a procedure which was by no means particularly agreeable. I was fortunate, however, because shortly afterwards it was the turn of another guest. The T'ien Kuan appeared again, performed his dance, very briefly and not without some malignant grotesque gestures. Then came the servants with the table, borne by four men, and on it lay a few paltry copper coins. Notwithstanding they called out: "We thank the great man Wang for his reward!" General hilarity ensued. On that occasion, I beheld for the first time the sudden blush of a Chinaman. He held his long sleeve in front of his face and soon disappeared from among the guests. I never discovered whether he had no money on him or if he intended to economize a little in secret.

The festivities lasted until late at night and continued on the following days. I took my leave, grateful for the impressive experience. The marriage of the prince incidentally turned out not to be a happy one, in spite of the beautiful festival. He died childless a few years ago, and today a small child, a nephew whom he adopted, sits upon the throne of the descendant of the master of the thousand families.

I had a curious experience on my journey homeward. As far as Tsinanfu the Chinese pupils and I made the journey together. After discussing the matter with the departmental official, I wanted to take a different road alone. There is a canal, the so-called Hsiaots'ing-Ho, from Tsinanfu running northward parallel to the Yellow River into the gulf of Pechili, into which it runs at Yang Kuo K'ou. From there I wanted to travel overland to Wehsien in order to join the railway there. The canal runs between high dams through a wide plain. Small flat sailing boats, which move at a great pace when wind and weather are favourable, can be seen upon it, and the journey was thus most enjoyable. The boat stopped at various inland Customs stations, which allowed the traveller to walk about on the dykes and to get a view of the country. The nearer one gets to the sea, the more frequently are strange windmills to be seen. They stand in flat salt beds and are pumping instruments for purposes of deriving salt from the sea water, by means of evaporation. Since there are no salt mines in China, all the salt there is either sea salt or else it is won from the salt works in the west.

The boat reached the harbour at last. I had been informed in Tsinanfu that the man in charge of the boat was in official pay and it was therefore only a question of giving him a small tip. Imagine my surprise when I stepped on land intending to take my money with me. I had about one hundred strands of coins. The boatman declared roundly that the money had to remain on board because it just amounted to the price of the journey. I explained the impropriety of his demand calmly, so that eventually he had no objections to offer and seemed prepared to refund, at any rate, a portion of the money, so that I could embark upon the rest of my journey. I had not, however, counted with the mentality of the Chinese woman. In China one can achieve one's purpose by the aid of reason with almost every man, because it is considered a disgrace if a man is not susceptible to the arguments of reason. Curiously enough a similar obligation is not imposed upon woman in China. She does not act logically, but from the depth of her feelings. My boatman had a mother, a horrible old woman. She could not be persuaded that money which was once in one's possession, rightly or wrongly, should ever be refunded. There is nothing in the world which possesses a greater power of swearing than a malignant old Chinese woman. The idea that she should part with a portion of the money made her malicious. Accordingly she took up her stand in front of me and began with a yelling voice to swear, choked only occasionally by tears of rage, and in spite of the aforesaid interruptions, she raised her voice again and again with renewed vigour. She simply let fly against the misdeeds perpetrated by the foreign devils upon poor deserted women. I stood there in amazement and observed the physiological miracle of her ability to continue cursing without interruption, without apparently ever a pause for breathing. She evidently continued to curse while taking in her breath, with the result that there was not the slightest opportunity for a reply. Her vocabulary, though extensive, was by no means equal to her requirements, and, for this reason, she was not in the slightest degree shy of repeating herself. Excited speech always exercises a contagious effect, and all kinds of people, among them very dubious figures, began to gather round us in an ever closer circle. Such coastal places are the homes of smugglers and thieves. Sullen murmurs were beginning to be heard and one or other member of the group stooped to pick up a suitable stone . . . when from the boat behind me, which flew the official ensign, a servant appeared and inquired into the cause of the uproar. I gave him my visiting card and explained the circumstances briefly. He spoke a few words very quietly and firmly, and the group was dispersed in the twinkling of an eye. He called the boatman and said something to him. The old woman disappeared, the man came again and threw himself upon the ground before me. He returned the whole of my money and would take nothing, as the honour that had been bestowed upon his boat by my presence was enough. I gave him a tip and went my way. The owner of the other boat asked me to come in, and I was indeed surprised when I was faced by a good friend, Taotai Fang Yen Nien, who had saved me in this manner. We passed the evening together in conversation. In the meantime a heavy wagon had been hired, in which I could continue my journey. On the way I had to spend another night in a small insignificant-looking inn on the roadside. As there were no large roads here, on which officials travelled, there were also no proper inns. The common room was a stable. I was allowed to climb up a ladder into an arrangement of mats which swayed suspiciously. The animals steamed beneath me. The people sat about for a long time relating all kinds of robber exploits which had recently occurred in the district. They also told a creepy story about a dead girl who had wanted to kill a sleeping guest. Eventually I fell asleep in spite of the noisy trampling of the animals and the monotonous conversation of the men. Neither robbers nor ghosts came to disturb me and I returned safely to Tsingtao.

8

THE HOLY MOUNTAIN

Not far from the birthplace of Confucius lies the Holy Mountain T'aishan, the Chinese Olympus. This mountain stands out from the oldest times of Chinese history, the highest peak in an extensive mountain range. It spreads itself with majestic calm over the region, and at its foot springs flow together from various directions. The clouds brood about its summit and it dispenses rain and sunshine over a wide area, because when its head is covered with clouds, which brood above it, then it draws more and more fog towards itself and the humid winds drive the clouds into cracks and hollows and rain descends upon the land. When it disperses the mists again, exhaling them, in tiny delicate clouds, so that they float gently away and disappear in the blue, the people know that the grey days are over. The sun shines again over the fields and at night the great stars flicker in the deep black sky.

This mysterious brooding has been observed through countless ages and thus it comes about that the spirit of this mountain is considered as holy, and kings and princes came from far away to offer their sacrifices at the foot of the range. The vital forces innate in these proceedings, the mysterious clarity of these powers, have always attracted me. Accordingly, there are temples in all places in China where the spirit of this mighty mountain is revered as the guardian of life and death. Popular belief declares the entrance of the lower world to be found in those temples. In Peking, for instance, there is a temple of the T'aishan, situated in front of the Eastern Gate, in which, especially round about the New Year, sacrificial flames burn day in day out and clouds of incense rise to the sky. In the wide courtyards, the various realms of the lower world are represented with their rulers, the domain of torture, fire, knives, and icy zones. The journey into the beyond is presented to the eye in terrifying pictures. It leads beyond the unhappy river into the lower world, in whose dull waters those unfortunate wretches appear and disappear who have failed by their deeds.

to open the way over the bridges. The road leads further through the village of evil dogs for whom bread is given to the dead, so that they may reach the promontory from which they may look back once more into their old home, which they have had to leave.

In those districts there is also the great wheel. When the souls have been punished and have done penance and have drunk the water of oblivion, they are driven into this wheel, which gives them a new being and then bears them again into one of the paths of life ranging from happy men down to the insects.

Births and deaths are solemnly announced to the spirit of the eastern mountain top, as the T'aishan is also called, with all the pomp of sacrifice. These are remnants of the very ancient nature worship of China, which in many forms and deviations has maintained itself to the present day.

At the foot of the mountain is the little country town of T'aianfu, which owes its entire importance to its proximity to the mountain. Here is the great and holy Tai Miao, which is dedicated to the divinity of the mountain. A secret mystery clings about the temple. Large, wide courtyards stretch out between mighty halls which are surrounded by a crenulated wall, whose corner pavilions of several stories are reminiscent of the forbidden city of Peking. Many monuments from far-off times stand there decaying in ruins. Emperors who have come here to offer their sacrifices to the holy mountain, ordered great tablets to be erected, engraved with long inscriptions. On one stone the picture of an ancient cypress tree has been cut. The picture was painted by the Emperor K'ien Lung himself. On another tablet there are the strange forms of magic signs which serve as a protection against the influence of demons. In the temple halls, on the walls behind the images of the gods, there are old frescoes, which have, however, been renewed from time to time. The abbot lives in hidden inner courts where blossoming bushes provide colour and shade. He has collected offerings from early days in his dwelling: one of the most curious is an old slab of jade, one end of which is cold and the other warm. The difference can be felt quite clearly. He also has in his keeping numbers of amulets and potent magic objects.

Today everything is in the course of inevitable decay. The walls are rotting, the roofs are falling to pieces, and many buildings and trees are mere ruins. The gates of the temple are closed all the year except in the spring during the time of the great pilgrimage. At this period the pilgrims come in crowds to offer their gifts. A gaily coloured turmoil throngs the wide courtyards. The scene is enlivened by a fair during which rubbings of the stone sculptures and all kinds of souvenirs are offered for sale as well as the usual goods provided during a fair. Soothsayers sit at their tables like spiders in their net. They spy out the passer-by who seems troubled with doubts. They beckon to him mysteriously: "The God has a counsel for thee." They manipulate their numbers and their signs and usually they manage to find something which has some relation to the life of their questioner who can then derive some information for himself. These fortune-tellers are to be found all over China. They are not all equally powerful. There are some, however, who appear to be endowed with the power of mediums. There is a man in Japan, for instance, who, in the year 1915, predicted in an unimpeachable manner, and in the main correctly, the end of the war, down to the dethroning of the German Emperor, which no one believed in at that time. The most famous soothsayers in China are those at the sanctuary of the Taoist magician Lü Tüng Tin in Wuch'ang near the Tower of the Yellow Cranes, some of whom have told the future with a truly appalling exactitude.

On the road to the mountain there are many stations which reveal wonders. In the small sacred courtyard of one sanctuary in the vicinity of the town there is a shrine in which are kept the mortal remnants of a Taoist who has attained immortality. His power of concentration was so great that he was able to preserve even his body from decay. He sat there for a long time without taking food. He had ceased to speak and was no longer concerned with the events of the world, listening only to the experiences of the inner light. Thus he remained seated and sits there to this day, dried up like a mummy but not decayed. At a later time his face was gilt. In spite of the gilding one can still see the expression of the man deeply lost in thought. The body has become quite small and has shrunk together. The skin has become a dark, deep brown, and his sinews and bones shimmer through with anatomical accuracy.[1]

Steps and pathways lead right up to the top of the mountain. Some of them are very steep and laborious. Those who are afraid of the effort can have themselves carried in a sedan chair. These sedan chairs are very light structures held together by straps made of leather. The bearers, who come from special families, are of an immensely powerful build. They proceed at a steady rhythmic pace and after a while they swing the chair from one shoulder to the other, which provides the inmate, until he is used to it, with a certain feeling of anxiety while he thus flies through the air. The carriers catch the bearing strap with great certainty on their other shoulder and continue with a firm and regular step. The hiring of these carriers is always quite an event. You have to arrange the price and the number of carriers you want with the greatest exactitude beforehand. These chairs are carried by only two men, but one has to hire three to five according to one's weight, and the men relieve each other at the various stations. One proceeds at a rapid pace through the plain in front of the town towards the mountains where the pace slackens as the incline begins.

The mountain is entirely submerged in an atmosphere of historical memories. In the whole of Shantung, and in an even wider area, you find at street corners or on the gables of houses, which are situated on roads leading in a direction favourable to spooks, the so-called T'aishan stones, bearing the inscription "T'aishan Shih Kan Tang," which means "the stone of Taishan dares to oppose." People have speculated a great deal concern-

---

[1] There are of course natural "explanations," which I am well aware of, for this as for other phenomena. What I want to give here is the experience of the T'aishan, the impression he has conveyed for thousands of years to the Chinese people.

ing these strange stones, which in reality do not emanate from the T'aishan at all, but have been made into T'aishan stones merely by virtue of their inscription. They are undoubtedly the remains of an ancient stone cult. Eventually the explanation was adopted that, in the case of these inscriptions, the people were not concerned with the stones as such, but merely that the holy Shih Kan Tang of the T'aishan was invoked as a protective spirit. It is a fact that such a Shih Kan Tang did live on the T'aishan who was equipped with magical powers, and occasionally other protective saints are referred to. On the other hand, there can be no doubt that in the popular belief it is the T'aishan stone which possesses magic and protective forces.

The mountain is not altogether bare, as most of the mountains are in modern China, ever since the kings and princes of antiquity have destroyed the primeval forests with their fire-hunting. The requirements of the ever-increasing population has exterminated the new trees which grew, and goats and sheep have taken care that no new growth can ever develop. Far up on the slope of the T'aishan there are holy trees. These are pine trees and cypresses which in the lower reaches, particularly in the neighbourhood of the monasteries, have formed themselves into groves and small woods, while, higher up, at the extremity of the tree-limit, they either stand alone as individual heroes, or in small groups, in their struggle against wind and weather. Some of them have been given personal titles, bestowed upon them by earlier potentates to whom they gave shade and protection.

All the roads are alive with pilgrims during the special pilgrim season. These pilgrims often come from far away in obedience to vows or to express their desire to the gods, for the T'aishan is inhabited by many divinities. Female as well as male gods are represented. At a fairly low level there is the Tou Mu Kung, the temple of the Mother of the North Star. This sanctuary is guarded by Buddhist nuns, who have not always preserved the full severity of their calling in the presence of their streams of visitors. Their nunnery is indeed surrounded by stout walls, and prickly branches on the walls are a warning to him who would attempt to scale them recklessly. Why should they scare him? The nunnery has, after all, a gate and doors through which the pious pilgrim can enter by a direct path. The old Mother of the North Star is a kindly goddess and her sanctuary possesses charming corners with exquisite views upon the mountain, and there are chattering brooks. The nuns have a sympathetic heart for the tired pilgrims. Sometimes, however, it happened that the boundary line between Buddhistic compassion for all living creatures and more worldly emotions became blurred. The nunnery became a centre of attraction for amateur pilgrims and a scandal for all pious souls. So one day a competent official appeared, who put things in order. The nuns were sent away to be married and a school was started in the nunnery. Times change, however, and though the school is still there today, the nuns have also returned and arrange their sanctuary beautifully once more.

There are also other sides to the mountain. It is terrible there during summer nights when the tempests rage and the water hustles along the mountain walls. For nights on end, one stroke of lightning succeeds another. The black and gaping night grows increasingly black through the alternation of the violet serpents which shoot across the sky or strike into the rocks with a crash. Many a summer visitor has had to feel the wrath of the gods, when the beams of the house in which he had sought shelter for the night began to sway and he was crushed in his bed beneath the thundering collapse of timber and tiles, while his dog whimpered outside the door, trying to reach his master, and frightened by the raging of the elements whose shrieking echoes are thrown from the rocks into the hut which men erect on the ground where dragons and the spirits of the cloud gambol.

The clouds often descend from the mountain tops to browse in the ravines and valleys. Torrents of rain fall and the wind whistles through the holes in the rocks and makes the ancient pines groan as it passes through their hairy branches and shakes them. The effect is as of a dance of ghosts. Then a wet white veil is suspended in front of the landscape; it penetrates cloaks and rugs, and again it will dissolve in parts, leaving its rags attached to crannies in the rocks, revealing vistas of deep valleys at sudden intervals. Then all at once the valleys are closed up again and a small strip of sun permits a view, somewhere through the air, of improbably distant green plains and the silvery course of rivers. The clouds float up and down and they cook, brew as it were, the weather to their taste. An eagle traverses a rift in the clouds and a croaking raven floats into a wall of fog in his slow flight. Sometimes the mists are absorbed and the rocks seem to advance, tall and steep upon the path. The road rises, glittering with humidity and dripping with sickering water. Soon a gate is reached, the gate where "one must leave the house behind." Once more you look down into the wide country. It is a small flat place surrounded by huts for the traveller's rest. They say that Confucius halted here when he climbed up the mountain with his disciples. The world is said to have seemed small to him from this height.

The path soon takes a turn. The steps lead solemnly and severely into the mountain. At one corner there is a pavilion with a bridge affording rest and a fine view to the traveller. A waterfall runs over the rocks and beneath the bridge. Inscriptions and verses which have been chiselled into the stone sing the praises of this landscape. Famous men from all ages have left their trace in writings on the rocks, which constitute a collection of poems and wise sayings. It is indicative of our modern age, lacking in piety, that an apothecary from Peking attempted to join this distinguished gathering. He had a long inscription carved in beautiful signs into one of the rocks to recommend his medicaments. Fortunately the inscription did not remain there for long. It was discovered by the official under whose care this holy district, protected by nature, stands and the irreverent merchant had to erase his advertisement at his own expense. Such severity is satisfying. Here at least is a place in which one can face nature and history undisturbed, where the ugly advertisements of cigarette manufacturers or of the swindlers who offer elixirs of life do not spoil the landscape, whereas they have covered the whole of China with a revolting mushroom growth of vulgar publicity.

The old times were not, of course, devoid of their own difficulties. Especially during the pilgrimage period, the mountain is full of beggars of all kinds, who demand their share in the feast of life. Hideous creatures with disgusting diseases crowd about you, pale children and horrible cripples crawl about; some of them throw themselves on the ground, so that you have to step over them; some have arranged corners in the rocks with piled-up stones, behind which they establish their dwellings. Some whimper in a broken voice, others beat their heads fiercely and ruthlessly against the stones until you give them something. Crippled limbs are extended to you. Blind men feel their way towards you, and lame children weep. Ossified people of incredible senility make dumb rumbling noises. And all, all of them want money, want sympathy, and when sympathy is not evoked, they have recourse to the horror of their aspect, from which one must buy one's freedom with a gift.

This host of misery which lines the pilgrim's path is a frightful experience. If one did not know that this misery is a highly organized trade, in which crippled are hired and advantageous positions are rented, it would be still more unbearable. Thus the impression of the grotesqueness of the strangest of all trades attenuates somewhat the inner revolt at the possibility of so much human suffering. It shows that life, even in the most horrible hell, adapts itself to make it supportable. You have to supply yourself with a sufficiency of small change so that you can hand a coin to every beggar. Woe to the man whose money runs out on the way! An efficient European can pass through the rows of beggars a stranger without giving anything. The beggars get accustomed to it after a few attempts and they accept such a European as they do an event of nature which crosses their path. If a tiger crossed the road, he would not give alms either. Once the traveller has entered upon the path of compassion, and has begun to give alms and should wish to stop half-way, he has to reckon, not merely with their greed, but also with the offended feeling of justice which will not permit unequal treatment. You are pursued by growling and yelling creatures who make you understand the despair which seized the men of antiquity when the Furies clung to their feet. "The gate of kindness is easy to open, but hard to close" is a Chinese proverb which has to be well considered in the whole of China, if a charitable man is not to break down.

Gradually you reach greater and greater heights, by steep paths beyond the tree level. There is a small tea-house near the "Five dignitaries," a few fir trees, beneath which an emperor found shelter from the rain. There are no longer five trees, for the lightning has lately felled one of them. From here the steep staircase leads to the Southern Gate of Heaven. The steps are small and almost as high as one's knee. Overhanging rocks threaten your path on the right and on the left and chasms open up below. Some of the steps give way when you stand upon them, and others are broken or at an incline. You must not suffer from dizziness if you want to enjoy the ascent, especially in damp weather, when the mossy stones grow slippery and drifts of fog float hither and thither. Owing to the fog the gaping chasms appear closed sometimes, only to open suddenly again, revealing profound abysses so that everything seems dizzy and uncertain. Chains have been fixed on both sides of the stairs for dizzy pilgrims, but they are not of much use as for long stretches they are broken and do not in any way induce a feeling of security. The best way is to proceed at a steady pace and, as it says in the fairy tales, "do not look about to the right or to the left, but straight ahead and you will be at peace." Eventually you arrive at the Gate of Heaven and enter in. At that place I once met a little old Chinese mother who climbed bravely upwards with her small bandaged feet and her pilgrim staff. I asked where she came from. She had walked many miles and yet she was cheerful, in fact she displayed an almost unaccountable exuberance. I inquired why she had set out upon this arduous pilgrimage. She replied: "It is not hard, the pilgrimage; I am now seventy years old and my life lies behind me. There is nothing I have to hope for or to fear; but that I have got so far, that the old Lord of Heaven has helped me through all these many years when I brought up my sons and grandsons and through all the misery and burden of life, makes me grateful. And at the end, I want to show this to him. I ask nothing and I avoid nothing. I am quite quiet, and so the journey was not hard." I often remember the cheerful old woman and her visit to the Lord of Heaven on the T'aishan.

If you go in at the Southern Gate of Heaven, you enter upon a very special district. A town of temples rises before you. First, there are the huts in which the bearers and the pilgrims spend the night, and then there are a large number of temples and holy places. The biggest temple is that of the old Mother of the T'aishan. Here very special forces preside. The spirit of the mountain is, as we have seen, the master over life and death. Just as death is announced in his temple so that the dead may find accompaniment into the beyond, so the old Mother of the T'aishan also has the power to give life. Women who wish for children, and especially for sons, come to her to sacrifice. The sacrifices are indeed varied. The altar is surrounded by a grille behind which the gifts are thrown. You can see heaps of pieces of money. Unminted silver and jewelry are also offered. The poor, who have nothing else, offer a piece of bread. The food disappears overnight. There are an enormous number of temple rats who have a good time of it, but it is a good sign if such an offering is accepted by the divinity. The gifts of silver and money are also removed from time to time. They are supposed to serve for the upkeep of the temple. Rich gifts of sacrificial vessels, entire chapels of bronze and gilt bronze tiles bear testimony to the life-giving force of the great goddess. Her powers are believed in not only in China. Many a foreigner has been driven to believe in her. From Tsingtao, for instance, a few German families made the pilgrimage to the T'aishan once, merely for the pleasure of the journey in the spring. When they came to the temple, they became exuberant and the women threw their gifts through the grille. You cannot play with the old Mother of the T'aishan. They returned home with their husbands and before the year was over they were blessed with strong healthy boys. The Chinese who heard about it greeted these happy events with special satisfaction.

There is a temple of Confucius not far from this miraculous place. It stands there somewhat deserted. It is as if the sage was not quite happy in this company. There was a time—now long ago—when the country folk made efforts to include him in the circle of the gods who dispensed happiness. They burnt incense and offered up sacrifices and the women came to him with their domestic troubles. The custom did not last very long for it was too contradictory to the significance of the saint. An Imperial edict forbade this kind of sacrifice and Confucius continued to be honoured as the illustrious example of wisdom and virtue and the noble teacher of the ten thousand generations.

Quite close to the top there is a deep abyss where a strange custom was practised for many centuries. Pious daughters, whose parents were ill or were the victims of other sufferings, came up here. They prayed for their parents for help in their need and offered themselves in sacrifice and took the fatal jump into the bottomless pit. This dizzy abyss has something mysterious and enticing about it and many a young human life has here come to a sudden end. The rock was popularly called "The rock of the sacrifice of life." A new and more humane period has put an end to these dark practices. It was forbidden to take the fatal jump and a wall was erected which made the abyss inaccessible. From then on, the place was called "the rock of the preservation of life."

The highest point of the mountain is surmounted by a temple. There is a stone wall round the very top within the temple courtyard, which is shut in by buildings on all sides. The real temple is on the north side. It is dedicated to the Jade Ruler, the Lord of Heaven. On the west side there is the dwelling of the priest, and on the east are rooms for the accommodation of visitors. Towards the back there is a more extensive hall which can only be inhabited during the height of the summer, for although the T'aishan is only 4,800 feet high, the top is pretty cool even when there is the greatest heat in the valley. Many a pilgrim, who only thought of the heat of the valley, has spent a frosty night up there.

When I was on top for the first time, the T'aishan was not yet well known among foreigners. Richthofen did indeed pass at the foot of the T'aishan, but his companions had not told him the importance of the place. Others had followed in his wake. Even in these days there were missionaries who spent their summer holidays regularly on the T'aishan. Notwithstanding, globe-trotters came from time to time who boasted in their travel books that they were the first Europeans who had climbed the T'aishan. Such statements are psychologically quite intelligible, for every globe-trotter likes, after all, to enjoy the sensations of a discoverer.

When I climbed to the top for the first time, clouds and fog concealed the mountain during the ascent. In the evening a mild spring rain set in, which drove the clouds like steam away into the blue air. At night the stars looked down from heaven, large and luminous, as if one were really nearer to them up there. The priests were old Taoists, who told mysterious sagas and fairy tales while the water boiled on the flickering fire and we drank steaming tea together.

Shortly before my departure from China, I made another excursion to the holy mountain with a few intimate friends. Much had changed in the meantime. The railway now runs close to it, and the modern hotel near the station provides comfortable lodgings. The temple walls and everything reminiscent of antiquity is more and more in ruins. The sanctuary of divine listening—Ling Ying Si—had been burnt down, and the bronze figures of the divinities stood in the open near the huge old trees in the court. The ascent was again damp and rainy. The evening at the top was cold and stormy. The wind howled in every key and shook the doors while we sat together over our grog. Frequently, cold drifts of damp clouds were blown in upon us. The priest had been changed. I wanted to talk to him again about the mountain and its secrets, but he had no mind for such things. He belonged to the modern school, and when he heard that I came from Peking, he was interested above all in news of the leaders of the modern literary movement and in their activities.

The night was restless and it rained in buckets, but the morning rewarded us for everything. We stepped out into the open and the fog was rent asunder suddenly like a curtain. Our vision extended as far as the horizon where the sun approached from behind red glowing strips of clouds, while white clouds hung in the folds over the mountain and the river flickered over the plain. It only lasted a moment and the curtain closed again. The clouds browsed once more and the damp wind blew them about.

On our way down we had another experience. On the previous day one of the leather straps of my sedan chair had got loose. I had told the bearers to put it right overnight. They had not done it, for they thought that it would still hold. It is sometimes an advantage in China not to know Chinese. You certainly lose in self-respect if you are condemned to hear the conversations that the bearers hold about you. You often feel sorry for these people for leading the undignified existence of weight-carrying animals. It is, however, merely a question of point of view; they speak together about the "burden" which they bear in a perfectly harmless manner. These burdens are judged only according to size and weight. They do not know the feeling that it is undignified for them, as human beings, to carry other men about. What they carry is not in the least considered as human.

While we were being carried at a rapid pace down the steep steps from the Southern Gate of Heaven (for just as the ascent was slow the descent was speedy) I listened to the following conversation. One of my bearers began to whimper quietly: "Today the steps are so smooth and I slip at every step; my shoes do not fit either, and on the top of it, my chap is too heavy. I think all the time that before the day is over I will have a fall."

There was a particularly wild fellow among the bearers who did not happen to be on duty just then and therefore walked alongside. He said: "Why don't you throw him over and let him have an accident? I don't suppose you'll get much of a tip from that one, anyhow." At that moment the depth became visible through a rift in the clouds. A swing—and my chair sat on the other shoulder of the bearer. "It's all very well for you to talk," my bearer began again, "but if I let this one fall, I shall fall with him, and apart from that, there is the responsibility."

"Oh, rubbish!" the other maintained, "you only have to let the leather strap, which as I see is practically worn through anyway, get a bit loose and then everything works of its own accord and nobody can say anything." "Get out of the road," my bearer replied, because the other had stopped in his path so that he very nearly tripped. "You only talk, but I really wish that we were down below, the leather strap is getting thinner and thinner and won't last much longer."

"Yes, it's cracking already!" a third bearer ejaculated and took hold of the sedan chair on one side to be able to lend a hand in case of need.

The ladies fortunately heard nothing of this conversation. Accordingly their peace was undisturbed, and we arrived at the bottom of the steps safely. We had hardly started along the level, when my sedan chair really gave way and collapsed. The leather strap had to be renewed, after all. That is always the way. Any one who has made the ascent several times becomes pretty hardened. It does indeed happen frequently that a chair breaks down on arrival at the bottom, but precisely in the worst places, where it is so steep that the head of the bearer in front is on a level with the knees of the one behind and where any break-down would be fatal, nothing happens. I have never heard that an accident has occurred.

It is always an experience to go up to this mountain. You continue to see its cloudy top rise up out of the host of the other hills and it seems as if it were revealing a secret every time: the secret of the connection between life and death in that great stillness whose symbol is the sign "Mountain" in *The Book of Change*. And one thinks of that other line: "I will lift up mine eyes unto the hills, from whence cometh my help." After all, the revelation of a secret is also expressed in these words.

9

CAVE TEMPLES IN YÜNKANG

LEAVES FROM MY DIARY

I

I WAS seated at a Chinese table in the lamplight of an inn. My travelling bed was already prepared on the resting-place built of bricks near the back wall of the room, which was, incidentally, quite clean. Outside, the clear autumn moon, which lights the wanderer on his way, hung in the sky. During the day, the railway journey had carried me two hundred and fifty miles. I had left the southern gate of Peking at seven o'clock in the morning. The journey took me at first all round the Manchu town with its walls and gates as far as the north-western entrance of the city, from where the train was to leave for Tat-ungfu in Shansi, the present goal of my journey.

I travelled first northwards through the plain to Nank'ou, where the mountain locomotive joins the train to pull it over the considerable height of the pass. At Ts'inglungch'iao, the bridge of the black dragon, the railway cuts through the inner ring of the Chinese wall and is the usual objective of the travellers who wish to see the Chinese wall. From there the journey proceeds through tunnels and rocky valleys, through stony plains and past bare mountains farther and farther along the caravan road towards the north-west. At three o'clock in the afternoon I reached Kalgan, the frontier town of Mongolia. The town lies in a wide depression between the mountains and somehow resembles in this way the situation of villages at the southern foot of the Alps. The houses are all made of clay: they are low and have flat roofs. The many inns make the town seem more like a caravanserai than like a proper settlement. At this place the outer ring of the Great Wall, the real protection against the wild populations of the north, comes quite close to the railway. From here the train winds along a clay valley between the range of the mountains towards the south-west. The river valley is very picturesque, especially at this time when everything is green and the wide river-bed is covered with a network of rapid rivulets. The district shows that it was once a region of frontier outposts. Everywhere on the heights there are towers from which fire signals used to be given, and in the valleys near the rivers there are military camps surrounded by walls and guarded by watch-towers which have fallen into decay years and years ago. The villages and towns are also surrounded by walls. All their fortifications have become superfluous long ago, since Mongolia belongs to China and invasions no longer take place. It is a quiescent volcano, which may, however, proceed to erupt once more, though such an event need not be feared in the near future. Mongolia has made itself independent. The Chinese troops of General Haü have been destroyed by the forces of Baron Ungern-Sternberg, and their bones are said to bleach still in the sun. Even the good fortune of this bold commander of a hired army turned. He was mown down by the Russian Bolshevists and killed. Mongolia had made itself into an independent republic under Bolshevik leadership. They issued a declaration to the effect that they renounced the idea of avenging the monstrosities perpetrated upon them by the Chinese.

II

YÜNKANG,
3rd of September

"Sleep not, sleep no more!
The horses neigh
In the stables, the servants are awake."

We got up very early before dawn and were under way when the city gates were opened. The cart with the luggage and the servants followed us. The town of Tat'ungfu is entered by the northern gate. Bridges and roads for modern traffic are in course of construction. The outer northern gate leads first of all into a large empty space. In the old times, when Tat'ungfu was a place of considerable importance for the frontier watch, this space was the northern suburb. The only remnants of those days is a temple structure on the north side. Today the entire place is cultivated, and in the autumn it is used for manoeuvres. The province of Shansi has a very competent governor who has maintained his position in spite of all the political changes; and his influence extends as far as Tat'ungfu, which is divided from the capital of the province T'aiyüanfu through wide ranges of mountains. Certain external failures are evident none the less. The old northern gate was no longer safe. To protect the inhabitants from this danger, it was walled up and another one was built next to it. This construction was to be modern. Thus, above the gate a building of several stories, meant to serve as a watch-tower, was erected and its appearance is of a specially selected European ugliness. As it can be seen a long way off, it lends its stamp to the town. Why does this age document itself of necessity with bad taste? The gate will only be beautiful when it is altogether a ruin. Into the bargain, it has been constructed with all the solidity of the massive ugliness of the European house of the 'eighties!

Friendly soldiers stood at the gate, inquired after our names and where we came from and allowed us to pass, and speeded us on our way with their good wishes. We then entered the town, whose activity is still quite old-fashioned and but little influenced by our modern age. Figures of dragons on the roofs display curious cock-crests such as can be seen nowhere else. Small lions of clay sit on top of the chimneys gazing pensively into the rising smoke. A live dog can be seen climbing about the roof, a dog who has learned to climb from the cats. The windows are often surmounted by rounded arches and decorated with delicate ornaments. Life pulsates in the midst of busy activity. The smiths stand in front of their doors and hammer their iron to a rhythmic beat. Merchants spread their wares on the floor. They have much fine fruit to offer: red apples and also peaches and melons of all shapes and colours and onions on long stems. All these products flourish splendidly in the high plain of Tat'ungfu, whereas the corn, which is sown in rotation without much manure, grows more poorly and to a lower height than in the other parts of China. In the region of the great wall they cultivate buckwheat, and here in the west, at a height of 5,000 to 5,500 feet, they grow oats.

The Chinese houses squat together in peaceful friendliness, though a few oddities of an ugly and European style rise from among them. Here live photographers, dental mechanics and the vendors of European and Japanese rubbish. Yet immediately next to such monstrosities you can find, for instance, a side alley leading into an untouched old quarter. There you can see a dragon wall from the Ming period built with marvellous coloured glazed tiles. The dragons are treated with freedom and vigour and the colours are of an harmonious magnificence which makes the wall into a first-class work of art. In front of it there are parts of stone lions whose archaic severity reminds us of romanesque sculpture. All these things belong to a ruined temple of San Kuan. The San Kuan are the Indian Trimurti Brahma Vishnu-Shiva, dressed up in Chinese Taoist garb. The main road leads to the south. There are four wooden gateways on which the governor has had proverbs of wisdom carved for the people to see.

You can read, for instance:

> "A true citizen should fear three things:
> He should fear God
> He should fear the law
> He should fear the report of men!"

From here one turns to the west and the next cross-roads is covered by a temple consisting of gates through which men pass from north to south and east to west. Those who pass through them are said to partake of the blessings of the divinity. The western gate of the town, through which one goes towards Yünkang, is in rapid process of decay. If sufficient means are found, a monstrosity similar to that above the north gate will probably be constructed. It is to be hoped that the money will not be found for a long time until, in the meanwhile, good taste will have returned in the domain of Chinese architecture. The corners between the inner and the outer gate, usually heaps of refuse, are here planted with acacias. Along the road there is an inscription directed against the activity of robbers and against the evil conduct of life.

As soon as you step out of the western gate, the wide plain stretches in front of you to the foot of the hills which are veiled in blue mist. The view over the wide fruitful plain is enchanting. The district is thinly populated. Whereas in Shantung, for instance, the villages jostle each other so closely that the extremities of the horizon appear to be sown with human settlements in the distance as much as in the immediate vicinity, you may wander here for hours before reaching the next village, and the settlements are surrounded by walls with watch-towers which lend them a fortified appearance. The road, which is filled by a river during the rainy season, has cut its way several yards into the ground as the result of the traffic of centuries. A path leads along the fields at the edge of the height. The downpours of rain frequently break away the earth and disclose her secrets. In this way during the last rainfall a human skeleton had been washed up which had lain hidden there along the path: I had to think of Chuangtse who also experienced an encounter with the bones of the dead and used them as a pretext for considering the mystery of life and death.

The plain extends far and wide. To dispel, as it were, the blue from the mountains one must shorten the distance that separates them from the beholder. The roads offer little variety: a ruined temple situated opposite to a village encircled by a wall, a large modern school building in the distance, a lonely farm also behind walls, and for the rest nothing but wide fields, some of which yield only a meagre crop. Caravans of donkeys and mules passed us on our way. A man called out to us that our carriage had preceded us and was waiting for us in the hills, whose blue has at last dissolved. Ringed rocks and scanty grass, a tower for fire signals in ruins, stand at the entrance to the hills. The stone path leads steeply up the river-bed and the sheep and goats graze on the slopes, and eventually we reach the huts of the little mountain village. There is a small inn at its farther end where our cart had stopped and the servants had already prepared refreshments of tea and fruit. The district provides small apples which are completely red and wonderful and refreshing watermelons. I was rather tired and therefore sat in the cart for a time, a proceeding which demanded a great deal of self-control, because one of the horses had a big open wound on his back and was consequently tortured all the more by the flies. It drew its burden in silence and suffered without people noticing it. The tortured dumb animals also long for rest and salvation.

The road led steeply upwards over the path beyond which we reached the valley of the Wu Chou River with its wide and violent course. There are coal mines near by. Both the banks of the river are formed by low but steep hills whose meagre growth of grass nourishes herds of sheep and goats which cover the slope in the distance, looking like thickly sown white dots. The path had been hewn on one side into the stone of the slope. The recent downpour of rain had torn large gaps into the road in many places so that the travelling carts preferred to ramble through the bed of the river.

At one place, where the bed of the river widens, there is a small picturesque temple of the divine protector Kuanti set against the vertical rock into which the elements have carved a few caves. The stone here is a conglomeration of rough-grained substance. In front of the gate of the temple there is a picture of the faithful horse of the god who in antiquity was a knight without fear or blemish. The little steed heals all ills. You need only rub that place on its body whose corresponding portion is diseased in your own body. In front of the temple there is a small place with tall rustling trees, which provide shadow and rest for the donkeys and their drivers. At the edge of the river there is a stage on which from time to time holy legends of the past and modern comedies are played in honour of the god, who is just able to watch the performance from his seat. These plays are also destined for the amusement of the inhabitants of the surrounding villages. The whole place, incidentally, is covered to the height of a yard with alluvial soil so that the stage, which used to be raised, now stands on level ground. Thus a few fields have been washed away from somewhere and deposited here at the whim of the river to no one's advantage and to the detriment of the former owner. Higher up on the road we encountered a village consisting of huts, vaulted like caves and covered with flat roofs, and there is also a theatrical stage whose pillars display the bowed heads of dragons as capitals, according to the model of the temple of Yünkang. A further halt is provided by a mountain temple of the goddess of charity Kuanyin, part of which stretches over the road in the form of a gate building. In front of it there is a marvellous dragon wall, made of beautiful glazed tiles of the Ming period. On the slopes in front of the dwelling of the youth who administers the temple there are fire-red geraniums.

III

Eventually we saw, in front of a wall which appeared to shut off the valley beyond us, a village and the temple of Yünkang. The remnants of a castle of the Ming period stand on the rocks which loom above them. Along the edge of the road the rock walls have been turned at first in isolated instances, and then in an ever closer sequence of caves, into stone figures.

Two high trees grow out of the courtyard of the temple, whose wide peacock-green roofs of glazed tiles seemed to be glued against the wall of rocks. On entering, the dogs retired shyly. A tablet announces that it is the temple of the stone Buddha which the traveller enters. To the right and to the left two colossal divine guardians threaten the visitor with their terrible expression. First the secondary priest appears, a young man who does not always lead the severely ascetic life, but refreshes himself on occasions with a drop of brandy. He looks after the luggage. The abbot comes out from the farther gate, a calm gentle man, and appoints a lodging for us in the inner courtyard in the immediate vicinity of the great hall of Buddha.

The courtyard lies there in the bright sunshine, and gay

flowers grow among the cracks in the tiles and bow to the sun-light. Two four-legged griffons with scaly bodies and hoofs stand on guard in front of the flowers and the temple. They are magnificent creatures. It is a pity that one of them once lost his muzzle and the other his entire head, and the damage has now been mended by new work in clay according to the old pattern. We rested a while in the cool room. Yünkang is noticeably cooler, even in the sunlight, than Peking. The monastery is situated probably not less than 6,000 feet above sea-level. In the circumstances it is not surprising that the kaoliang, which usually grows in China to a height of over three yards, stands here no higher than the rye does at home. The abbot told us about the recent rainfall which has carried away several of his fields during the last few weeks.

After we had rested and dined, we set about visiting the temple. Its history is more than a thousand years old. When the Tungusian race of the Toba, related to the Manchus, in-vaded northern Shansi, they founded a capital with the name of Yün Chung, which means "in the midst of the clouds." As a Chinese dynasty they called themselves We and ruled over a part of China under this name into the middle of the sixth century. The first rulers, determined and energetic men, for-bade their subjects the use of their indigenous costume, lan-guage and religion. The Tungusians were to become China-men in all respects. These rulers were the most ardent apostles of Buddhism and not dissimilar from the Manchus. In Yün Chung, the "rock of the clouds," hundreds and thousands of Buddhistic figures were accordingly carved in stone. Entire caves were cut into the mountains, whose walls were entirely converted into large and small statues of Buddha. This was a labour which lasted for years and new grottoes were started continuously. The visitor imagines that he can notice a tech-nical advance in the work as he moves from east to west. The figures become more delicate and suave. Curiously enough, inscriptions from this period are altogether missing, which ex-plains why this district attracted little attention from the scholars of Chinese antiquity.

The figures and grottoes are formed out of a coarsely grained standstone which lies upon a substructure of clay slate. Both stones deteriorate rapidly from exposure and the statues have therefore suffered considerable damage. Evidently temples had been built in front of the caves on the exterior of the mountain wall through which the caves could be approached, some of which were situated at a considerable height above the level ground. Traces can still be seen of holes which served to fix the structure of the roofs. These temples were later on destroyed, or else they fell into decay.

During the Ming period the district played an important part once more as a boundary and protective territory against the invasion of the Mongols. The remnants of the wall which have been preserved above the rock grottoes and the plateau date from this period. The aspect of these ruins is in its way reminiscent of a Roman castle. There had probably been a fortified camp up there. In the village itself there are also two gateways whose form suggests Egyptian pylons. Every now and again fragments of old porcelain are found in the ground.

The temple, which consists of two large halves, each of several stories which cover the interior of the hollowed-out rock, dates according to an inscription from the Ming Emperor Wan Li (1573-1619), and is particularly distinguished by its marvellous peacock-blue roofs. The edifice has been repaired on various occasions, the last time at the instance of a Mongolian prince, who also had some Mongol inscriptions carved into the place. As the stone is very soft, it decomposes even inside the cave where it is not exposed to the wind. The procedure of repair varies. Wherever possible, the painting is simply renewed and the damaged places are covered with clay. More serious damage is mended by covering the entire statue with a coat of clay and paper upon which, with greater or lesser taste, the previous lineaments are painted in colours and sometimes gilt. If the decay has progressed too far, holes are drilled into the stone to fix plugs which support the new coat of clay. If such a renewed coating falls off in the course of time then the decay spreads of course from the holes with particular rapidity. In those cases where the forms of the figures are melting away altogether, they are simply turned into a clay background upon which pictures are painted in colour. These paintings, just as some others, reveal, in spite of their relatively modern origin, a very good technique and their intellectual content is more powerful than is usually the case in such temple pictures.

In both temples there are galleries and bridges, often of a very dangerous kind, which lead to small grottoes, high up in the rocks. Some of these bridges can still be used with caution, others are in such a state of collapse that it is no longer possible to walk upon them.

To the east and to the west, there is an entire town of further grottoes, which are, however, in a more advanced state of decay than the temple grottoes. The eastern grottoes serve for the most part as nocturnal resting-places for animals and men who come this way. The walls are smoky and traces of fire are dispersed upon the floor. The western caves have been partly walled up in front and turned into regular dwellings for the peasants of the village. These people are born, grow up and die in view of the great remnants of the past, which watch in their holy stillness the petty turmoil of men with the same calm with which they watch the activities of the mountain dwarfs who have settled in other caves. In this way man comes and goes and the rocks remain. The rocks, however, do not possess permanence. Silently, one grain of sand after another slips down to the ground. Whatever wears away from the upper parts of the figures buries the lower portions more and more. While in this way the stone comes and goes, man remains. Not the individual, but the great forms and traditions from which the individual is formed. In the ancient days, when these rock temples were built, the Tungusian Tobas came into the land. They wore a different costume from that of the Chinese. They wrapped a cloth round their heads, and the rest of their garments differed also from the clothes worn by the people of the Middle Kingdom. Their rulers forbade the Tun-

gusian costume and wanted their people to resemble the cultivated men of the Middle Kingdom. They have passed away
with all their commandments and prohibitions, and others
have come and gone in the course of the centuries. If you travel
through this region today, you meet men whose appearance
still differs from that of the Chinese. They twist a cloth
about their head and wear peculiar outer garments which leave
the arms and the greater part of the chest bare. The women
wear the same dress, a custom which is unheard of elsewhere
in China. Where does this costume come from? Is it a remnant
of the traditions of the Tobas which has lasted longer than
the monuments of bronze and stone? . . .

Such thoughts passed through my mind as I sat in front of
one of the grottoes after sunset. Below me, in the village, the
smoke rose up peacefully from the small huts. Life proceeded
on its way with the regularity with which the seasons march
over the earth with their silent tread. The sky was lit with the
last colours of the evening. A Kuanyin sat in front of me pensively in her stone niche resting her head in her hand, and high
above me, in the clouds, two birds flew past who came from far
away, beyond the mountain. . . .

IV

YÜNKANG,
4th of September

The impression which the monastery temple made upon me
when the priest first led us into it cannot be expressed better
than in the words of Han Yü, whose poem "Mountain Rocks"
expresses the atmosphere of Yünkang extraordinarily well:

"The monk says that on these ancient walls
The Buddhist paintings are fine;
But when with his torch he lights them up
There is little to be seen."

I had a curious experience when I stayed alone in the rock
temple. As I entered it was quite dark, so that nothing could

be distinguished. When I had waited for a while quietly and had, as it were, collected myself, the mountain seemed to open its eyes. One image after another stepped out of the night, became alive and began to talk. The large images uttered deep powerful chords, the small and ever smaller ones resounded with a delicate melody, and eventually the room in the depth of the mountain was filled with a heavenly song of praise, which continued at a greater and greater distance more and more delicately right up to the greatest heights. When I had passed through this inner experience of an inaudible heavenly music, I understood why in the old legends they speak so often of cave heavens. These legends and sagas have found their last expression still in the "Peach-blossom-well" of T'ao Yüan Ming. I also realized why among the signs of *The Book of Changes,* the "Heaven in the midst of the mountain" occurs as a picture where it says: "Thus the nobleman learns many words of the ancient days and deeds of the past to advance his being." Have these things not been said as if in view of such a sanctuary in which the centuries look down upon us and widen and enlarge the soul? Curiously enough in this grotto the Gothic cathedrals seemed to loom up before me. They too possess the mysterious darkness which points the soul to itself, and they too have the melody which rises up from the voices of the stones. Gothic architecture also overcomes the weight of the stone and lends it life by turning it into a plant which grows upwards, stretching and twining so that everything turns into motion. Here in Yükang it goes a step farther: the stone exhales, not only life, but a soul. Here they are not plants in which weight and gravity are dissolved, but hundreds and thousands of human figures and faces, each one of which has a soul, and joins in harmony in the song of eternity.

v

> "The night is deep. At last we can rest,
> For the noise of the insects has stopped.
> A clear moon rises over the peak;
> Its beams enter at the door."

ınt to sleep and in my dream the secret of this temple
waı ⁊ealed to me. I saw the world in its progress; I saw the
watı low in the river, ever changing and yet ever the same.
Ofteı something lay in the way. Then the water would squirt
up, to be struck by a ray of sunshine which it caught and
reflected in gay colours. When I looked more closely, the
water of the river was stone, grey sandstone which was as soft
as water, changing and flowing. It was merely the times which
were different when the stone transformed itself. But I stood on
the shore of eternity and what does time mean then? The gay
colours of the rainbow were the images, hewn into the rock,
which glittered and shone. They grew dull and disappeared
like the forms which had shaped the waves of the water. I
found myself again in the grotto of the temple. Out of the
dusky night it gradually began to glow; figures grew out of the
stone and put on forms, and then they dissolved again into
sound. I suddenly felt a shiver pass over me. . . .

I awoke. Round about me everything was quiet, and only
the moon lay in a white strip upon the ground. I then remembered the song of Li T'ai Po:

"Close by my bed there shone a strange light;
Could it be hoar-frost shining on the floor?
I looked up: the moon was over the hill.
I looked down, and thought of my native land."

The temple bell rang deeply through the night as though to
question and to caution. I had to think about my dream and
then I went to sleep again, and only awoke when the crowing
of the cocks gradually penetrated the turmoil of my dreams.

VI

TAT'UNGFU,
5th of September

We got up early in the morning. It was perceptibly cold.
We wanted to renew the impressions of the previous day and
also to look at a few grottoes on the east side and take photo-

graphs. After dinner, of which we partook at an early hour, we started on our way back to Tat'ungfu. This time both of us travelled in the cart, which ambled through the river-bed. I have rarely seen a more dusty river. Barely two days had elapsed since it had rained last. The water was still running among the rubble which filled the valley, and already every whirl of wind, created by the increasing warmth of the region, covered us with clouds of dust and sand. The carriage was a model of its kind, indestructible in spite of incredible shaking and in spite of the fact that one wheel which had cracked had been patched up provisionally by being tied together with ropes. The servants followed on donkeys, which also carried a portion of the luggage. These Chinese travelling carriages seem to crawl along at an impossibly slow pace and yet they advance as quickly as an energetic walker, as I was able to observe when, for a time, we walked alongside because we were sick of being jolted to pieces. The return journey brought nothing new. The impressions of the previous day repeated themselves slowly in reverse sequence.

Evening drew on as we reached Tat'ungfu. In the inn we washed off the dust of the road and started on a small voyage of discovery through the town. We drove as far as the Hua Yen temple on the western wall. It is a Buddhistic temple of the Ming period of colossal proportions. It was already dark when we reached the temple. Our way led upwards through several courtyards. At one place two ferocious dogs were attached to bronze chains. They lay in front of the Hall of Meditation. Steps led up to a terrace at the end of which there is the main hall of the temple; on the right and the left there are small towers, in one of which a large drum hangs and in another an old bell which a monk struck just then for the evening benediction. The bell sent forth its deep tones peacefully over the widespread town, over all the roofs and gables which extend eastwards.

We stepped into the hall. The bronze Buddha figures loomed mysteriously out from the deep dusk of the background, while Arhats and Bodhisatvas stood along the side walls. A small tablet near the entrance bore the following melancholy verse:

> "Another day has passed,
> And that much shortened is your life.
> Thus it runs on along its brassy rails.
> Oh, friend, what do you gain by flinging yourself
>   into pleasures?"

Outside, the evening bell with its slow measured tones, red strips of clouds which had turned into a cold grey, and the dusk in the depth of the hall began to be oppressive. Thick clouds of incense rose into the air. Those present lay upon their faces before the hero, the conqueror, who had overcome the toil of life with calm. . . .

We returned to our inn. The streets were filled with crowds after the heat of the day. The women and girls, who cannot be seen on the streets during the day, come out at this evening hour, beautifully dressed and decked out. Students and pupils strolled by in the attempt to catch a glance or a smile.

When we reached the inn night had fallen and the inmates were in agitated conversation, because a man with his family had arrived and sought shelter in the inn. He said that on the very day on which he had been in Yünkang, a mutiny had broken out among the troops in a neighbouring town. They had received money from Chang Tso Lin, the ruler of Manchuria, who caused his enemies internal difficulties in this manner.

VII

NANK'OU,
6th of September

We were called to start in the morning before the break of day, while the cool air still swept across the roofs and the stars were slowly paling. The train leaves Tat'ungfu early. We found a comfortable compartment to ourselves, although a number of soldiers and policemen boarded the train. Our journey took us back again through a strip of valley which,

lying between barren hills, has in the course of the last generation been wrested from the desert by the peasants. The Mongols, who used to live here, retired at the approach of cultivation into a valley farther northwards. The entire railway can be
described as an advance of cultivation against the Gobi desert.
The colonizing power of the Chinese is incredible. The stream
of peasants and merchants pushes its way irresistibly towards
the desert. If no serious set-back occurs, the Chinese advance
is destined to open up wide stretches of the desert for cultivation. In such manifestations the great power can be seen
which is innate in the Chinese people, for they do not come
like parasites who batten upon the wealth of others, but as
colonists who turn the desert into tilled soil and make the
territory of robber chieftains into well-ordered and well-
directed districts for human habitation.

For a certain time we travelled along one arm of the great
wall which extends at the foot of the mountain on the north of
the railway across the plain, until it suddenly changes its course
northwards in a wide sweep over the mountains.

Eventually we came to Kalgan. A crowd had collected at
the station. Two captured robbers were on board our train
and they were to be condemned in Kalgan. This event allowed
an insight into the struggles of the frontier districts. The
advancing colonizers are surrounded and continuously alarmed
by bands of robbers which are known by the name of Hung
Hu Tzu even in Europe. It is a fight for life and death in
which there is no mercy. The two robbers were laid in chains
which were fastened at their feet with a large wooden block, so
that they could advance only slowly with short steps. Immediately in front of the station there were carts in which they
were placed under strong military escort, to make every attempt
at escape impossible. I was able to look into the face of one of
them as he passed. He looked like a caught tiger. You could
see that he would kill these soldiers mercilessly if he had the
chance, just as he went to his condemnation without hope for
grace.

This was our last impression of the frontier district. From

Kalgan the railway winds south and east, and soon we approached the mountains where the inner circuit of the great wall crosses the railway line. If one were to attempt to describe the gigantic structure of the great wall which follows along the ridge of the mountain to lose itself in the distance on the horizon, one would have to compare it with the boundary lines built by the Roman Empire against the northern countries of the Barbarians. Both are systematic means of safeguarding the "world" against the wild and uncontrolled element in the masses of the population that live "beyond." They are protective means executed with superlative skill. There is also another parallel: the final result that these artificial means were eventually of no avail against the attack of the natural forces which were active in those peoples. Just as the Teutons eventually seized the Roman Empire, maintaining themselves as the ruling class, but themselves though victors were vanquished by the more advanced civilization, so the Mongols and other races broke through the great wall repeatedly, and they too were fitted into the great Chinese culture system which better than any other has known how to melt the most heterogeneous races into the harmonious entity which the China of today presents to us.

There is nevertheless an essential difference between Rome and China. The seed of the Roman world empire was, after all, the city. This was the reason why, in spite of the assistance of ever-widening circles, the Roman Empire died of bloodlessness as it became over-civilized, and consequently only its empty form was inherited by future generations. The kernel of the Chinese power is, however, the homogeneous mass of the large peasant population. They are the powerful roots of its strength, and from this soil new and healthy successors enter the ruling classes, if and when over-civilization corrupts the society and with it the state. This explains why China has remained so vital for thousands of years and has outlasted even the change of her ruling dynasties.

VIII

PEKING,
7th of September

We beheld quite a different picture of the past magnificence
and splendour of the last national Chinese Dynasty, which fell
in the year 1644, when we rode from Nank'ou, where we had
spent the night, to the tombs of the old emperors of the Ming
Dynasty. The road was long and we therefore started at an early
hour. We were called at four o'clock while the chains of the
fretting donkeys rattled. Uncertain lights trembled outside
and the air was cold and sharp as we rode into the night. The
stars glowed in the sky, from which strips of black clouds
seemed to hang. Shooting stars could be seen beyond the dark
masses of the rising mountains. The sure-footed animals found
their way in the dark. They climbed on tortuous paths through
the stone rubble which lay about everywhere. Our journey
led us across rivers and over steep slopes until we came to a
high plateau after passing over the black mould of tilled fields
and through sleeping villages. The dew of the night still hung
on the trees. A cock crowed in the distance. The intermittent tones of mourning for the dead penetrated the night.
Gradually the stars sank in a wide arch in the west and a cutting wind announced the dawn which glimmered in the east.
At last we came round the side of the mountain, which had
moved over nearer to us, and we found ourselves beneath the
regular undulations of the hills in a round basin which seemed,
at the uttermost ends of the earth, to have opened its arms to
the tombs. As we approached the great gate, with its seven
divisions which stand at the entrance of the road leading to the
graves, a red cloud rose from the sea into the golden light
which had suddenly broken out in the east. The tops of the
western mountains were already luminous with a purple radiance. The light seemed to descend the slopes to the nearer hills
which awaited it in a grey green twilight. Eventually the burning glow of the sun poured itself out over the first of the red

mausoleums which seemed to lean, surrounded by close black groves of cypresses, against the mountain-side. Then the light advanced from one mausoleum to another until eventually the last corner of the valley was bathed in sunshine. In the meantime we had ridden probably for an hour upon the long road which leads, through many a gate building between stone figures of animals, towards the main temple. The road is reminiscent of the roads for the spirits which approach Egyptian temples. The largest funeral construction is that of the Emperor Yunglo (1403-1427) who, in his day, moved his residence from Nanking, the "Southern Capital," to the "Northern Capital," Peking. As we dismounted from our donkeys, we were bathed in the first rays of sunshine. A man was called from the vicinity, who opened the mighty wings of the doors for us and then left us to our own devices. Among these immense decaying temple buildings we felt as though we were in fairyland. Pine trees and cypresses, among which an undergrowth of oak stretched upwards, had stood for centuries in these courtyards. Little birds flitted in their branches and chirped continuously like the departed souls of whom Homer tells us. In front of the real funeral hill there rises a two-storied building which contains the marble funeral tablets. No steps lead up to it, but a steeply rising vaulted passage which twice bends round a corner, and is built in such a way that a strange echo repeats every sound made by the approaching visitor. Everything is in a state of decay. The one-time gorgeous sculptures, sacrificial vessels, in the ancestral temples have been replaced by others made of cardboard, and their decayed condition is a cruel sermon on the corruptibility of earthly splendour.

No one who sees the way these graves are laid out will escape a magnificent impression. There is something imposing about the manner in which an entire mountain valley has been transformed into an immense piece of architecture in which the veins of the rocks and the rivers have been included in the building of the cemetery. It is a different thing from the will of the Egyptian Pharaohs who raised the pyramids as artificial mountains to defy the plain, and it points to a no less noble culture to build the resting-places for departed rulers in harmony with heaven and earth in the way in which this has been accomplished with such rare skill in China.

CHINESE COUNTRY LIFE

A T the time of the first edicts of reform, by means of which
it was hoped to bring about a change in the entire educational system, I happened to go a good deal into the country,
because in China people were somewhat at a loss as to how to
arrange the new schools. I was therefore asked to take over the
organization and management of such schools in towns and
villages for a while. The school in Kaomi and a few village
schools in the district were especially consigned to my care.
While the Shantung railway, which now connects Tsingtao
with the capital of the province Tsinanfu, had not yet been
built, I had to travel to the interior on horseback. My way led
round the bay of Kiaochou. The district near the bay which
used to extend much farther into the mainland is for the most
part flat. Along the shore dams had been built at intervals containing salt deposits, in which sea salt is gained by means of
evaporation. Salt plays a very important part among the products of the Tsingtao region. The fields are planted with the
utilitarian plants of northern China: millet, sorghum, wheat,
soy beans, sweet potatoes, and also maize and peanuts. There
is also a considerable production of fruit, especially pears, per-
simmons and zizyphus. The peasant homes of the district are
for the most part made of granite and porphyry; the walls are
primitive and frequently put together without mortar and
merely stuck together with clay. The roofs are either covered
with straw or rounded off flatly with clay covered in chalk.
Life in such a Chinese fishing village is anything but comfortable. The buildings are all bungalows. From the courtyard,
to which the threshing place is attached, one enters by a double-
winged wooden door without a handle whose only means of
shutting is a bolt on the inside, directly into the central room,
whose floor consists of compressed clay. A ceiling can be
found only in wealthy houses, and usually the construction of
the roof lies here. On one side, in the background, there is the
fireplace, above which hangs the coloured picture of the house-

hold god. The smoke from the cooking usually has to find its way out of the house by its own devices unless, at most, a small broken chimney opens up a way for it. All the houses face south and contain in the central room no aperture except the door, which, for this reason, is usually kept open all day. Only the north wall contains a broad low window, which is bricked up in the winter and serves to create a draught in the summer. To the right and the left of the actual room there are two inner rooms which are accessible through openings generally shut off by curtains. These interior rooms have south windows with wooden grilles which are pasted over with paper in the winter. Against the back wall there is a bed built of stone and the flue of the fireplace passes through it, so that in winter you sleep in a heated bed. If the clay of this masonry is not air-tight, you have to pay for this warmth by putting up with a good deal of smoke. There is very little furniture in such a peasant's house. The kitchen utensils and other objects of use are kept in the central room. There is a crude table near the wall and a few stools, and that is all. The stone bed, the k'ang, is the place of predilection of the female members of the family. There is usually a small cupboard at the foot end of the k'ang in which clothes are kept, if they are not stowed away in chests. The bed is frequently shut off by curtains. Counterpanes are used to lie on as well as for covering purposes, and one's head reposes on a Chinese pillow, which is really a support for the neck. Near the window there is a rectangular table with a few chairs. The table displays the bowl in which they grind their ink; there is also a brush and paper, a calendar, and probably a letter-writing manual. On the whole, the rooms are smoky and cold in winter, and they are only bearable because of their sheltered position, especially on days when the north wind blows. In the summer, especially in the rainy season, there are other troubles, sweltering heat, clouds of mosquitoes, which are supposed to be driven away by the choking fumes of artemisia herbs, and there are other insects which cannot be driven away by any kind of smoke. In addition, there is the constant danger that the clay of the roof and the walls may melt in the rain, and that consequently a greater or a smaller portion of the house is liable to fall in. The clay is indeed covered by a coating of chalk for protection against the rain, but where a place is not sound, the rain, which often falls in torrents, penetrates mercilessly and causes wholesale destruction.

The fishing trade practised in these villages on the bay of Kiaochou gives a meagre return, and is dangerous. In earlier years, when the bay was visited regularly by swarms of herring, the situation was different. There were fishes in plenty, in fact so many that poultry and pigs were fed on them, and the large quantities which could not be eaten at all were used as manure for the fields. These times are over long ago. The long narrow fish are salted and dried, and their taste is appalling to a cultivated palate. Apart from other kinds of fish, the people also eat crabs, shrimps, cuttlefish and jellyfish. The fishing trade has lately suffered considerably from the competition of Japanese fishing trawlers, whose enormous catches are very disastrous.

Apart from fishing, the people live by agriculture. Tilling the soil is very laborious as there is a scarcity of animals. Sometimes you can see the wooden plough drawn by men. The whole family joins in the work, and for this reason the blessing of children is much desired, for they can help in the work. During the summer, at harvest time, men, women and children can be seen at work. The radiant sky stretches overhead and men and nature grow into a vast unity. In the dry season, the people live almost entirely out of doors. The heat and the mosquitoes make the house unbearable. They build huts on the fields. In the upper portions the women and children are housed and the men of the family sleep on the level ground. In spite of the extreme poverty of the north Chinese peasants, who are agriculturists, in a climate which produces only steppes, and where either the rain is insufficient or else summer downpours cause inundations, the people are yet contented and simple, which proves how well Confucius knew the way to make men's lives harmonious by means of his ethics.

The solemn mountain tops of the Laoshan look over the

plain. Beyond the bay the Perl Mountains greet one in the
west, and between them you see green islands of trees formed
by the villages in the midst of the wide and swaying sea of
corn. Such an evening is described in a few lines by an old
poet:

"From the edge of the hills I see the mist advance;
Through the bamboo-leaves I watch the setting sun.
A bird skims the gable of my thatched roof;
Clouds pour out, as though through the windows of the house."

Towards evening, the travelling horseman beholds the
battlements or the walls of Kiaochou. The fate of this city has
been very varied in the course of history. It is situated in the
south of the plain which, in the form of a broad strip running
from north to south, links the peninsula of Shantung with the
mainland. This peninsula is mountainous throughout. The
Laoshan rising straight up out of the sea to a height of 3,500
feet, and the Shengshan, its counterpart in the north, form the
outposts of the peninsula. In the earlier days the district lay
beyond the sphere of Chinese culture. The mountains were
regarded as the mysterious residence of conjurers and fairies,
and many an emperor who sought the lozenge of immortality
has made a pilgrimage to this district. The Peng Lai mountains in the north, where the "sea market" can be seen rising
from the mist of the sea on occasion, was considered to be the
meeting-place of the immortals, and it was from there that
once upon a time the knight Ts'in Shih Huang Ti went out with
his famous expedition of hundreds of boys and girls who were
to look for the island of the blessed. The peninsula offers
many dangers to navigation. The rocks of the outrunners of
the Shantung mountains have caused the shipwreck of many
a vessel when the typhoon raged. For this reason a canal, the
so-called Chiao Lai canal, was built in the Mongol period.
This canal starts from the Kiaochou bay and goes northward
past the departmental town of Laichou to end in the gulf of
Pechili. This canal not only shortened the route for the ships
coming from the south to proceed to the northern capital, but

also saved them from the danger of a stormy voyage round the
Shantung hills. Kiaochou lay in those days immediately on
the shore of the bay and was a flourishing port. The junks ran
in and out and the merchandise was piled up in the town.
Near the town itself the temple of the Queen of Heaven was
erected. She is the goddess who appears to sailors when the
storm drives through the sea. When the horizon is full of dark
clouds, thunder and lightning, when the storm and the sea
threaten to crush the ship, then seamen invoke the Queen of
Heaven for help in the hour of their greatest need. She then
hangs out her lantern and on the waves approaches those who
are in distress and calms the storm. The crew of many a
saved ship has hung up a small wooden junk in the temple of
the goddess in token of gratitude. The temple still stands
outside the walls of the town in the southern district, but the
sea has receded a long way. Kiaochou has become an inland
town, at a distance of some hours from the bay, which is connected with it by a flat stretch of sand. The canal in the north
has fallen to pieces. The larger junks cannot advance far beyond the middle of the bay, where they have to cast anchor and
land their merchandise in flat sampans. Along the deserted
shore, next to a lonely pagoda upon a little hill, lies the port of
Kiaochou Japatur, which transacts the meagre trade which
still continues to be routed via the bay of Kiaochou. Since the
harbour of Tsingtao has been built near the entrance to the
bay, most of the trade has gone there. In the town of Kiaochou,
as in all large localities, regular market fairs still take place, and
the population forgathers from all the four corners of the
wind. The people start long before daybreak from their homes
with goods or fruit, which they sell at the market to be able
to purchase the necessary tools in exchange. These markets
usually take place at intervals of five days; they are in the
country the almost exclusive means of traffic in merchandise,
except in so far as commercial travellers go from place to place
and offer their wares. The market offers incidentally the best
opportunity for exchanging the news; and the most sensational
rumours are frequently related there as facts. If an epidemic

of rumours, which never represent the facts, but always only moot the tendencies, flits through the land, then you may be certain that they originated in such market-places. Newspapers of the Western kind have been more frequent only in the course of this century. On these occasions quarrels are sometimes also settled, and the culprit may be condemned to provide a meal with wine, in the course of which all those concerned take their fill and become cheerful and friendly once more. Sometimes, however, when a peasant, after doing good business at the market, has partaken too freely of what is not good for him, evil spirits, who do all kinds of mischief, appear to him in the darkness on his homeward journey. Such stories were told even in the old days. In Lü Ru Wei's *Spring and Autumn Annals* the following story is told:

"In a village there was a curious devil who delighted in assuming the forms of the sons and brothers of other people. An old peasant from the district had one day gone to market, and returned from it drunk. The devil assumed the form of his son, apparently to lead him home. But he annoyed and worried him terribly on the way. When the old man reached home, his drunkenness had disappeared. He taunted his son and said: 'I, your father, have never been lacking in love to you. What was the reason that you plagued me so on the way home, when I was drunk?' His son sobbed, beat his head on the ground and said: 'This is a spook, it was not thus, for all that time I was busy in the east. You can ask the people along the road.' His father believed him and said to himself: 'Ha! ha! this is surely the curious devil. I have heard of him before. Tomorrow I will go to the market again and drink more than ever and then I should like to meet him and will surely kill him.' Next morning he went to the market and became drunk. His son, however, was afraid that his father might not be able to return alone, and went out from the village to meet him. When the old man saw his son, he drew his sword and stabbed him to death."

Kiaochou is today a quiet town. The walls are crumbling

away, the gates are in decay, and the memory of the past broods over the wide fields which today fill large portions of the walled city where houses and streets used to be. The crickets sing in summer in the willow trees, and the larks sing in their cages, which are carried out early in the morning into the open by the bird lovers.

There is also an old myth about the fairy Maku which tells that she is still young, although the sea has thrice been turned into mulberry gardens, and that the mulberry gardens have then again been dipped below the surface of the sea. Today the land rises again out of the sea and becomes first a sandy plain, then steppes, and at last agricultural land. Harbour towers are set back in the mainland and new places appear from nothingness, as for instance the German harbour of Tsingtao, which used to be a poor little fishing village until the railway came and the mammoth steamers, the big roads and the factories. Kiaochou sank back into the oblivion of a little provincial town and the times changed again. At one time German soldiers dwelt in magnificent barracks on a hill outside the town of Kiaochou. They went away again, and the forest grew round the barracks, while slowly windows and roofs, doors and bolts, fell off and were removed, so that the place is today only covered with undergrowth and ruins. All the activity and the hubbub has passed away within the span of half a human generation. We understand the attitude to this transition, of which Laotse said:

"All things arise in turmoil.
I remain quiet and behold how they return whence they came."

From Kiaochou, the road leads up country to Kaomi. This town is the sleeping city of the fairy tales. Its walls rise at the top of the hill, full of the old burial groves of the so-called "old town" near the banks of a small river. The district is level and at a low altitude. North of the town there used to be a large lake, which has dried up in the course of the centuries, and continues its ghostly existence only upon European maps. The citizens took care that the railway was kept at a considerable distance from the town. Accordingly it was necessary to take one's departure almost a full hour before the train leaves. While one is in the city, one is farther away from alien influences. At the time that I used to go to Kaomi there were still people there who had refused even to look at the railway. It was then that I saw the solemn veneration of Confucius for the first time practised, as it used to be in China in those days. On the north wall a wooden tablet was erected with the temple symbol of Confucius about it. In front of it, there were, to the right and to the left, two candelabras and two vases, in the middle a vessel in which sticks of incense were buried in white glowing ashes. After I had expressed my veneration for the Master according to the Western tradition of bowing three times, the master of the ceremonies, who first pronounces the litany and then conducts the ritual, came to the front. Teacher and pupils kneel three times on square cushions and touch the ground on each occasion with their forehead. That ends this ceremony, and the solemn welcome of the teacher by the pupils takes place. By their reverence for the great Master, the teachers attain to the dignity which entitles them to be honoured by their pupils. It is a peculiar part of these proceedings that if a pupil does reverence before the man, whom he wished to honour as teacher, the teacher replies by performing the same ceremony. Everything is based on mutuality. There is no slavish onesidedness, but only free mutual respect. This old Chinese custom of thus placing school life upon the basis of reverence as being the most fruitful human stimulus, has always struck me as very beautiful and impressive. In the process of such veneration, the accidental personality of the man in question is not particularly exalted, but what is honoured is merely the mental or spiritual quality in whatsoever is above us and in whatsoever is below us, and the pupils who are united by affection to the same teacher thus also show reverence for whatsoever is our equal.

Among the missionaries there was at that time a good deal of discussion as to whether the veneration of Confucius was not something heathen. I confess that I can regard this tradition only as beautiful and exalting. The reverential attitude is at all events an advantage. Wherever this attitude disappeared nothing which could possess as a symbol an equivalent expressive value comes to replace it. The inner freedom of the people concerned is in no way disturbed. It is not a sign of higher piety or of profounder freedom if one denies a man worthy of reverence, whom one happens to meet by the way, the honour which is his due.

Discords and intrigues lamed the power of decision. Many of the ablest people retired, according to their wealth, to the enjoyment of their opium pipe or the handy bottle. The revolution came, and with it the whole of the aristocracy ceased, for the time being, to exercise their previous influence. The revolution introduced an entirely different system of management. The Manchu régime in China had been built up upon a condition of equilibrium between local self-government and centralized bureaucracy. The organs of self-government were the Shensi, or the wearers of girdles as they were called. They had to show a certain consideration for the various guilds, but on the whole the power was theirs, provided they were united and considered the interest of the population. The central government was represented by a district official whom the Portuguese used to call Mandarin, and the English used to call magistrate. These officials had judicial and administrative duties. The district officials were nominated directly by the Emperor. It was a strict law that no officer could hold a post in his own province. By this means an effort was made to avoid the danger of a cohesion amongst the lower sections of the system against the central government. The district official was subject to, firstly, the departmental officer, and then to the governor of the province, all of whom were representatives of the central government in Peking, and stood under its control. Nevertheless, one or two powerful men succeeded in acquiring for themselves a certain independent power in the provinces, which explains why the false description of viceroy became current in Europe as a description of the governor of provinces or the governor-general. Li Hung

Chang, Chang Chü Ling, and later Yuan Shih K'ai, were examples of this type, but even they were dependent eventually upon the court and could be transferred and deprived of their power when such action became for any reason necessary. This system in which the interests of local and central government found satisfactory expression, was efficient as long as the various officials occupied their post for a certain period, so that they were able to make themselves genuinely familiar with local conditions and requirements, and could therefore collaborate productively with the representatives of the local population. Since the purchase of appointments became more and more popular under the Manchu régime, it was necessary to allow the numerous expectants, who had frequently borrowed considerable sums for the payment of their patent, sufficient opportunities to enable them to recuperate the capital they had invested as quickly as possible. The result was that individual offices were frequently filled, for years at a time, by substitutes. These substitute officers, who knew that they would scarcely remain at their post for more than a year, were able at best to deal with the routine work, always with one eye to making as much as possible by charging all kinds of expenses in order to climb the ladder of advancement as rapidly as possible. In this way, haste and insecurity entered into the public life. Nothing was done thoroughly. Everything was patched up somehow and resulted in slovenliness and superficiality. These circumstances were the main cause of the collapse. The officials were, on the whole, not nearly as corrupt as people in Europe thought. The population which was ready at any moment to make difficulties and protest if an official wanted to enrich himself at the expense of the taxpayer, in a really unreasonable manner, would never have put up with it. The system had ceased to be effective, because the necessary determination was lacking on the throne.

This double system of central and local government has now ceased to function. Since the revolution the officials are eligible even among members of their own provinces, which has changed the whole position. Local co-operation has become the basis of their work. The relation of the province to the central government has become far more loose than heretofore. The taxes are spent in the provinces. The central government only disposes of the Customs money and the receipts—all of them pledged—from the salt revenue, the railways, etc. When the conditions, which have at present become untenable owing to the constant interference of the foreign Powers, are consolidated, China will become a loose-jointed federal state.

The conditions in the provinces and towns repeated themselves on a small scale in the villages, with the difference that the village official, who is a member of the village community, was the responsible personality *vis-à-vis* the district official, just as the beadle, the Tipao, carried the responsibility as far as police matters were concerned.

I had a good deal to do with the organization of elementary schools in the country. The process of adapting these institutions to modern conditions was not an easy one. A Chinese village school was in the past something very different from what we call a school in Europe. The educational authorities of the central government had no connection whatever with the schools. The government merely held the examinations for the various grades, and it was left to the competitors how they chose to prepare themselves. All the schools were therefore private institutions. A teacher could, for instance, begin a kind of boarding-school, which would be attended by pupils from the immediate or the more distant vicinity, according to the teacher's reputation. The pupils then shared the life of the teacher with whom they worked at their literary education to prepare themselves for the state examinations. The preliminary studies were generally made in the country; the village authorities either provided superfluous rooms in a temple, engaged a teacher and the children came for lessons, paying small sums for the maintenance of the teacher, or else large families instituted family schools held in their ancestral halls. Sometimes several families clubbed together and then engaged a teacher for their children.

The teacher was responsible for looking after the children

the whole day long, from sunrise to sunset, unless he was relieved during a midday interval, if the children did not live
with the teacher, or the teacher did not live in the home of the
pupils. The actual teaching, of course, could not last the whole
day. The pupils would participate occasionally in the domestic
labours of the household at certain hours, and at other times
they would be occupied with learning and writing. The
teacher would then go through the lessons with each individual pupil, his first function being to show him the pronunciation of the characters which constituted the text the
pupils had to learn. The boy would then seat himself and
memorize his task in a loud voice and in a singing rhythm. As
the tasks set varied with the length of the lesson and the talent
of the pupil, the noise of the concerted memorizing voices was
truly deafening to an unaccustomed ear. The Chinese pupils
have sound nerves. Without being disturbed, each pupil sings
his lines while his neighbour emits altogether different tones.
One of these old Chinese schools sounds, even at quite a distance, like a hive of bees in the act of swarming. When the
pupil has learnt his text by heart, he walks up to the teacher
to say it to him. When he does so, he has to turn his back to
the teacher, which looks most curious. There are two reasons
for this procedure, firstly, it made it impossible for the pupil
to glance secretly at the book which the teacher held in his
hand, and secondly, the proffered back was immediately ready
to be plied with the ruler, in case the pupil hesitated or showed
himself in any other respect lazy.

Writing was taught in a similar manner. The teacher painted
the characters on a large scale upon a sheet of paper in Chinese
ink. The paper was then covered with a transparent sheet, on
which the pupil copied the outline of the characters with ink.
The teacher then corrected this performance; lines drawn
through the painted character meant that they were bad, and
rings were considered as praise. The Chinese characters are
very difficult to write, because the brush has to be moved with
a light and easy touch. For this reason, writing has always
been considered as an art in China, and scrolls of handwrit-

ing by famous painters are no less sought after than their pictures.

Chinese writing was originally a hieroglyphic picture-writing. Gradually the characters were used as signs for syllables and qualified by signs to indicate their category. You differentiate between pictorial conceptual and phonetic characters, according to the nature of their composition. The pictorial signs are, for instance, a circle with a dot in the centre, which means the sun, a semicircle means the moon, etc. . . . The conceptual signs are composed of several pictorial signs. In this way, two trees means a grove, three trees means a forest; a woman and her son means good, a woman beneath a roof means peace; a pig beneath a roof means a family, birds in a nest mean the west or evening.

The phonetic signs consist of one half which indicates the sound (phonetic component), and a categorical sign (the radicals which indicates the category to which the object belongs), for instance T'ung means together. T'ung with a categorical sign for "metal" means "a metal which is pronounced t'ung," i.e. copper. T'ung with a categorical sign for "tree" means a "tree which is pronounced T'ung," that is to say, a Pawlownia Imperialis. Or Ch'êng means to complete. Ch'êng with the categorical sign for "earth" means "something of earth which is pronounced Ch'êng," i.e. the moat of a town.

The Chinese language is monosyllabic, so that its grammar contains a syntax and no conjugations. The number of syllables which exist is very limited; there is, for instance, no "r" in Chinese, and syllables end only in vowels or in "n" and "ng." The first sound consists only of simple consonants. The limited number of existing syllables is of course by no means sufficient to provide a special pronounceable expression for every idea. In the case of the written language this provides no difficulty, because every concept has a special character. In the case of the spoken language, however, there is the possibility of expression because many characters are pronounced in the same way. The language has therefore found the solution of differentiating syllables of similar sound by a variety of intonations. In this way, "Hao" pronounced in a questioning tone means "beautiful," pronounced in an authoritative tone it means "to love." Nevertheless, misunderstandings occur not unfrequently. In case of difficulty, you either write the word on paper with a pencil, or make the sign of it in your hand.

The new Chinese writing and the everyday language is so formed that such misunderstandings occur far less than they used to.

The old Chinese schools have developed more and more in the last centuries into an external activity which confines itself to developing the sheer faculty of memory in the pupils. The curriculum is limited for the most part to literary and historical subjects. Even the old literature of wisdom was treated largely merely from the point of view of its usefulness for the examinations which, since the Ming period, had become more and more formal. There was a definite form of essay consisting of eight parts, which was the form into which the treatment of the subjects taken from the four holy books had to be compressed. The man who was able to handle this set form skilfully passed his examination, even if the ideas contained in his essay were quite superficial. It also happened quite frequently that people cheated at their examinations. There were all kinds of essays in small books which one could hide in one's sleeves, and they contained in diminutive print a compendium of the entire subjects set for examination. It was simply a question of finding the right subject in the index. If the candidate chose the wrong one, he might hand in the most perfect essay and yet fail. The most magnificent arrangement of the kind was a beautiful silk examination cloak whose white silk lining was covered from top to bottom with closely written examination essays. A handkerchief was supplied with it which contained the subject index and an indication as to where the essay in question could be found in the lining. A brief indisposition on the part of the candidate sufficed to enable him, having retired to a quiet place, to cut out the particular part from the lining and to pass the examination with distinction—if he was

not caught. On the whole, it may be stated that the commandment "thou shalt not be caught" was obeyed in China with
great conscientiousness.

In these circumstances a teacher in a village school enjoyed
a fairly comfortable existence. In his household he had the
service of his pupils at his disposal, and the pupils had to attend
to what they had to learn, also by themselves. He merely listened and punished those with a ruler who were lazy. On hot
days it happened frequently that the teacher slept as fast as a
beadle during a lawsuit. The learned professor also often had
a small jug of liquor standing by his side, the contents of which
he caused to disappear gradually in small cups. From time to
time he would probably beat a pupil to keep himself awake. If
nevertheless he fell a victim to his sleepiness it often took up a
long time of continued recitative sing-song on the part of the
pupils before they noticed it, just as the old heathens continued
to sacrifice to their gods long after the gods had died.

It was therefore a real necessity that the whole school system
should be put upon a sound basis. This was done by abolishing
the state examinations and introducing instead public schools
with a definite curriculum. There was of course a shortage of
teachers. Japan was drawn upon first, not always with good
results because, naturally, it was not the best Japanese teachers
who could settle down in a Chinese town. I knew one of them
who, in the physics class, only dealt with acoustics, which he
taught his pupils by playing all kinds of popular songs on a
badly tuned harmonium. Similar instances may have occurred
in other places. Abridged courses and institutions for the preparation of teachers were established, in order to give the old
teacher a modern varnish. Ch'uan Hsi So, which means normal
school, were called by the people Chiraniso, i.e. clothing institutions, and Shih Fan Hsüo T'ang, which means a school for
teachers, they called Ch'ih Fan Hsüo T'ang, which means eating school, in order to indicate that the allowances paid to those
who attended the schools were the most important part of the
institution. Today these conditions have changed altogether.
Nowadays, even those who have passed through the pedagogic

university of Peking do not despise going to the villages as teachers, in order to do thorough work for popular education. China is making rapid progress in the number and quality of its schools.

I had a good deal to do at that time with the institution of those village schools, which involved frequent and lengthy journeys. At a station, for instance, I would be awaited by the mule cart of the head of the school, an old friend of mine, who was bent on doing something really substantial for the school of his native village. I had to spend the whole day being jolted over hill and dale, in the dust of the road and the heat of the sun, along the Chinese country road, until I reached my goal at night. These journeys made me perfectly familiar, from my own experience, with the ancient torture of tying people to the wheel. On arrival, my first business was to get my belly, which had been shaken to its foundations, into proper working order. For this purpose, my touching host had usually prepared a lavish meal, accompanied by a kind of rye brandy. In the country, in China, there is no such thing as a luxurious cuisine. The meat, usually chosen, for my sake, to be beef, regarded by the villagers, in my opinion with perfect justice, with abhorrence, was high, and rendered unpalatable by a preparation of oil extract from beans. The shrimps were old and smelly, and the black eggs were really not quite fresh, although they were barely a few weeks old. The bean cheese tasted rancid, and the brandy was adulterated with fusel-oil. In fact the dinner was to complete whatever the jolting of the journey might have failed to achieve. After a more or less unpleasant night, spent in the midst of mosquitoes and other animals, I was nevertheless usually able, next morning, to inspect the school and its lively youths, with their avidity for learning. In the light of the sun, the burdens of the previous day were then quickly forgotten.

My old friend was the very pattern of a pious kindly patriarch. As long as he lived, order reigned in his family. His house was strongly reminiscent of the family of that model father in which, many centuries ago, nine generations were represented simultaneously, and who lived in such harmony that even the dogs followed their master's example.

This old patriarchal form of family life, in which the piously revered ancestors form a vast community with the living successors, still exists in China in the country, and will continue to do so for a long time; for China is, in its mass, a peasant people, and peasant people have sound and enduring traditions.

THE OLD MEN OF TSINGTAO

IN the passage of years a certain intercourse has come to be established between Tsingtao and the back country. The antagonistic atmosphere which made itself felt during the occupation of Tsingtao, and subsequently rendered any intercourse between the governor of the province of Tsinanfu and the German governor of Tsingtao impossible, had disappeared. The Chinese governor, Chou Fu, broke the ban and made a personal visit in Tsingtao. He acted on the supposition that more could be achieved on both sides by mutual trust and goodwill, than by distrust and isolation. The Germans did not at first know how to act in view of this new situation. The "China connoisseurs" among the colonists there are usually people who always prophesy the worst, to be able to say afterwards, "I told you so!" for if their quacking warnings were in vain, nobody would remember them afterwards, and it looks more knowledgeable if one is pessimistic. These people had therefore expressed the idea that there was a certain intention behind this visit, to take at any rate moral possession of the German protectorate. In consequence, the colonists were anxious. On the other hand, a friendly visit could not be refused. The offer of a visit was therefore accepted—not without taking certain secret precautions. When the governor Chou Fu came, his crude candour and his healthy sense of humour soon cleared the air of such thoughts. A friendly and neighbourly intercourse developed between Tsingtao and Tsinanfu.

The two cultures came into contact. In view of the great distance which separated them in those days, a number of queer misunderstandings occurred.

Public life in old China is conducted exclusively by men. Women were not present at dinners; at most, public singers were admitted for the entertainment of the guests. The foreign ladies in Tsingtao were far too interested in the Chinese guests to miss the opportunity of seeing them in their magnificent gold-embroidered garments, with the horseshoe applica-

tions on their sleeves and their pigtails beneath their Mandarin
caps crowned with gay crystal buttons. In this way, it came
about that modern European clothes—the men in swallow tails
and the ladies in evening dress—came into direct contact with
the old Chinese Mandarin costume. The Chinese gentlemen in
their gorgeous costumes and with their harmonious and ample
movements looked imposing in European company. Of course
there were occasional misunderstandings. In China there is a
custom that at table one wipes glasses and bowls before use,
and even the chopsticks are cleaned as a matter of precaution.
As a result of old habit, it sometimes occurred that one of these
gentlemen wiped his wine-glass with his handkerchief. The
lady of the house was horrified. The butler asseverated that the
glass was clean. The lady commanded the glass to be brought
and found that, on the edge, where the guest had wiped it
with his handkerchief, it was dull, but otherwise impeccable.
Misunderstanding also occurred in the other camp. Two
Chinese guests, for instance, held the following conversation:
"How is it that the foreign ladies are dressed this evening
quite differently from their usual attire? Just look, above their
breasts the flesh bulges out all round, down to their backs,
where they do not wear a single thread, and only the smallest
remnant of sleeves seems to be left. On the other hand, their
skirts are so long that they drag on the floor for more than a
foot. What can really be the reason for being so naked on the
upper part of the body and so concealed in the lower portion?"
His neighbour, who had travelled in foreign parts, replied:
"That is what they wear on feast days; only the higher orders
are entitled to dress themselves like that." "H'm, I see,"
was the reply, and the conversation turned to other subjects.

Or else it might occur that a few ladies from Shanghai happened to be staying in the house of a friend. They did not wish
to miss the chance of seeing the Chinese dignitaries at close
quarters, and they therefore declared themselves ready to play
a few violin pieces with piano accompaniment in the presence
of the company, which consisted only of men. They played

very well, and every one clapped to express approval. At the end of the evening, one of the Chinese guests inquired: "Do you mind telling me how much you pay such girls for the evening?"

Later on, when the refreshments led to more intimate intercourse, many a diplomatic duel was fought, in which each combatant held a champagne glass in his hand. A high Chinese official was famous for his insensibility in the matter of drink and was therefore dreaded on account of the ruthlessness with which he disposed of a less able victim by continually raising his glass to him. There was a Japanese professor who was his match. With a friendly smile he always drank when the Chinaman did and had his glass filled again and again—with sodawater. The old gentleman eventually took up two glasses simultaneously and continued to drink, but he left the diningroom and sank into an upholstered chair. A catastrophe was anticipated with excitement and anxiety. Such things, however, are impossible in China. At the critical moment, a secretary entered with a telegram to announce that his excellency's aunt had just then passed away. Sobbing, the old gentleman was led away by two servants, for it is the requirement of piety to collapse when such a blow is dealt and to move only supported by servants.

One of the most curious members of the colony was a camel, which had been imported from Mongolia when it was a tiny foal. It had been a present to the mess-room of one of the regiments and was kept as a pet. Later on it used to be dressed up, when transports of troops, which were returning home, had their farewell celebrations, and on these occasions the camel behaved in an unseemly manner, after the manner of camels, until at last it became so big and so wild that one day, seeing artificial flowers on a lady's hat in a rickshaw, it pursued her through the whole town in order to graze on her hat. Thereupon it had to serve as a beast of burden in the Laoshan district, and was killed when war broke out to prevent its falling into the hands of the enemy.

These comfortable days in the small colony were succeeded

by others of a more serious order. The Chinese revolution began to raise its head. Tsingtao remained quiet, whereas storms were raging everywhere else in the Chinese Empire. I shall never forget the moment when one day, working in my study, a Chinese visitor was announced. One of my friends entered somewhat excited and evidently upset. He was a man with whom I used to talk about the secret Taoist doctrines. He had been commissioner for education in Tsinanfu. I valued him exceptionally highly on account of his strong quiet personality and his thorough mastery of Chinese literature, and I was therefore surprised to see him pale and harassed. In the meantime he had been director of the arsenal in Shanghai. He and his secretary, an old friend of mine, had escaped with the utmost difficulty from the mutinous soldiers, and they had made their way to Tsingtao. The German authorities saw themselves faced by the important question of what attitude they should take up towards such men who had escaped. Happily, they took the right attitude of keeping the protectorate open to members of all parties who sought refuge there and who were prepared to submit to the rules and regulations of the place. In this way, a new period began for Tsingtao. The contact with the Chinese officials, and later the foundation of the German-Chinese High School, provided a basis for intellectual intercourse. After the first guest had been received in a friendly manner others followed, and what used to be, once upon a time, a fishing village on the shore of the eastern sea, became the place where the most important personalities of the old Chinese Empire met. Many of them settled down and took up their summer residence in Tsingtao permanently, even after they accustomed themselves to the new state of affairs and took an active part in the direction of the young republic. In Tsingtao, at that time there were ministers, generals, governors, high officials of all kinds, scholars, and captains of industry, and the ways of intellectual Chinese life met upon the hitherto deserted shore. All kinds of cultural and scientific manifestations resulted from the presence of these men. Regular meetings took place in the rooms of the magnificently equipped club of the merchants' guild of the Yang Tse provinces. Scholars and officials were present from all parts of the Chinese Empire, from Mongolia and the Kansu province, from the far west down to the most southern province of Yunnan. The men who were the bearers of intellectual influence streamed together from all sides. Apart from the men who stayed permanently in Tsingtao, important guests came on long or short visits, so that Tsingtao afforded an opportunity at that time of making the acquaintance of the most distinguished representatives of the old culture, such as could not be found anywhere else in China. Those days in which scholars and statesmen of all parties lived together are reminiscent of many high-water marks in Chinese history when scholars and artists met, as, for instance, the meeting of the scholars in the Pavilion of the Orchids, which the poet Wang Hsi Chih describes in the following words:

"Though different the ways of men
  As together they fling through life, some fast encircled
  With small familiar cares—utterly incurious
  Of things under another roof; others striving outward
  Lodge wildly truant thoughts
  In realms beyond the waking world; yet leaving, taking,
  Patient, passionate, each finds some means to stay
  (By pleasure sought without or fancies hid within,
  By hope or resignation) the thought that Death
  Already meets him on his way."

I had regular meetings with a smaller circle of representatives of various mental tendencies. We met over a Chinese dinner with its various delights, and bowls of hot wine—Chinese wine is drunk hot—were not lacking. Moreover, the circle of our friends contained members who were strong drinkers. An old Mongolian prince, who had the scar of a deep cut on his neck and had passed through many experiences as governor-general of the western provinces of Shensi and Kansu, a kindly, powerful and important individual of extraordinary large calibre, showed the greatness of his nature, also when he drank. He drank on a liberal scale. When we played the finger game, by means of which one can condemn the opponent to drinking, if one is his master in intellectual perception and speed of decision, he was by no means anxious to be victorious, although he excelled all. He used to say: "In one case I gain in respect, in the other I win a beaker of wine, which is also not to be despised." When he was in a good mood, he would tell of his experiences among the Mohammedans of the west and of the living Buddha, beneath whose influence these regions stood. Many a strange and mysterious fact was revealed in these conversations concerning the night of magic in those parts. He was the man who had fled with the Empress-Dowager dressed up as the driver of a cart when she left her capital in the costume of a Chinese peasant, and he could tell many a story of the hardships and adventures of that victorious flight. He was still in contact with the provinces whose wealth in coal and minerals awaits exploitation even today. Many an evening we built castles in the air, but eventually the war broke out, which put an end to all our plans.

The most extreme contrast to him was presented by a lean professor with long finger-nails from the Yangtse district. When he played the finger game, he unwrapped, as it were, his fingers with cunning hesitation, just as a snail stretches out his horns, and he used to say what his figures were only after his opponent had long finished. It must be said, in excuse, that he could stand very little wine and always became cantankerous and even venomous when he was under the influence of alcohol. One day I told the story of the Chinese doctors who always hang out lanterns at night for the souls of the patients who have died under their treatment, and I mentioned that one man had gone to a doctor where only one of these lanterns was burning, but then, he discovered to his horror, that this doctor had only practised for one day. General hilarity ensued, because this story belongs to the well-known stories concerning Chinese conditions which are known in Europe, but not in China. Our lean friend, however, who practised medicine in his leisure hours, became quite savage when some one asked him how many lanterns for the spirits he had hung up outside his gate.

A former minister of education belonged to our circle, and he was distinguished by his humour; he was really a man of profound seriousness, but he chose to assume unbridled be-haviour. He belonged to the secret saints. Such people appear in China at a transitional period when a dynasty falls. At such times you find former princes and courtiers among monks; you find among beggars and robbers even, desperate men, who used to be officers in the army, and you find quiet scholars in meagre huts; former ministers of high rank, you find as restless wanderers, as wild poets or painters who wash down their misery in wine. You find them among scurrilous jesters and men of the world who consciously waste a life which has lost its significance for them. The minister in our company was one of these. He was always ready with a joke and the unchallenged leader in the matter of drink. It was rare that a meeting took place in which he took part, at the end of which he could not point to several victims who had been goaded on by him. He himself became always more cheerful and unbridled. He was well known for his beautiful handwriting. To this day, one can still see gay inscriptions of firms all over Peking, which were painted by him. He took no money in payment, but an exquisite dinner in the company of a singer. Even when he was nearly blind, he wrote his long rhythmic poems on strips of paper. There were many forgers, who used his name in order to find a market for their meagre efforts. I found, for instance, in an inn, such forged inscriptions, in the extreme north of China. He only laughed when he heard about it and said: "Those who know me will not be deceived, and the others are not worth anything better." Once I met him in a serious mood. It was on the occasion when the Japanese with their twenty-one conditions seemed to rob China, during the war, of the last remnants of her liberty. He broke into tears and cried like a child. I tried to comfort him, but he would not listen: "It is our fault that things have come to such a pass, it was not given to us to protect the dynasty, and now

I throw my life away, because it is worth nothing any longer."
When the evening came he drank more vigorously than ever,
and resounding laughter filled the room until the last candle
was snuffed out, and the drunken guests swayed on their way
home.

The winter is the special period of sociability in China. People forgather and talk and play chess and look at old pictures
and handwriting. People also improvise poems by way of competition. Such gatherings are called "Unions for melting the
cold." They begin at the winter solstice and last until Lady
Day. A dinner is held every ninth day. I find the following
entry in my diary, relative to one of these dinners: There
were eight of us, the number of the immortals in China.
Besides myself, there were present a former finance minister
and his brother, a director of the arsenal (the man referred to
above), a Taoist abbot, a geomancer, a merchant, and a student.
The abbot was over 70 years old, and had gathered round him
four generations of pupils in his monastery T'ai Ts'ing Kung
—a monastery full of strange myths, situated at the place
where the Laoshan mountain falls into the sea. Nevertheless he
is fresh and active and lively in his mind. He and his pupils live
a simple and purely vegetarian life in the monastery. The day
is spent in divine service and the reading of the holy writings.
He also plays the k'in, the old Chinese zither, with its uncannily floating magical tones. In his capacity of abbot he comes
in contact with the visitors to the monastery, both Chinese
and Europeans. He told very funnily the story of a large-
hearted missionary who had visited him and with whom he
had conversed for hours about the highest problems of human
life. The missionary was much delighted to find that their
view had so much in common, and in the midst of the most
enchanting conversation, the visitor had suddenly wanted to
make him a present of ten dollars. The abbot regretted that
he was unable to accept his gift, because he could really do
nothing with the money; clothes and food were provided by
the monastery, and he did not need other luxuries. Recently,
when Taoism had to be organized like a church, under the

republic, he was elected as the president of East Shantung. He had, however, resigned his office again. He said that it had involved so much worldly business that had nothing to do with piety, and apart from that, there were plenty of younger people, who regarded such offices as an honour. We spoke about life in the monasteries. His view was that the main thing was a devout piety and a conscientious and kindly conduct of one's life, in which event all the saints stood as protectors with their miraculous powers by your side. In his heart of hearts, he would have liked me to become a Taoist, and he even lent me several of the most potent and sacred sutras, which he usually conceals carefully from any alien eye. The books are disappointing. They contain so much superstition, and what is best in them is borrowed from Buddhism. It is quite certain that the old gentleman has not acquired his sober piety from them. It is difficult to get him to speak about the problem of mystic meditation. He told me that it took up much time and easily led to self-exaltation, and in any case, what could be gained by it was not susceptible of being judged by others. He was able to give an account only to himself of the inner progress made by its virtue.

The other Taoist of our circle, the former director of the arsenal, provided a striking contrast to the old monk. That such a man can occupy such a position is only possible in China, and what is more, he managed the arsenal well. He is a highly educated scholar whose knowledge of the whole of Chinese literature is rivalled only by very few men. In spite of the fact that, like all scholars, he is a Confucian, he occupies himself a good deal with Taoist meditation, for the better conduct of his life, and when he hears of any one who can help him in his efforts, he tries to make his acquaintance. He has a preference for mountains and stones. A mountain, according to Chinese philosophy, is an animated being, which operates in silence. The mountain exhales clouds and brews the rain; it covers itself with grass and growing trees, and all that lives finds something for its purpose in it. Thus he is kind in his gifts and yet quiet and old. The generations pass and each one of them takes from him what it needs. This is the reason why Confucius has said: "Men of knowledge love water, which changes eternally, but the kindly love the mountains." The Laoshan, near Tsingtao, is just the very mountain for the Taoists. Every now and again you can find at a point, with a particularly beautiful view, stone seats, or an epigram chiselled into the rock. When you examine it closely, you find that it was made by our arsenal director. He does not talk much. He hardly said a word the whole evening. Intellectually, however, he follows all that goes on. He is a man with a strong personality and a powerful will. He writes very little, although he is an excellent stylist, but what he does write has to be perfect, so that it can be shown to the succeeding generations.

Another personality is that of the former minister of finance. He combines a refined attractive nature with a calm clarity of vision. He did the new Chinese republic a considerable service at a difficult time by raising a big loan, and in the course of this task he had to conduct infinitely difficult negotiations, and suffered a great deal of unpleasantness, which his refined reticence concealed to perfection. He possesses remarkable talent for organization. His retirement from the influential position into the quiet calm of Tsingtao was due to the fact that he found too few cultivated people at work in Peking. His younger brother is extraordinarily vital in his nature. He is intelligent and his mental activity, as it were, bubbles over. What the man can produce in half an hour in the way of telling remarks would cover the requirements of another man in this direction for many years. He shows a lively interest for the new problems and has occupied himself a good deal with Christianity.

As to the geomancer, it is first of all necessary to correct the ideas which exist in Europe concerning geomancy, to be just to him. What distinguishes this man is a keen eye for the subtleties of relations in terms of landscape. I was present when he was selecting the site for a house. He discovered at a first glance, as it were, a spot in the entire neighbourhood, which afforded on the one hand the most harmonious setting for the house in the landscape, and would provide, on the other hand, a well defined and satisfying view from the house. The art of building into the landscape has produced those master-pieces of architecture which excite the admiration of con-noisseurs, for instance, in the Imperial tombs in Peking. A certain truth is also to be found in this penetration into land-scape conditions for purposes of human dwellings. A healthy situation, which is also aesthetically satisfying, creates in the long run values for the inhabitants of a house, which must not be underestimated, because in our mechanical age they are so often disregarded. This art of feeling your way into your sur-roundings must of course be distinguished from many excres-cences of popular superstition, such as the doctrines of wind and water which are met with, especially in South China. Our geomancer comes from Szuch'uan and has practised his vision for the beauties of landscape from early youth in the midst of big mountains.

The merchant has been a friend of mine for many years. A man with a straight and open nature and a genuine aspiration after truth, and although he has occupied a series of influential positions he always valued his clear conscience higher than money and property.

The young student, the nephew of the minister of finance, is a representative of young China, and he completes our circle. In spite of his youth, he has passed through hard experiences and has therefore gained in seriousness and independence of his individual personality. Life has brought him many a prob-lem already which used to be unknown in earlier days in China. The conversation turned upon present conditions in China. The manifestation of nationalism which has come with the revolution in China is regarded as the power of darkness. "What appears at first," said the geomancer, "is a setting of the sun, a victory of the negative forces. When the destructive forces have attained their zenith, a new light will no doubt begin to shine, just as the new day begins at midnight. But in China the night is just beginning to fall." "The old Jews," I threw in, "had a beautiful custom—they began the day at sunset. This is a symbol for their faith in God's power, which they always regarded in the hour of darkness and universal catastrophe as something which was about to come." "This view is also compatible with our *Book of Change*," replied the geomancer. "The evening is the zenith of the powers of darkness, from then on the more they manifest themselves the more they exhaust themselves." "And the coming God" (Ju Lai), added the student, "is the highest description which we have in Buddhism of the nature of divinity."

The conversation changed from the subject of Chinese conditions to the consideration of universal problems. The minister of finance thought that militarism, like a vampire, was threatening to swallow all the forces of the people. "What was so great in Confucius was that, for him, mental values counted primarily for the establishment of the order of the states of the world. The state exists for the sake of the people, that is the principle whose application or disregard determines whether a Power flourishes or decays. In Europe there is a danger that, owing to misunderstandings, the army, in itself a means for the protection of the state, will not only suck up the powers of the state, but may bring about a state of affairs in which men are judged only according to their capacities for a military purpose. It would be calamitous if China were to be drawn into this whirlpool, because if the Western people are able to adopt such erroneous policy, owing to their momentary wealth, for a certain period China can only be saved by extreme economy and by taking human beings as seriously as possible."

We then spoke about the future. The abbot mentioned a book containing all sorts of prophecies, after the manner of Nostradamus. It contains curious pictures to which poems have been added, but they are all in irregular sequence. It is impossible to understand the meaning of the pictures and verses before the event to which they refer takes place. When the event has occurred the prophecies fit them in the most astounding manner. The sequence of the pictures and verses is not in chronological order. "Nevertheless, one must not regard these prophecies too mechanically," threw in the geomancer. "The effect of the powers of the universe acting together brings about, as it were, the formation of knots from which certain tendencies for the future develop. Any one who understands the forces which happen to be operative at the moment, can probably see tendencies beforehand. These tendencies are, however, never decisive for any given detail. Human liberty permits us to alter and change all sorts of things." The abbot thereupon told us that he knew of other prophecies, according to which, before long, a new kingdom upon earth will begin. It will be different from everything that has existed heretofore. It will encircle the whole world for the first time and not confine itself to one half. The salvation which is to come is to come for all. It is to manifest itself in the love towards men, also towards the lowly. He who is to bring it will be surrounded with divine authority so that people will believe him without a struggle. This hope, concerning which we were all of one mind, cast a kindly light over the rest of our conversation. "In our age," said the geomancer, "individuals of all kinds and conditions meet in the truth, but only in absolute stillness. This common truth is at present still a secret. The right expression will have to be discovered for it, before it comes to exist for mankind."

At this point the brother of the minister of finance asked apparently out of the blue, and yet in continuance of our thoughts, whether Christianity would be the future religion of China. "Certainly not in the form of the churches which exist today," I replied; "these churches were all founded in very special circumstances. Not one of them possesses the entire truth of Christianity. They are necessary structures, temporary buildings, which cannot be transplanted without further ado from one region to another. But Christ is more than the head of a church, and more than the founder of a religion. He is the divine representative of humanity, which represents in Him, as its head, a unified entity. This humanity is of cosmic significance, and will surely materialize in China as well as in Europe." "In this way, the future points back to the past," said the geomancer. "In *The Book of Change*, the great unity is

spoken of which preceded all separation and caused it. The unification of what is separated signifies perfection." We then
talked a good deal about the curious Chinese book which contains so many unsolved secrets. The student and the abbot had
disappeared quietly in the meantime, and the hour was already
far advanced when the director of the arsenal rose with a laugh
and said, "Usually a Chinese dinner does not take so very
long." "Well, it was only half Chinese," the brother of the
minister of finance remonstrated. "The food came from China
and the wine from Germany." The snow fell in silent flakes
from the sky, when the guests had separated.

These meetings led to the effortless foundation of the so-
called Confucius union, to which a great number of Chinese
officials, besides myself, who were living in Tsingtao, belonged.
Money was collected and a library was built in which a fair
number of precious Chinese works were brought together; a
study and a lounge were arranged, in connection with the
library. The idea was to save for the future the treasures of
Chinese culture, which were in great danger at that time. It
was hoped to establish contact and collaboration between East
and West in intellectual matters by means of translations,
lectures and scientific publications. Writings by Kant were
translated into Chinese, and Chinese classics were rendered into
German. It was hoped that Tsingtao, which was spared from
the storm of the Chinese revolution, would be the place in
which, in the picturesque stillness between mountain and sea,
constructive work could be done. The hope of the participants
ran high, when the foundation-stone was laid of the building,
which was to be completed in the course of the summer 1914,
when events took a different turn from what had been expected. The war broke out just as the building was completed.
It has survived the bombardment without being injured.
During the war, when hundreds of German women and
children were interned in Tsingtao, the library became, as it
were, the living-room of the German community of Tsingtao.
Lectures, festivals for the children, concerts and theatrical performances were arranged, so that the long period of waiting

was made tolerable, and intellectual stimuli were provided to help those present over the sadness of these years. In this way the building served a cultural purpose none the less, and revealed itself as a fair gift from Chinese culture to the interned Germans. Before the dark clouds discharged themselves I had a queer dream. An old man with friendly eyes and a white beard came to visit me. He called himself "Mountain Lao," and he offered to initiate me into the mysteries of the old Mountain. I bowed before him and thanked him, whereupon he vanished and I awoke. About that time, the old Governor-General, Chou Fu, with whose family I was on friendly terms, made me a proposal. He said: "You Europeans only work on the surface of Chinese culture. Not one of you understands its real meaning and true profundity. The reason is that you are never in touch with the right Chinese scholars. The retired village teachers, whom you have as professors, understand only the outer shell themselves. It is therefore not surprising that such a lot of rubbish is taught about China in Europe. How would it be if I procured for you a teacher whose mind is really rooted in the spirit, and who will initiate you into its profundity? You will then be able to translate all kinds of things and write others yourself, so that China will not always have to be ashamed before the world." No one was, of course, more delighted than I was, and a letter was sent to the professor. I prepared a suitable apartment for him in one of the buildings. A few weeks later he arrived with his family. His name was "Lao," his ancestors came from the region of Mount Lao, from which the family had derived its name, and he resembled, in every detail, the old man who had visited me in my dream. We set about our work. We translated a certain amount and read a great deal, and daily conversation initiated me into the profundity of the structure of Chinese culture. Master Lao suggested that I should translate *The Book of Change*. It would not be easy, but he said it was not as unintelligible as it was usually supposed to be. He declared that it was a fact that its vital tradition was on the point of expiring. He, however, had had a teacher who was still fully imbued with the old tradition. His family was closely related to the descendants of Confucius. He owned a bundle of the holy milfoil poles from the tomb of Confucius, and he still knew the art which had also become almost unknown in China of working out an oracle by their aid. Accordingly we proceeded to work upon the book. We worked accurately. He explained the text in Chinese and I made my notes. I then translated the text for myself into German. I thereupon translated my German text without the original into Chinese, and he compared it to see if my translation was correct in all particulars. The German text was then gone over to improve the style, and it was discussed in detail. I then wrote three to four other versions and added the most important commentaries. Before the work was finished the war broke out, and my reverend master Lao returned with other scholars into the interior of China. The translation lay there unfinished. I was beginning to fear that it would never be completed, when I received an unexpected letter from him asking if I could put him up as he wanted to return to Tsingtao to complete the translation of the book. My joy can be imagined when he really came, and the work was then completed. After that I went on leave to Germany. My old master died during my absence, after he had put his testament into my hands.

At that time many guests came for short visits to Tsingtao. K'ang Yu We came once for a few days to discuss the position with former officials who held monarchist views. Ku Hung Ming came frequently for shorter and longer periods, always appearing suddenly like a meteor, full of thoughts and whims, cursing and swearing at the new era, the revolution, and the foreigners, who were to blame for everything. At the same time he would give a survey of Chinese culture, reveal the profoundest insight into the wisdom of the saints, and paint imaginative pictures of the mental activities and literary products of the old days, and then again he would draw superficial parallels between Chinese and European men and periods. His bad temper came back. He was dissatisfied with everything. There was not a single creature whom he did not find fault with, and by this means he did a lot of harm. Even the plan for the reconstruction of the monarchy which was forged in secret, at that time, broke down owing to petty quarrels. Ku Hung Ming was absolutely determined to be minister for foreign affairs, and his determination caused a good deal of bad blood. The more thoughtful people turned more and more away from the conspiracy, some made their peace with Yuan Shih K'ai and the republic, and eventually the whole movement ended in adventure.

Some important visitors came to Tsingtao from Europe. The man upon whom Chinese culture made the deepest impression was Count Hermann Keyserling. At his request I put him in contact with a whole row of important personalities. Some of them were high officials and some of them scholars; the majority were Confucians, though Taoists and Buddhists were also represented. Count Keyserling has described his impressions of this dinner in his *Travel Diary*. I only wish to add here that I have rarely played the part of interpreter with so much pleasure. Whereas usually meetings between Europeans and Chinese hardly ever got beyond raising a friendly glass to each other, or confined themselves to the most superficial and conventional conversation, a real contact was immediately established, owing to the almost uncanny mental agility and faculty for adaptation on the part of the Count, with the result that the conversation turned upon essentials. The Chinese were not a little impressed by Count Keyserling. Years afterwards president Hsü Shih Ch'ang, who was present at the party, still inquired after him. The impression they derived of him was that of a significant, very vital man, in earnest about learning something of Chinese culture. He was met more than half-way on all sides, for nothing opens the heart of Chinamen so much as the genuine desire to arrive at a mutual understanding. Of course they do not speak of their deepest and ultimate knowledge very easily. A certain shyness always holds them back. The conversation turns on subjects which are generally accessible, and the man who has the right vision will deduce the profounder element out of the being and personality of his interlocutor. In the history of old China many examples are given of two men who need only be in each other's company to understand each other about the profoundest principles.

After my guests had dispersed, Count Keyserling stayed with me and discussed his experiences. He had been deeply impressed by the quiet clarity of vision of these old gentlemen and by the ultimate simplicity and largeness of their nature. He considered, however, that the element in which the West was superior was its vitality. He had gained the impression that the Chinese nature was not a match for Western vitality. I told him that I could only wish that he could make the acquaintance of Ku Hung Ming, for whom I claimed that in vitality and nervous staying power he was second to no European. As accident would have it there was a knock at the door, and Ku Hung Ming entered to announce his visit for the night. The frugal evening meal that he had ordered was not yet ended, when the fire of conversation, as it were, showered sparks, as the result of what may be called the mutual power of induction. When the Count said anything Ku Hung Ming could hardly wait his turn. He spoke and wrote in Chinese, French, German, English, all mixed up. Every thought and feeling which fills the heart and the conscience of the Eastern prophet, the history of the entire world and the divine plan of creation, the soul of the Far East and the savage preying of the West. He unburdened himself of all these things to the Count. The drinks had eventually come to an end. The morning twilight shone through the windows. The floor was covered ankle-deep with pieces of paper which were covered with Chinese and European proverbs, suggestions, bons mots, and quotations. Hu Kung Ming rose and went to bed, and Count Keyserling confessed that here, indeed, a Chinaman had faced him who had a full measure of vitality.

These days in Tsingtao also came to an end. Dark clouds had been gathering on the horizon for some time. The war broke out at last. It was as if a trumpet call had rent the air, and all that blossoming life was dispersed. The ancient teacher of the young Chinese Emperor had recently paid a visit to Tsingtao, and he had travelled with a few friends into the Laoshan mountains with all their fairy tales, when the declaration that Tsingtao was in a state of siege came like a flash of lightning. . . . I had the greatest difficulty in obtaining the freedom of people who had been arrested on the open road and then to get them safely on the railway, which took them back to Peking. When war was declared in Europe the flight of the more timid people began already, but the more thoughtful remained. People believed that Germany would be able to hold Tsingtao. Several friends among the Chinese gave warnings, even then, that Japan was only waiting for the right moment to declare war, and eventually the Japanese declaration of war was announced. There was no holding out any longer. Even the Government expressed the wish that the Chinese guests, in so far as they did not wish to participate in a siege, should go to more protected regions. The rush for the railway was indescribable. Together with my friends I organized a branch of the Red Cross with the approval of the German Government. The first function of the organization was to help non-combatants to get away in safety. The attempt was successful, thanks to the intelligent collaboration of the various offices and departments concerned. In the first days of the war it added no little to the difficulties that the monsoon set in, bringing with it such rain, as it were the deluge itself, that the railway line was flooded and so damaged that all transport by land had to be stopped. A rich man in Shanghai ordered a Chinese steamer for himself and his family, with the approval of the militant Powers. He had also permission for a few Chinese to be allowed to join the boat. An incredible throng resulted from this permission. The steamer had hardly come alongside when it was boarded by thousands of passengers. Scenes of indescribable excitement took place. A merchant stood on deck, but his luggage could not be carried through the turmoil by the porters. He saw it in front of his eyes, but he could not get hold of it. He yelled, issued orders, threatened—nothing availed. Eventually he jumped continually three to four feet into the air. I had never seen a man in such a state of hysteria. When the owner of the ship arrived with his family, it was so full that I had the utmost difficulty in finding him a place. In the end, however, this last ship was dispatched in safety.

There were some curious people among the refugees. I remember in particular a certain Hung Shu Tsu. He had been accused of the murder of the leader of the southern party of the republicans, Sung Kiao Jen, and he had fled to Tsingtao. He was a heavy, corpulent man. He had immediately sought the house of a Civil Servant, because he felt more secure there. He was the picture of an evil conscience tortured by the furies. He could look no one in the eyes. His dry tongue continually licked his withered lips in a vain attempt to moisten them. He lived in constant fear of being expelled, in which case he was as good as dead. The fear created by the war proved in the end to be stronger still. He came to me to ask me to get a ticket for him. I asked him if he did not feel more secure in Tsingtao. He did not think so, and said that he was prepared for all eventualities, as he had obtained a certificate from a German doctor that he could not be beheaded, because he had a large swelling on his neck. Eventually his destiny overtook him, nevertheless. The son of the murdered leader found him. He was then prosecuted and condemned to death by hanging, in spite of the medical certificate. This procedure was not all good for him because, in the course of the execution, his head came off and the body fell heavily to the ground. This fact created a great legal difficulty, because, according to Chinese ideas, the severance of the head from the body is considered a much more severe punishment than mere hanging, owing to the unpleasant consequences in the next world. The family of the victim brought the matter to court, and it is said that they obtained damages, and also that the head was subsequently sewn on again.

Those days passed like a wild dream. Only a few of my friends remained behind. Prince Kung and Kao T'ien Yuan, who stood faithfully by my side during the whole duration of the war, helped in the management of the Red Cross and the conduct of the Chinese schools. It was a queer contrast how all the turmoil was succeeded by the stillness of death, interrupted only by the booming of the guns, which resounded uncannily in the empty streets. Even after the terrors of the bombardment were over and Tsingtao had been conquered by the Japanese, the old life did not return. A few professors did indeed continue to live there, while others came for a brief summer holiday, but it was a new period. The old men of Tsingtao had been dispersed to the four corners of the world.

THE PRINCE

PRINCE KUNG was also among the visitors who took their residence in Tsingtao. He was, by adoption, the grandson of the famous Prince Kung who had conducted the affairs of state for a certain period as senior of the Imperial household under the Empress-Dowager. The old Prince Kung was distinguished by his great objectivity, knowledge of affairs and impartiality. The old Empress did not love him. He had opposed her personal plans too often. This was also the reason why the young Prince, who had shared with Prince P'u Lun the best chance of being nominated as the successor of the Emperor Kuanghsü, was rejected during the secret council by the Empress-Dowager immediately before her death.

He was a man with a proud, upright nature, accustomed to command, unapproachable, but also incorruptible. He was one of the two princes who had refused to sign the renunciation of the Manchu Dynasty to the throne. He had managed after many difficulties to reach Tsingtao after he had sold treasures and valuables of his household in order to obtain the means for resuscitating the old dynasty. These treasures went for the most part as desirable collector's pieces to America, and the assertion that a work of art emanated from the collection of Prince Kung constituted for a long time the habitual recommendation with which the merchants of Peking tried to raise the price of their goods.

The Prince lived at first in the profoundest secrecy in an out-of-the-way beer tavern in the neighbourhood of Tsingtao. A young Manchu who had accompanied him even cut off his own pigtail as a precaution. Prince Kung himself could never take this step, but wore a broad well-cared-for pigtail as a sign of his dignity to the very end.

Later on he bought a house in Tsingtao, and then he sent for his family in Peking. His mother, who was already old, but enjoyed an extraordinarily well-cared-for and youthful appearance, was one of those severe active women, possessed

of that uncanny and restless energy of which the house of the
Manchus knew other examples, as for instance that of the
Empress-Dowager; her authority over the family was unqualified. The wife of Prince Kung was a Mongolian princess
of uncommonly delicate charm, but she was an invalid. The
hardships of the journey and the tremendous excitement of the
past, all the fear to which she had been exposed, all the misery
she had endured, the iron severity with which her mother-in-
law had treated her, had broken her strength. When she
reached Tsingtao, she was completely deranged. At first an
ugly shed had been rented for the family of the Prince until
the newly acquired house could be made habitable. All the pri-
vations and strange surroundings caused violent maniacal outbursts. The Prince asked me to spend the night near her in case
anything should again happen, and I did so. Next morning, I
took her to the Chinese hospital where I arranged a place to receive her. There she gradually regained her equilibrium. Little
by little her old self peered out again from the night of mad-
ness and she revealed herself as a woman of the most extraordinarily charming personality. A certain freedom in her nature,
which is a peculiarity of Mongolian women, compared to the
Chinese of the old tradition, made a closer acquaintance possible, in the course of which she showed herself to be not
only clever and refined, but also gracefully witty. She was a
talented painter. To this day, I treasure as a valued memento,
several pictures delicately and yet vigorously painted by her
in brush and ink. A certain melancholy of course rested upon
her like a shroud of clouds, which would rise or fall from
time to time. This was due partially to her physical illness,
which would not perhaps have been incurable, but to which
she eventually succumbed, because the etiquette of the family
did not allow her to entrust herself to an able European
physician.

At first the Prince occupied himself very much with political
plans. As a faithful vassal, he wanted to help the young Emperor again on to his throne. Yuan Shih K'ai, who had spies
everywhere, saw to it that these efforts were frustrated.

The Prince showed no great insight in the choice of his tools. His agent, who was responsible for looking after his income, was a pock-marked lanky Manchu slave who defrauded him terribly. The Prince owned immense stretches of land and he could have lived royally on his revenues from rents. Year after year, the agent sold large quantities for his own account, and he concealed the absence of revenue by attributing it to drought or to inundation, which were blamed for the failure of the crops and consequently made the collection of the rents impossible to their full extent. A great many books and antiquities were also smuggled out of the Peking palace of the Prince, before and after the great sale had taken place. When the thefts assumed such dimensions that the Prince was obliged to dismiss him, the agent to revenge himself set fire to the palace and a large portion of it was burnt down. This practice of burning had always been resorted to by the eunuchs of the Imperial Palace when their misdeeds were discovered, and they used to set fire to the rooms from which they had stolen to make a proper investigation impossible.

The experience of exile had a beneficial effect upon the whole nature of the Prince. He became more simple, more human; more accessible without losing the dignity into which he had been born. There was something straight and uncomplicated about him, which, although it prevented him from being able to cope with the realities of life, often made him quite touching in his almost childish inexperience. This state of affairs was due to the seclusion from the world in which princes grew up within the palace walls where they had intimate intercourse with no one except eunuchs and servants. Even the *citoyen Orléans*, among the Manchu princes, Prince P'u Lun, has kept to this very day something of this awkwardness, although he has been accustomed for a long time to participate in drinking bouts with Chinese friends of all sorts and to stay there until early in the morning, or to clink glasses with Europeans of the most variegated classes in the Wagon Lit Hotel in Peking. One could frequently observe that the princes took little thought in the choice of their companions.

There were not only all kinds of Chinese elements who pushed their way in, and many of them belonged by no means to the best society, but a most curious mixture could be noticed among many of the foreign friends of the princes. Apparently, they considered the step they took to meet other people on a footing of equality at all as so great that they did not or could not distinguish among this set, which was new to them. Such a state of affairs has something to justify it. Only it was noticeable, that there was not only a delightful and complete absence of the sense for middle-class distinctions, but they also frequently lacked the feeling for distinguishing between degrees of quality. This was a mistake which took its own revenge, because in the place of the uncomfortable but efficient people they gathered the comfortable flatterers about them.

In my own intercourse with the Prince and his family I had nothing but good and agreeable experiences. We often plunged into deep conversation about Buddhism, which was the real religion of the Manchu Dynasty in spite of the outward display of Confucianism. He told me with pride how the race of the Manchu had acquired its name from the protective saint Mancusri, the Bodhisatva who had divided the night of ignorance with the sword of recognition and who had been a pioneer of all those who strove from darkness towards the light.

One day when he visited me, he induced me to play a few European pieces on the violin. I attempted to show him the highest aim of the spirit of European music. This attempt interested him and he said that it coincided with the real significance of the best Chinese music. He then sat down in a corner and on his flute he played the melody which has been played from immemorial times in the temple, in honour of the tilling of the soil in Peking, when, in the spring, the Emperor drew the plough with his own hand and cut the first furrows. The evening darkened. Inward pictures appeared before me and deep emotions seemed to come with the simple tones of the flute floating from far-off worlds. This melody will probably be forgotten, for who bothers about it today? It is nevertheless a precious memory to have cast a last glance into these worlds.

Occasionally he would talk of former rulers whose pictures he had had occasion to see in the Imperial Palace. He would speak, for instance, of the last Ming Emperor, who, in the midst of the chaos of the revolution and invasion, in the year 1642, had hanged himself in despair, together with his faithful eunuch, on an old cypress tree on the Coal Island. He said that he thought the Emperor was really a Christian. The Prince had himself seen a picture in which he knelt before the cross. Sometimes he would recall pictures of the great rulers of his own race for the material of which he drew upon his own memory. He would describe the tall haggard K'ang Hsi, with his thin pointed beard on the end of his chin and his sharp protruding eyes, or the fat and gorgeous K'ien Lung or his predecessor Yungtshung who had himself portrayed in shimmering armour and wore a curiously twisted and upturned moustache beneath his glittering helmet. From this external peculiarity, the Prince deduced a certain inner relationship to the Kaiser.

Occasionally, though rarely, he spoke of the Empress-Dowager. When he did so, one felt in his remarks the respect, bordering on fear, which she knew how to inculcate into those who surrounded her. He spoke of the immense capacities which enabled her, right up to her old age, to conduct her audiences during which the most important affairs of state were decided by herself and with the greatest circumspection. Such efforts involve, purely physically, extraordinary freshness and vigour, for these audiences all took place at an early hour in the morning, and at daybreak everything was finished. In those small hours of the dark morning many an important decision was taken, and the old lady held her ministers and princes in her hand with the accustomed assurance of a ruler. The Prince related how he trembled when he had to deliver a report. Everything had to be related in such a form that it satisfied her, for otherwise she easily became angry and was terrible in wrath. On the other hand, it was not permissible for any one to contradict himself, for her ever-present memory watched like an eagle. If any passage occurred in the report which was not quite clear, she was immediately ready to question how this point was consistent with an assertion that the reporter had made perhaps a year ago. Woe to him, if he did not succeed in explaining any query to her complete satisfaction.

On the other hand, she had a clear vision of what took place in the audience chamber. If, for instance, an old and venerable dignitary was ill at ease, while he knelt—all the reports delivered before the throne were pronounced in a kneeling position—she noticed him and would allow him to stand up. She was also quite capable, if the man in question displeased her, of making him feel extremely uncomfortable, out of sheer malice, by making him kneel a long time.

The Prince also spoke a good deal about her relation to the unfortunate Emperor. He never talked about the Emperor himself; nor did he mention how severely he was imprisoned for a time, in the Summer Palace (Wan Shou Shan). It must have been terrible. The walls by which the Emperor was cut off from light and air, in those days, speak for themselves with sufficient clarity. A naked sword lay in front of the door, on a stone in the courtyard, and any one who attempted, in any way, to approach the Emperor could expect a certain death. Nevertheless, those days of terror passed away. The old Empress enjoyed the summer in the Wan Shou Shan at the foot of the western hills in the company of her circle. The palace had been rebuilt at her order out of the ruins and destructions of its former perfection. The palace is situated on the slope of a hill. The buildings near the slope at the back are still in ruins and are now cut off by a wall. Its distinguishing feature is the great tower-shaped terrace surmounted by a sanctuary dedicated to Buddha, for the Empress was a pious Buddhist. The terrace affords a wide panoramic view over the K'unming Lake, in which the palace reflects itself, and above whose various branches fantastic bridges are stretched, whereas sanctuaries and little tea-houses adorned with flowers and grottoes and artificial rocks stand on the little islands, much in the manner in which they can be seen in the parks of European palaces of the eighteenth century.

Here the Empress enjoyed the peace of the country, surrounded by Court ladies, eunuchs and relatives. Excursions were made on the lake in gorgeous boats and on these occasions jesting and laughter were not forbidden. The days of a dangerous youth lay behind her, and in gentle wisdom she delighted in the activity of her surroundings. Occasionally an expedition was made to the marble ship, a hideously ugly contraption, being an imitation of a European paddle steamer, which has been converted into a tea-house. This monstrosity had cost a great deal of money, but the Empress enjoyed it as a curiosity much as she enjoyed the tigers in the zoological gardens. In this form, she could support European boats; they were at any rate harmless.

In this country seclusion, into which the pagoda of the jade mountain and the buildings in its vicinity, also for the most part ruins left from fairer days, seem as it were to send their greeting, she pursued her hobbies. She had a special passion for clocks and watches. Any one who wanted to give her pleasure, added a specimen to the large collection of watches which she had gradually brought together. She also had a special affection for a certain kind of red apple, of which there were always whole mountains near her, and above everything, she adored her peonies. The fragrant large tree peony is after all the queen among flowers, equally gorgeous because of its size and delicate fragrance, its multitudinous tones of colour which run through the whole scale from delicate white and the palest green to lilac and scarlet red. Near the Summer Palace, there is a special hill of peonies on which one bush jostles another and their gorgeous blossoms open the festivities of the year.

The Empress also painted these pet flowers of hers with great pleasure. She could use a brush with skill and ease. She used to present her pictures, after they had been provided with the large Imperial seal and with a dedicatory verse, to the friends of her preference. Later on she employed two painters to make these pictures for her, and in this way it came about that the Chinese art trade is by no means poor in pictures by the Empress-Dowager, all of which bear the genuine Imperial seal! Among the arts, she had a special preference for that of the theatre. She was pleased to escape from the noise and turmoil of the day into this fantastic world of heroes and fairies. The Summer Palace possesses its own stage on which the most famous singers of the capital gave their performances in the wonderful old silk dresses belonging to the Imperial wardrobe.

The whole Court forgathered to see these performances. Even the Emperor was allowed to witness them when the wrath of his aunt had abated. He remained a lonely prisoner even in the midst of these festivities. The Prince used to describe how the Emperor was carried in, seated in a gorgeous sedan chair, without saying a word, and merely pointing with his finger to the place to which he desired to be carried. Thus he would sit there during the performance. The tradition of the Court forbade most strictly that his dignity should be infringed by any one present addressing a word to him. The courtiers sat on either side at a respectful distance. As soon as the performance was over he would take leave of his aunt, and then he would be carried away again, in silence, as he had come. "The Empress-Dowager," continued the Prince, "was not quite so particular as far as her own person was concerned in the matter of etiquette, and she would continue to remain seated, and to chat with one person or another, as the case might be. The Emperor, however, was surrounded with reverence, as if by a wall." It can be imagined that this splendid isolation was bound to affect the unhappy prisoner, and it can easily be understood how these continual humiliations—for he had to express his gratitude again and again to his kindly aunt—corroded his spirit, so that eventually he passed out of life with that grimace with which he recommended Yuan Shih K'ai to execution.

We can also understand equally well how far from the world, and surrounded by the atmosphere of the ancient knights which made the past seem so alive, romantic notions germinated in the head of the young princes and an entirely different world was apparent to them from the hard and alien world of reality, which manifested itself disagreeably again and again, until it destroyed, with a cold hand, the whole fairy tale of the Summer Palace. Today, the Summer Palace, Wan Shou Shan, formerly the hidden resting-place of the hidden Imperial Court, is shown to foreigners for an entrance fee which is exacted at the various gates. Poor haggard Manchus drag themselves about. The entrance fees are substitutions for tips, but an attempt is made to wrest a few coins from the visitor and these poor creatures then tell of the secrets of the past in a muffled voice. The foreigners, however, run about everywhere, gaping through the dusty window-panes into the bed-chambers of the Empress; they crack their jokes about the bronze storks, and in exchange for money and persuasion they induce the servants to steal one of the little riders made of glazed clay which form a ledge in a portion of the roof which can be reached from the steps. They then depart, having hidden the object with much ado in their pocket, delighted at these stolen Chinese antiquities; while the servants place a new one on the roof, which they then steal for the next visitor who has an inclination for antiquities. The visitors ascend through rock grottoes, puffing and blowing until they reach the temple of the Buddha where they drink tea and spit the shells of the melon seeds down over the wall. They are then rowed about on the lake, and in the marble ship whose splendour they duly admire, they drink a second cup of tea, and finally purchase souvenirs and picture postcards.

At the entrance gate of the Summer Palace there once stood a bronze dragon, who watched over the entrance in company with his brother. He has fallen from his pedestal and broken his legs. He lies there helpless on the floor. He cannot protect the palace any longer. A lady prods him with her parasol: *Sic transit gloria mundi*—.

The Prince, as has been mentioned before, spoke rarely of these things and, when he did so, it was without pleasure. The memory of those distant days, when power and beauty were the ornaments of his life, was disagreeable to him. He had gone into exile, of his own free will, because he no longer desired to live in that China which had been wrested from its Emperor, because it had ceased to be his home. He had left his glorious palace, at the foot of the Coal Hill which belonged to the most famous monuments of yore. He had abandoned his summer residence in the splendid Tsia T'ai Si temple in the Western hills near Peking. He had parted from his treasures and his beloved books. He had taken in Tsingtao, a lightly built summer villa, in which he and his family found only the most meagre accommodation. I still remember the touching pleasure with which he showed me his newly constructed pond of gold fish with its fountain and the attempts to convert his wretched little garden into a park. In the course of time, he was obliged to give up even his two-horse glass carriage, because his means were insufficient. He bore everything with great matter-of-factness and without a murmur. It was hard, nevertheless, and while he was in Tsingtao he never abandoned hope altogether of returning home one day, from his exile.

At the outbreak of war he showed how great his determination was to assume the burden of exile. At that time, all the Chinese guests had abandoned their retreat in Tsingtao and had gone partially into the interior of China and partially to the foreign settlement of Tientsin. Prince Kung alone remained. He preferred to put up with the siege of Tsingtao, rather than return to China while it was a republic. As long as the European powers alone participated in the war, his decision gave no cause for anxiety, because in the circumstances Tsingtao was, at the worst, exposed to the danger of an occasional bombardment from the sea. After the Chinese visitors had all left in peace, he visited me daily to talk about the events in the European theatres of war. He wrote a war diary and was firmly convinced of Germany's ultimate victory. One day we talked about wonders and signs. He inquired whether the appearance of a comet had not yet been announced in Europe, because such a war could not possibly take place without such a sign in the sky. I told him that such news had not been received and I attempted to explain to him that, in Europe, the people were persuaded that comets were natural manifestations which had no kind of connection with human events. (The age of astrology had not yet dawned in Europe.) "Curious," said he; "a comet ought to appear and it ought to be visible in the sky in the west." After this conversation there followed a long period of terrific rainfall and the sky was covered day and night with thick clouds. One evening when the sky was clear again, a comet really appeared in the west. I had to think of the prophecy of the Prince, but he had discovered the comet too. A few days later, he came to me again in the evening. He pointed with his gaze to the western sky. "And what do you call that?" he asked seriously, and with a special significance in his voice. "That is a comet," was my reply. "And it stands in the west, exactly where it had to stand," he replied. It would have been difficult to convince the Prince that the comet had no kind of connection with military events.

When Japan entered the war, he became a little anxious all the same. His house faced the sea, and was therefore particularly exposed to bombardment. Accordingly, he was most grateful when I gave him the use of a house in the patch of land belonging to the Chinese Red Cross. He moved in with his family and left merely a few servants to guard the villa on the shore. The grim days of the siege followed and they were so rich in experiences that one would not care to have missed them in spite of all the danger and misery. Apart from the Prince, another Manchu had stayed in Tsingtao, a man who rendered me very considerable services, both in the management of the Red Cross as later on in the reorganization of my work for the schools. The three of us met frequently. My scientific work was not interrupted even during the bombardment and I found the assistance of my two friends most precious. The Prince occupied his free hours by working at his war diary and by copying the Chinese *Book of Change* from an old printed edition, of the Sung period. This book, at which many a saint of an earlier day had worked during hours of great trial, now helped the Manchu prince through the difficult hours of the siege. For sometimes, when the bombardment was at its height, his nerves threatened to get the better of his courage. His former absolute conviction that buildings on which the flag of the Red Cross was flown were exempt from every attack began to be shaken.

It must be conceded after all that the forces of destiny are stronger even than the Red Cross. This is a fact which revealed itself also in Europe. Accordingly, towards the end of the bombardment, our buildings also came under fire. It was a piece of good fortune that most of the Japanese grenades failed to explode, for otherwise not one of us would be about today. When the house in which Prince Kung lived received a few direct hits no power could hold him any longer. He and the whole of his family disappeared one night. He took refuge in a house that belonged to General Chang Hsün, but even then he was not destined to be at rest. He had hardly moved in when the explosion of a shell destroyed one entire wall of the house. In this case, he also escaped with nothing worse than the fright. Later on he had photographs taken of himself and his two sons, standing by the ruins, and he also preserved a few pieces of shell on which he had inscriptions engraved, in memory of the occasion.

After Tsingtao had been taken by the Japanese there were a good many doubtful elements in the locality. The Japanese authority prevented serious plundering only by means of absolute iron severity. It goes without saying that the Prince, who was in hiding, was in considerable danger at that time. A former Mohammedan antique dealer, who also belonged to the dubious elements, came to see me shortly after the occupation of Tsingtao and inquired after the whereabouts of the Prince: "If I knew where he lived, I would be better able to protect him. There are all kinds of fellows here who are after his life." I saw through him at once. An attempt at blackmail on a large scale was what he had in view and so I did not, of course, give away the address. A little later when the Japanese had provided the Prince with a guard, I informed the Mohammedan in detail. He smiled with a bitter sweet expression: "In that case he will not need my protection any more." But he disappeared.

The Japanese were exceedingly accommodating towards the Prince. He was allowed to return to the house near the sea and was provided with a constant bodyguard. It is curious to think how often he had changed his abode during the siege of Tsingtao; the terror of war had pursued him everywhere and when, eventually, he returned into his own house it was absolutely intact. No one would have thought it possible.

At times he was in money difficulties. His Chinese estates produced less and less revenue and sometimes it was by no means easy for him. The Japanese offered him various means of making money, but he renounced them. The first offer he had was to take over the opium concession. This was an excellent proposition and brought in money. Prince Kung had been the president of the committee for the suppression of opium, and the man who, when he occupied this position, had always shown himself severe and quite incorruptible, refused the Japanese offer in the following terms: "I am an Imperial prince. To my regret I am unable to do anything in the present circumstances for the Chinese people, but I will never lower myself to the extent that I should support myself by a trade which is ruining the Chinese people." The Chinaman who exploited the concession afterwards, became a multi-millionaire.

Later on he received another offer, namely the management of the sewage of Tsingtao, also a very remunerative undertaking. He refused the offer with a smile. He stayed in Tsingtao, nevertheless, not only during the whole of the war, but as long as the Japanese were in control. It was not until Tsingtao was given back to China that he went away and settled in Port Arthur, where he is to be found to this day.

I have described the fate of this prince at some length, because it is characteristic of the whole of the Imperial household. An ancient era takes its leave. Its days are irrevocably of the past and it had to be so. The general conditions of the

times and also the particular circumstances attendant upon
the ruling house being of alien origin combined to bring this
about. China is today no longer a monarchy founded upon a
religious basis in which case the nationality of the ruler is of
no importance, as long as it is appointed by heaven and dis-
charges its trust faithfully by means of a sound and just government. China is today a nationalist republic and it is one of
its principles, on the one hand, that no alien may interfere with
the Government and, on the other hand, that every Chinese cit-
izen has the right to participate in the Government according
to his station.

The odd fact is the nature of the transition. Heretofore,
when a dynasty had lost the authority of heaven and the inclination of the people a revolution broke out when the measure
of the sins of the rulers was full and its success proved the
revolution to be divinely ordained. The new dynasty had removed the old one and a new era began. The greater the
mental power behind these changes, the greater was its
effect, even in the future. Dynasties which were founded by
truly good and great men lasted longer—especially if every
now and again, the spirit of the ancestor returned in one of the
descendants—than those which were merely the consequence
of the momentary fortunes of war. The beginning of the
Manchu rule was very peculiar. The Ming Dynasty had used
up its original forces during the long and extravagant government of the Emperor Wan Li. A few weak though good-
natured rulers had succeeded him, but they were unable to prevent the downfall. Revolts broke out, and the last Emperor
came to an end. The Manchus had come, as it were, to help
him, and during the struggle against the revolution they
occupied the empty throne. In this way, the transition from
one dynasty to another took place in a much milder form than
usual. This fate was now to be the end of the Manchu
Dynasty. The Empress-Dowager had made considerable demands during the long course of her reign upon the still
effective power of the merits of the first rulers, K'ang Hsi and
K'ien Lung, but these merits had on the one hand been partic-

ularly great and on the other the government of the old lady could not be regarded as purely negative. During the revolution, the store of good works had not been exhausted altogether, and for this reason the destiny of the dynasty was not so hard as it might have been. The Emperor renounced his prerogative of government, but he remained Emperor with all the insignia of his rank and with a very respectable annuity from the coffers of the republic.

Circumstances eventually proved themselves to be the strongest masters. The public coffers were empty, and consequently the Imperial revenue was paid with more and more delay until it finally ceased. The Emperor himself is a young man, intellectually wide awake, and he had acquired thoroughly modern ideas under the guidance of an English teacher who was also highly cultivated in Chinese matters. The modernity of the young Emperor was often the cause of considerable shock to the old gentlemen at Court and to the older princesses with their conservative views.

It was not only the fact that he visited the temple of his ancestors on a bicycle and practised this sport also near the Summer Palace, but he enforced all kinds of reforms most energetically. He dismissed at one fell swoop all of the eunuchs in spite of the energetic resistance of his Imperial aunts. The dismissed servitors sat for days, with all their goods and chattels in front of the palace gates, before they departed. Shortly after his marriage the Emperor also sent the superfluous Court ladies back to their parents to provide them with an opportunity of getting married elsewhere. Finally he entrusted the English teacher with the reorganization of the management of the Imperial Summer Palace.

The sands were running out and evil indications made themselves felt. Fires broke out, three in one night, and they were interpreted as being unfavourable to the dynasty. The financial crisis became greater and greater. New treasures had to be sold continually. Dissentient voices were heard which disapproved of those not strictly personal possessions leaving the country.

Then the Christian general completed the dream. When the power was in his hands, he expelled the young Emperor and his family ruthlessly from the palace of his ancestors. What will happen now is doubtful, though one thing is certain: that here a piece of an old tradition with all its faults and insufficiencies but also with all its beauties and its nobility glides irretrievably into the past.

BEGGARS, THIEVES AND ROBBERS

I WAS not very frequently in touch with beggars, thieves and robbers, but my experiences, such as they were, were nearly all comparatively pleasant. Politeness towards guests and foreigners is to this very day held in such esteem that one can observe that this courtesy, even if it was not by itself decisive, played at any rate an important part in the intercourse between these people and strangers in so far as other considerations did not prove themselves to be more cogent.

The social strata to be discussed here are, of course, well organized like other classes, and they are certainly more disciplined than in Europe, where frequently a certain competitive jealousy seems to predominate among the various professions of this underworld. Such an organization also requires a moral basis. The ancient philosopher, Chuangtse, tells a pretty story of the necessity of the moral properties of an efficient robber chieftain.

The companions of the robber chief asked him one day: "Does a robber also need morals?" He answered them and said: "Why! of course, without morals he cannot manage to achieve anything at all. He recognizes by intuition where something is hidden: that is his greatness; he has to be the first to get it, that is his courage; he has to be the last to get out, that is his sense of duty; he has to know whether it can be managed or not, that is his wisdom; he must divide fairly, that is his kindness. It is absolutely impossible that a man who is lacking in one of these five virtues will ever become a great robber."

But speaking quite seriously, it must be confessed that, while membership of this lower anonymous section of the outcasts of life necessarily stunts certain regions of the soul, which are required for a well-ordered social life, it does not throttle all the better feelings of men. This is true particularly of beggars who have dropped out of society far more frequently owing to external circumstances than through their own malignity. The family system in China brings it about that every man has a firm foothold in his class and he can always resort to it in all kinds of unfortunate situations. The position is very different when owing to journeys into foreign parts, epidemics or the migration of entire villages during years of famine, this connection with the man's family is lost. Charitable institutions are by no means lacking in China, but the public care of the poor is not organized anything like as systematically as in Europe, precisely because the cohesion of the family or tribe takes its place in most cases. The outcasts have therefore a bitter life. The most that they can hope for is to find shelter here and there. They have to provide for food themselves and the miserable rags with which they cover their nakedness. I was once in a workhouse in Tsinanfu. It was winter and the day was cold. The unfortunate inmates sat huddled together in the corners of dusky rooms blackened with smoke in so far as they were not engaged upon begging excursions. In the middle of one room a coal fire gleamed dimly and an immensely old man squatted by its side. His powerful, well-formed head was bald. His eyes had a far-off and empty look; he held his trembling hands over the coals and he answered all questions with a dull "ooh." The others said that he was well over one hundred years old, and that he had forgotten the present and conversed only occasionally in a horrible manner with the shadows of the past which seemed to throng round the fire.

The beggars constitute a regular guild. They used to have a beggar king, recognized by the municipality, and the ordinary beggars had to pay him tithes and he controlled the work and the distribution of the available means. To this day, in the larger towns, individual streets which contain shops are canvassed regularly at certain hours. The larger firms relieve their customers of the unpleasantness of being pestered by beggars by the payment of fixed sums. Other firms prefer to pay these sums themselves after a corresponding period of waiting. The individual beggar has to spend a good deal of time in saying his verses before they throw him his copper, otherwise his fellows would come too quickly and the fixed sums available would not be sufficient.

Once a man has sunk into these depths, it is difficult to help him. He is exhausted and he lacks the power of rehabilitating himself. If, for instance, you give such street beggars warm clothes in the winter, you may behold, to your surprise, that he has sold or pawned them the very next day. When I once questioned such a beggar on the subject, he replied with touching sincerity: "I am not ungrateful, the beautiful warm clothes were a great blessing and also I got a good price for them. I must go about in rags, no matter how much I freeze. If I am well dressed nobody would give a single copper and I cannot satisfy my hunger with warm clothes."

Naturally enough you meet with a good deal of degradation and spiritual defects among these people. Dull desire is the only emotion which animates them. They beg, or beat their head upon the floor, or run after a carriage without allowing themselves to be stopped by anything. Nothing but the act of throwing them a coin brings them to momentary rest. The fate of these creatures is terrible when they fall ill, and excite the sympathy and abhorrence of the spectators by the exhibition of their horrible sufferings. In former days, large crowds of these dehumanized and tortured creatures used to sit at the southern gate of Peking. When Yuan Shih K'ai assumed the reins of government they suddenly disappeared, but no one ever discovered what became of them.

You can also sometimes find sages and saints among the beggars. You are sometimes struck by a look issuing from beneath touselled hair and deep folds expressing such a profundity of suffering and gentleness in endurance, that one would like to sit at the foot of such a beggar and ask him to reveal the secret by which he has endured such torment. But the beggar sits there quietly and waits. He does not grow impatient, even if thousands pass him by, and then if some one gives him anything he thanks him with a quiet kindly smile, so that you feel as though he had given you something far more valuable than the wretched coin you have put into his bowl.

Once a small boy ran by my side with begging eyes. I gave him a piece of bread and meat from my travelling provisions. He thanked me, and put it, without attempting to eat it, into his bowl for alms. I asked him if he did not care for alien bread. His little face lit up: "It is a special treat, but I have an ill mother at home and am so pleased if I may bring it her."— "Have you eaten something yourself yet?" He replied, almost apologetically: "No, not yet today, but I am young and do not need it so much. I will find something for myself all right."

When many years ago, an aged beggar died in the province of Shantung, it appeared that in spite of his extremely wretched manner of life, he had saved quite a considerable sum. It was money for which he had literally starved. He directed by means of a will that his fortune should be given to a kind of school for the poor, so that at any rate a few children might, after his death, be saved from the fate of spending their lives in the streets as beggars. In the circumstance it is intelligible that in Chinese fairy tales and in Chinese art old beggars of repulsive appearance are often really powerful magicians and sages, and also that the great magician Li Tie Kuai assumed the appearance of an old cripple and was not ashamed to show himself in the form and the company of the eight genii among whom he found acceptance owing to his magical powers.

A special category of beggars in China are the very numerous blind. They distinguish themselves in contrast to the often suspicious and cunning deaf by a quiet gentleness. They usually play the lute or some other instrument as they go through the streets, earning a trifle in this way. In one hand they carry a stick with which they feel their way with remarkable deftness, and in the other they carry a small bell-gong whose regular beats request passers-by to make way for blind men. The blind are usually treated with friendliness, and there is a general readiness to assist them. I shall never forget the blind man who passed me in the streets of Suchou. It was in the spring and he played on a small Chinese violin, one of those primitive instruments which are held in an upright position and between whose two strings a bow of horsehair generally produces shrill and shrieking tones.

I have often been asked whether China possesses any music. I then remember perhaps the moving theatres with their cymbals and castanets or the twanging guitars and the harsh tones of the violins which accompany singers in tea-houses, or else the moaning autumn flute above the reed-covered lake; but all these things are of no account. That there is music in China, I have known since I heard that blind fiddler on that spring evening in the fair town of Suchou.

Even in China, of course, all the beggars are not such ideal musicians. In Peking I once saw a scene whose horrible comedy was almost reminiscent of a picture by the Höllen Breughel. I was driving along the willow-lined canal, which forms the boundary of the old Imperial town. Close to the former temple of the Tartars, near the little acacia wood in which from time to time the spirits of the hanged call for a new victim, which you can see one morning hanging from a tree, there was a turmoil of people. The newspaper boys had left their papers on one side to join the crowd; other idlers, who thronged closer and closer together, surrounded a chaos of curses from which clouds of dust flew up into the air from time to time. When I came close I saw a blind beggar in the midst of his tormentors. Somehow or other he had quarrelled with a few good-for-nothings, who laughed at him and threw handfuls of dust into his face. The blind man was in a towering rage. He opened his white and empty eyes wide and raved while beating about him with his stick and his guitar. The laughing crowd fled before his blows and new clouds of dust enveloped him. With a yelling voice he cursed and insulted those who stood about, but his crude insults were so grotesque in their unlimited exaggeration that they only called forth rollicking laughter. Needless to say, such scences of a town mob out of control are revolting. Nevertheless, it must be said in honour of the Chinese that a few quiet words sufficed to bring the whole crowd to its senses. Reason won the day so quickly that it is not conceivable that it would have been possible to

restore such a mob to order anywhere else in so short a
time.

Whereas the majority of the beggars are the passive section
in the underworld of society, the thieves and robbers represent
the active parties. It has been mentioned already that among
them there exists a definite system. On the whole it may be
said that in China, trifles, especially those which the owner does
not use or neglects, disappear, but serious thefts occur far more
rarely than in Europe. During the period before the war, you
could as a rule leave your front door open, even at night, without anything being stolen. It was only once, about the New
Year, that my servants caught a poor little thief who wanted
to fetch something for himself at night, so that he could also
have a little pleasure during the special festivities of the New
Year. He trembled as he stood before me while I questioned
him about his intentions, and I have never seen any one run
away more relieved than when under severe threats I provided
him with some food and a little money to enable him to return
to his own home. He swore he would never return again, and
kept his oath.

The thieves who do not steal in secret, but in the open, are
more dangerous. In the place where the fir-covered heights of
the Laoshan plunge into the sea, there stands in the midst of
bamboo groves the Taoist monastery of T'ai Ts'ing Kung,
famous for its peonies and camellia trees. The monks distinguish themselves by the seriousness of their conduct of life
and by their pious practices. The abbot was a good friend
of mine with whom I often used to sit together on summer
evenings plunged in deep conversation or listening to his playing the old mysterious cithara. The monks were very friendly
towards Europeans. A special guide to receive the guests had
been appointed by the abbot to minister the intercourse of
foreign visitors. This man often came to me in Tsingtao to
bring me the greetings of the abbot or to present me with a
marvellous stone, a mysterious priest's staff, whose upper
portion ended in a curiously shaped animal head grown from
roots, a magical wand to frighten away evil spirits. He arrived

on one of these occasions in an excited condition. There was something uncertain, something of the expression of a fox in his face. I suspected nothing, because as usual he handed me the visiting card of the monastery with the greetings of the abbot. He had come to buy a revolver and cartridges, because lately robbers had frequently disturbed the monastery. I was glad to procure the weapon for him and gave it to him as a present to the monastery. I cautioned him never to make serious use of it, but only to fire off shots to frighten the robbers, and this he promised to do. As a matter of practice we shot at a target. He turned out to be a remarkable pupil as he hit the bull's-eye at the first shot. As he had instructions from the monastery to undertake a lengthy journey, he asked me to lend him one hundred dollars which I handed him readily. He took his leave with great friendliness and promised to arrange immediately for the repayment of the money. Thereupon he departed.

I waited weeks and months, but nothing happened. It was then that I remembered the fox-like expression in his face, and after a good deal of consideration I sent a messenger to the monastery to inquire with the greatest circumspection if the revolver was satisfactory. Then the whole thing came out. The monk who used to receive the guests had become re-calcitrant and had joined the robbers. For this reason, he had equipped himself through my assistance. He had also borrowed money from other patrons of the monastery, but to obtain a useful weapon he needed European assistance. The T'ai Ts'ing Kung monastery behaved incidentally very decently and generously. The "borrowed" hundred dollars were repaid fully, in spite of all my remonstrances, because the man had come with a visiting card from the monastery on the strength of which he had been given money.

The method of friendly borrowing is often practised by clever thieves in China. It was still in the days of the Empire when the following incident occurred on the occasion on which a new governor-general was appointed in one of the provincial capitals. The old governor waited for his successor to hand over the seals. An elderly gentleman called on the pro-vincial treasurer, introducing himself as the father of the new governor. He informed him that his son would follow him immediately, and that he himself had gone ahead to raise an advance of a few thousand taels in order to pay for the ex-penses involved in paying for the new appointment. The treasurer offered him tea and conversed with him, and the visitor was perfectly informed about everything. In the mean-time the new governor was announced. He entered, and greeted the treasurer and his father in the most courteous manner. After a few words had been exchanged the old gentle-man got up and said: "You have no doubt all sorts of official business to settle, and I do not wish to disturb you; I merely request the payment of the advance we have spoken of." The treasurer put the required advance at his disposal out of the coffers of the province. The old gentleman departed, accom-panied in the politest way by the two others. When the two men were seated again and had exchanged the usual etiquette, the treasurer said: "Your father is still vigorous for his age." The governor heaved a sigh and said: "Yes, he was in the full possession of his mental powers right up to the end."—"How do you mean? what do you mean by the end? Has he retired from business?"—"Well, you see, he died three years ago." The treasurer began to doubt the faculties of the governor.— "But he was just here!" The governor felt that there was some-thing uncanny in the situation. "When?" he asked; "what did he look like?" "Why, the gentleman who has just gone away!" —"But I don't know him," replied the governor. "But you were so deferential to him and allowed him to sit on the seat of honour," said the treasurer.—"I did that, because I saw with what deference you treated him." The treasurer after a little pause began again somewhat timidly: "Then I suppose he did not ask for the advance at your instruction?"—"I never dreamt of an advance," said the governor greatly perturbed.—"Oh! well, then he was just a swindler." The treasurer called cash-iers and guards in great haste, but it was no use. The old gentleman had taken the money and had disappeared without any trace. Similar experiences are unfortunately not confined to the treasuries of Chinese provinces.

Tsingtao had been taken by the Japanese. I had managed the Chinese Red Cross during the siege of Tsingtao, and after its surrender I was allowed to remain at liberty for this reason. The Chinese wounded continued to be attended and Chinese friends supplied me with money for this purpose from time to time. This fact must have become known somehow. One evening as I sat in my house reading a book—the servants had just gone to bed—a peculiar-looking Chinamen suddenly came over the verandah, through the door, into my room and looked about him with great curiosity. Before I could make out what he wanted, a few others followed him. I asked in Chinese what they were about. For answer, two of them, pretty evil-looking fellows stepped behind me and tied my hands on my back in the twinkling of an eye. The third stepped behind the table opposite to me, pulled out a revolver, aiming it at me and said: "What we want? We want to shoot you." I suddenly had the absurd sensation of feeling myself the centre of a novel of adventure, and the situation struck me as less dangerous than funny. Accordingly I asked them why they wanted to shoot me. "You have received 2,000 dollars today and we want them," was the reply. I remarked thereupon that it would hardly seem necessary to kill me if that was their sole object. After a short discussion, in the course of which one fellow was in favour of dealing with the matter gently, they saw my point. I told them that though I did not have 2,000 dollars, I did not see that I was in a position to withhold whatever money I did possess. They then asked for the key of the safe and which letter had to be used to open the lock. In the meantime, one of these fellows removed my gold watch-chain and watch. The watch was not of great value as my gold one had stopped and could not be repaired at that time in Tsingtao. But I was sorry to lose the chain. The robbers fortunately took no interest in my pocket-book which contained a fair sum in bank-notes. Meanwhile one of them had opened the safe and fetched out the money-box. They then began to bargain again. They pointed out that they now had the money and would surely take it away with them, but it would really be a pity to smash the box. They argued that the key without the box would be useless to me, but most useful to them. I saw the logic of this argument and showed them where the key was kept. They unlocked the box and were rather disappointed not to find more money in it. It was now my turn to bargain and I said: "The money in the right drawer is my money and it is at your disposal. The money on the left belongs to the Red Cross and is destined for the care of Chinese wounded. I should be glad if you would leave that there." This argument did not appeal to them at all. "We are Red Beards [1] and don't bother about the Red Cross." There was evidently nothing to be done in that direction. I inquired if they would care to have a cup of tea, but they were in a hurry. They now wanted to put a gag into my mouth and tie my legs together. The gag, which was sewn out of a pretty dirty piece of blue cloth and was evidently filled with sand, made a most repulsive impression. Who might not have had it in his mouth before? I thereupon became very grave and said to them, that I did not wish to be gagged in any circumstances. They again held a short council of war, and the gentlest among them remarked that I had really been very polite and they did not wish to be monsters. Accordingly, they decided not to gag me, but said that I must not do anything against them for at least half an hour. The most forward among them tied up my legs, nevertheless, though imperfectly, and said that if I moved a muscle they would shoot me dead from outside, where their companions were waiting, and indeed I did hear a dull noise outside the door. Thereupon they left the house. Their visit had apparently taken rather longer than they had anticipated. In the end I could not stop myself from calling after them that I had 2,000 dollars all the same. They immediately rushed back. "Where are they?"—"At the bank!" I replied

[1] "Red Beards," in Chinese Hung Hu Tzu is the name of a Manchurian band of robbers who have the habit of attaching red beards to their faces in their expeditions. Later on this name was used for street robbers of all kinds.

with courtesy. This announcement damped their interest to a marked degree, for the bank was kept under a Japanese guard and protected against thieves. They did not stop any longer, but disappeared into the dark.

At this moment help came from all sides. My dog, who all this time had remained as quiet as a mouse behind the stove, rushed out barking loudly as soon as the robbers had disappeared. When I reached the room of my valet, he quickly untied my fetters. They were marvellously solid silk cords in the Japanese national colours, white and red, and firmly twisted together. A friend who used to visit me in the evenings arrived. Quite by accident he came on this evening, half an hour later than usual. I had to tell him the whole story. In the meantime, I had sent a servant to notify the Japanese police. A strong contingent arrived and proceeded to make a most conscientious report: What was my name, when was I born, surname, Christian name, date of birth, place of birth, as well as the date of the death of my parents and also their names and all the various dates in reference to my wife and my four children. Then I had to give reasons why my family was not present in Tsingtao. (I had taken them to safety just before the bombardment which did after all involve the risk of their lives.) I also had to state what had been stolen. I had to give an accurate account as to why I wore a less valuable watch on a more valuable chain. The fetters had to be produced, and in spite of my earnest entreaties to be allowed to keep them in memory of the occasion, they were rigorously removed as the *corpus delicti*. Thereupon the police departed.

Next morning they wanted to arrest all my servants and to pump them full of petroleum so that they should confess the theft. I had the utmost difficulty in getting them released, though I was convinced that they were in no way connected with the event.

A member of the Chinese secret police who had come with the Japanese from Manchuria to Tsingtao undertook to get to the root of the matter, but he was dismissed when his research pointed to clues which were not destined to disclose only

Chinese robbers. At that time, certain very doubtful elements turned up in Tsingtao who had come in connection with the Japanese army from Manchuria, the home of the Hunghutses, and they had formed a limited company for the purpose of robbing the wealthy Chinese of the neighbourhood. Later on they were not allowed to continue to rob in Tsingtao itself, but they did continue to ply their trade in the vicinity during the whole of this period and in many cases people did not get off as lightly as I did. A number of murders testify to the activity of this horrible financial enterprise.

In the meantime, the Japanese Government heard of the affair, and I had to appear before the military authorities. I was treated with the greatest courtesy and the Government gave orders for soldiers to mount guard over the property. Some Chinese friends hired a few solid watchmen for me who encircled the house all night and beat with heavy sticks upon the floor to frighten undesirable visitors. One day, when I had gone out for the evening, I tried to enter my property on returning home. The guard rushed out of his hut, screaming and shouting and confronted me with fixed bayonet. I had the greatest difficulty in convincing the guard that I was the inhabitant of the house, and not a robber. Eventually, he seemed to trust me and allowed me to pass. An instant later, the two country watchmen leapt upon me with their sticks and would almost have knocked me down if I had not managed in the nick of time to convince them of their mistake.

And thus the adventure ended. I remember with gratitude the kind and humane treatment which the Japanese authorities gave the Germans in Tsingtao. Nor was I visited by any more robbers while I was there.

The plague of robbers became specially bad as a result of the war. The large number of workmen and soldiers who had been sent to France and to Belgium did not like the idea, when they came back, of returning without further ado to private life. In so far as they did not join the troops of the various generals, they became robbers on their own account. The bands of Lao Yang Jen wrought particular havoc and the

name of the leader, "old foreigner," indicated where he had
learnt his trade. He has burnt down whole villages after he
had previously robbed them. The men were usually killed and
the women and girls were taken along as slaves. At certain
times he owned large districts and the admirable armed equip-
ment and military discipline of his people enabled him to
oppose regular troops successfully. In the end he was murdered out of jealousy by one of his followers and it was subsequently possible to disperse the band.

Whereas these robbers resemble the ancient type of high-
waymen, a different band, resembling rather the kind of limited
liability company of robbers such as Bernard Shaw has occasionally described, formed itself to practise this trade. They
had made a fortress for themselves in that dangerous corner
of the country where the province of Shantung and Chihli
meet. There is a mountain there which might have been
created for such an undertaking. It rises almost vertically and
only a tiny footpath leads up along its walls. On top the mountain is level and can be used for agriculture. The story goes,
that to till the fields on top, small calves were carried up to
grow to full size on the mountain, because a full-grown animal could not possibly climb the path. There are a few houses
on the height would could easily be fortified in such a way
as to resist any attack. Here were the headquarters of the
robbers and they had instituted a proper diminutive state. The
young chieftain had learnt in Europe that mere devastation,
though amusing, was not really remunerative, and that the
elementary principle of sound finance was the seizure of property, taken in such a way that no attempt at concealment was
possible on the part of the former owner. The seizure of
property, called Pang piao in Chinese, was understood by them
to perfection. They placed themselves in possession of the rich
people of the neighbourhood, or of their dearest relatives, and
maintained them as guests in their fortress until a sum com-
mensurate with the wealth of the man concerned had been
paid. On the whole, they behaved in the most mannerly fashion, only they would stand no jokes if the money did not come.

Eventually the leaders of the troops in the neighbourhood would stand this state of affairs no longer and they decided to make a regular expedition against the robbers. The robbers, however, in their difficulty, prepared a great coup. They made an attack upon the Peking-Hankou express. They tore up the railway lines near Lin Cheng. The train which passed the place after midnight was brought to a standstill. As soon as the train stopped, they opened fire on it mildly to intimidate the occupants and then they stormed the train. The staff were rendered helpless and the train was plundered rapidly. The passengers were then compelled—just as they happened to be, for the most part in sleeping attire—to set out on a long excursion with the robbers in order to reach a spot beyond the possibility of pursuit. In the process the most touching scenes occurred. The wife of an American millionaire had put all her valuable diamonds into her shoes. As her walking tour took a long time, and led further and further into the mountain, she had to confess that even the most beautiful jewelry is a burden, when worn beneath the soles of your feet. Accordingly she took advantage of a brief halt and buried it under a stone. The honest finders had to take considerable trouble before they had turned over all the stones in the described place, though they eventually found the jewelry and returned it to its owner.

The former passengers, in so far as they did not suffer from illness and disease treated their imprisonment as a kind of sport, especially as the robbers were really most agreeable and spoke good French for the most part, which they had learnt in Europe during the war. Nevertheless, they could not be persuaded to set their former allies at liberty. At the end of several days' marching, the prisoners were brought to the hiding-place of the robbers where they had to remain for the next few weeks. Only the ladies, who inspired the robbers with the profoundest respect, were set free before long. Then the negotiations began. An armistice was declared and according to its terms the regular troops had to retreat some twenty miles. Conditions were made; befitting ransoms had to be paid, the robbers were to be pardoned and given the option of entering the Chinese army and positions in the higher command were demanded for the leaders; in addition, the representatives of the foreign powers were to guarantee the proper execution of the conditions, as the robbers did not feel unqualified confidence in their own Government. The Chinese Government was in an extremely difficult situation. On the one hand, there were the robbers who threatened to kill the foreigners if their bidding was not done, and on the other, there was the diplomatic corps. The foreign representatives held the Chinese Government responsible and threatened with progressively increasing indemnities for material and spiritual damages and notably the spiritual damages amounted to very considerable sums. Whereas on the one hand the Chinese Government was hotly pressed, their hands were tied on the other by preventing them from taking any forcible measures against the robbers.

There developed regular diplomatic negotiations between the robbers and the Chinese authorities in the presence of Europeans and Americans. They met at a neutral place. They invited each other to dinner. A regular postal service was instituted with special "robber stamps," which were of the greatest interest to collectors. Photographs were taken of the young and good-looking chieftain whose interest for photographic apparatus was such that suddenly a camera had disappeared. In short, the negotiations were conducted in the most delightful manner and the robbers eventually obtained what they wanted; the commander of brigands became the commander of a brigade, and as many of his men as felt inclined were assimilated into the regular army. They formed a special section which was incorporated with the Shantung regiments. The more reputable robbers, of course, preferred to retire with their earnings into private life, or else to seek employment with a different band of robbers.

The robber chieftain of Lin Cheng was not the first who rose with rapidity from being a robber to the position of a general, but this one was not made of the right stuff. He and his men apparently did not understand their new position, which they had obtained by the intermediation of the foreign representatives. They could not resist robbing just a little bit every now and again. The authorities were eventually compelled, in spite of all efforts, to proceed to summary execution.

The appearance of robbers in China is always the symptom of transition periods. When the old order has passed away, when failure of the crops and increased prices make life unbearable, it happens that the wilder elements of the population, who are not prepared to surrender themselves to their fate without resistance, desert their normal calling, and in their new capacity as robbers increase during these periods the burdens which weigh down the people anyhow. It is not a proven fact that these elements are always the worst. They are simply those who prefer the function of the hammer to that of the anvil. Frequently the factor of a religious movement is added and the band of robbers becomes a secret sect. During periods of transition between two dynasties, it has already happened that such secret sects have played a certain part. The sect of the White Lotus, the Sect of Brothers, the Union of the Three and others made a name for themselves at such times, which was the combined result of fear of their monstrosities and a secret terror of their magical powers.

P'u Sung Ling tells in one of his stories, which deals with an old magician, about the miracles of the sect of the White Lotus. The magician had an apprentice who indulged an illicit love with the pet slave of the magician, who noticed what was going on, but kept it to himself and said nothing at all. He told the apprentice to feed the pigs. He had hardly entered the pigsty when he was turned into a pig himself. The magician called the butcher to have him killed and sold his meat. No one heard any more about it.

At last the father of the apprentice came to see what had happened to his son because he had not come home for a long time. The magician sent him away by telling the father that his son had left long ago. The father went home and inquired everywhere after his son, but he could not obtain any news whatever of him. One of the fellow pupils of his son knew about the whole story and told the father. The father sued the magician before the magistrate who, in his turn, was afraid that the magician might make himself invisible and did not dare to arrest him, but reported the matter instead to his superior and asked for one thousand armed men. The soldiers surrounded the house of the magician who with his wife and his son were seized at the same time. They were locked into wooden cages to be delivered to the capital.

The road led through the mountains, and when they had gone half-way they met a giant who was as big as a tree, had eyes like saucers, a mouth like a dish and teeth a foot long. The warriors trembled and did not dare to move. The magician said: "That is the spirit of the mountains, my wife can chase him away."

Accordingly the soldiers did as they were told and released the woman from her fetters. She took a spear and went towards him. The giant became angry and swallowed her lock, stock and barrel. The warriors were more frightened than before.

The magician said: "If he has slain my wife, my son must deal with him." They released the son, but he too was swallowed up in the same manner and the warriors did not know what to do.

The magician cried with rage and said: "First he has killed my wife, then my son, would that he were paid out for it! But no one can do it except myself."

So they took him out of his cage, gave him a sword and sent him ahead. The magician and the giant fought together for a while, but in the end the giant caught hold of the magician, put him in his mouth, stretched his neck and swallowed him down, and then he went away cheerfully. It was too late when the soldiers realized the trick the magician had played on them.

The famous novel, the story of the three kingdoms, begins with a description of a rising caused by such bands of robbers who possessed secret magic powers. The difference between the present times and the past is only this: that while the early robbers occupied themselves with black magic the modern ones occupy themselves with the Western practice of war. In this respect, it may also be observed how times progress incessantly in China.

MISSIONARIES IN CHINA

THE function of the missionaries is the subject of consider-able discussion in China. Most of the foreigners in China who are not directly concerned with them, are convinced that the missions only do damage, that only charlatans are attracted to them, that the missionaries merely rob their followers of their old culture without giving them a new one, that conse-quently all the Christian servants are impertinent and good-for-nothing, that the work of the missions is a vain labour of love. The missionaries, on the other hand, have always been prepared to resist these charges; they used to deny their oppo-nents especially the right of regarding the missions, with their higher aims, merely as a training school for servants and nurses. The globe-trotters who write books about China are in a most unfortunate position. They form their judgment according to the company into which they get at first; for it is after all impossible to arrive at an independent opinion in a few weeks or months. As the missionaries used to be, apart from the Customs officials, almost the only foreigners who spoke Chinese and came into close contact at least with a portion of the Chinese population, a new attitude towards the mission grad-ually developed. People frequently saw in it a means of edu-cational propaganda. America in particular recognized this side of the question at a very early date and spent considerable sums for this purpose. In many instances American industrial magnates and merchants took a great interest in the missions and established commercial relations through the intermediacy of individual missionaries. On the other hand, it would, of course, be unjust to imagine that the importance of the Amer-ican mission was confined to its activity in matters dealing with the politics of trade and cultural propaganda.

The problem of the missions in China is very complex. Missions have shown two sides from the earliest days in all the countries into which they have penetrated: a religious side and a cultural side. When St. Paul decided to journey from

Asia Minor to Europe to help the Greeks and the Romans, he brought with him no stimulus of a cultural kind. It is far more probable that he had no appreciation of the profoundest significance of Greco-Roman culture. What struck him in Athens was the superstition of the people and it was with difficulty that he saw a point of contact for his message in the "altar to the unknown God." What he brought with him was purely religious: the message of the Christ, who is the spirit desirous of filling the hearts of those who believe in Him, the living knowledge of God which may be found within the experience of man as opposed to the ethnic religion which seeks an external God. This religion thus entered, as it were, into a union with the Greek mysteries of salvation, the teachings about a saviour which were current in Asia Minor and Egypt at that time; with Roman organization and Greek philosophy and so became the Christian church. When this Christian church came to the German countries, it had all the power of cultural superiority. It forced the Teutonic culture and its gods into the background and was victorious in virtue of its cultural and intellectual superiority. The missions in Africa bring with them to their task the same advantage even today.

In China, the missions are not faced with a weaker or less developed culture, nor do they confine themselves, as did the original Christian missions, to the purely religious domain based upon the assumption of a common culture. A double struggle began: an attempt was made to proclaim the true God in opposition to the Chinese "idols"; an effort was made to save the poor souls lost in sin from the quagmire of their corruption and from the hell which awaited them. In the process it naturally happened that the missionaries regarded everything which differed from their own customs as subject for condemnation. The kindly saints and protectors who had helped many a worried soul out of his misery, the great and kindly Bodhisatva Avalokiteshvara, who looked down compassionately upon all human suffering and was revered under the name of Kuanyin, the true, courageous and noble protector

Kuanti, and many others, were all made out to be devils or despised as lumps of clay. Innumerable sermons were delivered with the object of stressing the torments of hell, from which these poor souls could be saved only by believing in the Christian dogma. This side of the teaching of the missions, for which in particular the most uneducated missionaries of certain revivalist sects could never do enough, was, of course, the most difficult undertaking, since hells are known in China, compared with which the horrors invented by the Western imagination were a mere bagatelle. It is only in reference to eternity that the Christian hell is of greater malignity, because even the most ghastly Chinese inferno comes to an end one day and a new birth in the evolution of life provides new possibilities of salvation.

A further difficulty in arriving at a mutual religious understanding arose from the fact that, especially in earlier times, the missionaries considered it one of their main duties to discuss and prove the errors of the heathens. Accordingly all kinds of errors and imperfections in Confucius were hunted out laboriously. It was desired to discredit him and his doctrines as much as other religions. An attempt was made to interfere with the fundamental principle of Chinese ethics, filial reverence. What was recognized as the highest duty in China, the veneration of ancestors, was branded as idolatry. Not all the missionaries worked along those lines, but it cannot be denied that especially in the early days of the evangelical mission, this kind of missionary doctrine was practised with great enthusiasm.

It is not surprising that such missionary methods led to many conflicts. The cultivated section of the Chinese population regarded it as presumptuous that the missionaries, guests upon Chinese soil, did not hesitate to drag into the dust what was precious to the souls of the people as its holiest and highest possession, and that they did so without any provocation. Everything which had been laboriously built up by the highest wisdom and goodness, by the saints of ancient times, was wilfully to be

destroyed. People were not prepared to stand that. Many per-
secutions of Christians can be attributed to these causes.

Many a pious missionary had no idea what obstacles he put
into the way of the Gospel when, for instance, after making
what was revolting music to Chinese ears upon the horn in
order to attract the visitors at a fair, he offered them salvation
in his sermon, having first of all damned everything which had
been held holy for thousands of years. I remember the surprise
of a certain missionary at the devilishness of the Chinese when,
at a fair at which he had thus blown his horn, he first had to
listen to laughter and jokes which threatened to be followed
by a few stones, before which he had to fly with his horn over a
wall to avoid seeing, as he thought, the persecution of Christians end in the spilling of his own blood. Or what must the
Chinese, for instance, have thought when a solitary missionary
lady, who had hardly learned more than a few words of Chinese
in the course of a few weeks, made her first missionary journey
into the interior and patted any man she met on the shoulder
and said: "God loves you, I love you too"? To nothing but the
unparalleled good education of the Chinese, the lack of charm
of the lady and the hidden power which protects the pure mind
of simpletons was it due that she was not molested.

Another impediment to the mission in China is the great
difference which in Christianity separates theory and practice.
A Chinese Christian once told how he had first come in contact
with Christianity. A missionary had delivered a sermon in the
market-place before a great crowd about the duty of loving
your neighbour. He had said that you must offer the other
cheek if you are struck on the one, that you must offer a man
your coat if he takes your cloak and so on and so forth. This
was quite reminiscent of the old Chinese saints, one of whom
had said to his pupils: "What do you do if a man spits in your
face?" The pupil replied: "I simply wipe it off." The master
said: "Even that is not enough, because even by that you
might increase the man's rage instead of overcoming it; let it
dry and do not bother about it."

Some man then wanted to see whether the missionary was

really in earnest about his doctrines. He stepped towards the preacher and firmly removed a small table which stood in front of him. He who had been so gentle hitherto, now became angry. While previously he had spoken in oleaginous tones, he suddenly acquired a perfectly natural, almost screaming voice; and, seizing the little table by one of its legs, he ran after the man, threatening to prosecute him before the court and showering all sorts of abuse upon him; nor did he let go of the table until the man turned round with a laugh and said: "There, take your table, I don't want to steal it; I only wanted to see whether you were really serious about your sermon. Now I have seen that your words had no meaning and that is all I wanted to know." The man became a Christian later on, none the less. This does not prove, however, that such occurrences are harmless. Owing to such incidents the national hatred which showed itself during and after the war, not only decreased the inclination towards the Christian people and their representatives, but also enormously lowered the Chinaman's respect for them.

Another very grave difficulty for the mission is that people so often mix up civilization and religion. Religion is primarily only concerned with the relation of the soul to God, and secondarily with man's relation to his neighbour; but it has nothing whatever to do with power and wealth, possessions, machinery and inventions. When the purely religious revelation did not prove to be as effective as had been expected, the mission did not evade taking "the flesh into its own arms," which means to say that it dragged all these things into the sphere of its activity. As a proof of the truth of Christianity, they proclaimed that the Christian states became more civilized, powerful and rich as they became more Christian. They told of the excellence of the school system in Europe, of the splendid police, of the strength of the armies and the fleets, of the electric light and the machinery. In fine, they painted the picture of the paradise of Western conditions as the direct result of Christianity. On such occasions, it was not customary in this connection to speak of the hovels in the capitals, the misery of the workmen and the mental impoverishment. All these things were done for the most part in absolute sincerity. These people were quite naïvely so sure of their own superiority that they recognized at every step the need for salvation among the poor heathens, particularly when one saw them not only quite contented with their poor circumstances but even filled with an inner peace; or when they saw the little children naked in the heat of the sun and playing about in the street with a single red rag round their little bellies. All this was before the war, which in its glaring contrast to the former songs about culture, presented rather an impediment to the missions. In spite of this fact, a missionary of the old school called a meeting and the subject of discussion was: "What religion is best suited to make a state rich and powerful?" He had indeed to face the following question: "When our revered Master Mongtse came one day to King Hui of Liang, the king said to him: 'Since a thousand miles are not too far for you to come to my court, you have surely some advice to give which will profit my state.' But Mongtse replied: 'Not so, O King! He who seeks profit spoils the state. Search first for love and duty, and profit will be added unto you.' And now, Mr. Missionary, you have come many thousands of miles to offer to our country advice to make it powerful and wealthy. Is this not just the opposite of what Mongtse did when he stood before King Hui of Liang?"

Let us now inquire into the successes of the missionary activity. They vary according to the different personalities and the method they employ. It is evident that if a man with a limited field of vision comes to a country like China and begins by challenging the whole of its culture with its thousands of years of tradition, stigmatizing it as the work of the devil, even though he has the best intentions in the world he will not find support among the upper intellectual strata. In consequence, the first men who attached themselves to the missions were the people who were outcasts. The mission offered financial advantages—it provided free board and education for its pupils and the parents were often paid an indemnity if they sent their children to the missionary institutions. Proselytes can be made everywhere by such a method! Little girls who had been deserted by degenerate parents were bought; foundling homes were instituted in which young girls were fed, clothed, educated and married, and these institutions were soon used by poor parents as the best method of providing for their girls. Teachers, often of very doubtful quality, found occupation, even though poorly paid, as preachers and evangelists. These "teachers" received sometimes less pay than a cook or a nursery maid. In addition, the missions—frequently with the best intentions—interfered in the legal proceedings in which their converts were involved, who often succeeded in representing as persecution of Christians what were in reality attempts at blackmail on their part. The missionary, ignorant of the facts, used his position as a foreigner, behind whom stood the power of the foreign gunboats, to induce the local magistrates to give judgment in favour of the Christian party against their better knowledge. Such a state of affairs attracted the doubtful elements of the population.

I was a witness of the following occurrence. A genuine and cultured American Christian missionary told me of a case of persecution of a Christian in a village which I happened to know. I also knew the local official and mentioned the matter to him. He had already examined the question in detail, and the papers were complete. There had been an attempt on the part of several individuals belonging to the place to commandeer a piece of public property for their private use, and when they met with opposition they went to the mission, became Christians and attempted to interest the missionary in the case, which they presented as an act of robbery on the part of the non-Christian population. The official said he was prepared to allow the missionary an insight into the records relating to this matter. When I informed my friend of the facts, he was very disappointed. He did not conceal from me that he thought I had been deceived, and believed firmly in the assurance of the Christians. Nevertheless he allowed himself to be persuaded to investigate the matter once more on the spot. He came back disgusted. "I would like to box the ears of every one of my Christians," he said. "They have all deceived me behind my back." This was one case in which a particularly well-meaning missionary was enlightened owing to the coincidence of particularly fortunate circumstances. How many instances must there have been in which this was not the case?

In the interior, I myself was asked one day what the entrance fee into the evangelical church amounted to. When I asked the man what he meant, he explained that he was in a difficulty because he was threatened by a lawsuit and would therefore have to join a church, but he was not sure whether he would join the Jesu Kiao (the evangelical church), or the Tien Chu Kiao (the church of the Lord of Heaven, i.e. the Catholic church), or the Tieh Lu Kiao (the railway church). He thought he would prefer the railway church, though it was dearer than the others, but on the other hand its procedure was far more ruthless (at that time the railway in Shantung was being built from Tsingtao to Tsinanfu). This shows the attitude which existed in those circles.

Naturally enough these methods provided peace neither for the Chinese people nor for the missions. It was a *circulus vitiosus*. The missionary brought pressure to bear on the local official in favour of his Christians, and threatened him with gunboats or other diplomatic means of intervention. The official gave way and oppressed the people in favour of the Christians. Eventually, when the misdeeds had accumulated, the population would rise in some sort of local revolt; they would burn down the mission buildings, and every now and again they would kill the missionary. Then the foreign powers interfered, dispatched gunboats, executed sanctions—the occupation of Tsingtao was, for instance, one of these sanctions—and everything started from the beginning again.

The Christians were not, of course, always the only people to be blamed; but the whole system was to be condemned. St. Paul was beaten, locked up and stoned without any power avenging him. The missions in demanding worldly protection and frequently getting more than they asked for placed the whole thing on a wrong footing. When we remember into the bargain that the missionaries had obtained the right of settling down everywhere in China, acquiring property there and practising their activity by a falsification of the Chufao treaty between France and China and that this right was subsequently claimed to be legal by all the other powers for their nationals, one can understand even better the profound opposition of the Chinese people against the missions as shown at present in the anti-religious demonstrations.

A very curious situation arose when, about the turn of the century, the American, Mott, conceived the idea that the world had to be evangelized in the course of this generation. This idea had a contagious effect among the Chinese missions. The centenary of the evangelical mission was about to be celebrated by doubling the number of foreign missionaries. Prayer-meetings positively jostled each other. It became a battle cry at home so that a young man could no longer ask himself if he had a call to join a mission, but whether he could produce a serious reason for being allowed to stay at home. Almighty God was positively threatened with mass meetings in order to induce Him to bring about the doubling of the staff of the mission. He did not do it. When the centenary occurred the number of missionaries had nothing like doubled itself for all their prayers. The people concerned ought to have stopped to consider why God had not heard their prayers, and, if they had done so, the enlightenment they would have gained might have led them to reason: but nothing of the kind was done. The question was simply dropped and although they had, as it were, measured faith solely by the granting of prayers, they behaved, all of a sudden, as if nothing of the kind had even been attempted. They continued, of course, to inebriate themselves with big figures; and no statistics had ever been more devastating in their effect upon the home circles than those emanating from the missions. All that was registered under the title of Christian really went a little too far. As a result of this mass production system, certain people came to China as missionaries who were totally lacking in the holy conviction of the earlier generation. There were men among them who regarded their profession as a business; others who spent their time in meetings, holiday resorts and committees. It was shown one day, to everybody's amusement, that a missionary who would attend all these congresses conscientiously would find at most one month in the year in which to attend to his mission duties.

None the less, there were also refined and noble people who did their work all the time. Special reference must be made, in this respect, to the activity of the various American, English and Swedish university missions. Valuable Christian and educational work has been achieved in a free and sympathetic spirit. Especially is this so since the revolution, which has made Christianity a fully recognized religion in China; since the mischievous policy of the gunboats has been put into the background; and since the mechanical routine of preaching has been replaced by an intelligent development of educational activities complemented by hospital work.

It would also be unjust to assert that the Chinese Christians were only the inferior specimens who had turned to Christianity from unworthy motives. On the contrary, there is a considerable number of Christians among them who are deeply religious and who have adopted the teachings of Christ and attempted to practise them in their lives: members of former secret sects who sought to attain eternal life, ended by joining the Christian church. Young people with a Western education adopted not only Western culture, but also the religion which is its basis. The result is that in China today there is a native Christian community which plays an important part in public life, and to which not only Sun Yat Sen and Feng Yu Hsiang, but the important leaders of young China belong. But just as Sindar Singh in India is a Christian appalled by the European transgressions of real Christianity, the indigenous Chinese church is liberating itself from erroneous influences. The church is financially self-supporting and during the war, for instance, the vast majority remained strictly neutral. I have often heard it said that the Chinese Christians wish to hear the gospel but not national propaganda for one of the parties fighting in

Europe. The greater part of the Chinese church regarded the war as a terrible falling away from the principle of true Christianity.

In the act of becoming more independent from the foreign missionary activities, they have established a closer contact with their compatriots. The Chinese church is today no longer a body alien and hostile to the majority of the Chinese people; but it plays an active and productive part in the general life. Similarly the Christians are beginning to co-operate with each other. Christianity was brought to China by a countless number of different sects and nations who fought and abused each other. How many battles have been waged by missionaries concerning the proper translation of the expression "God," and the various clerical usages and customs? The fury which animated and divided the opponents was in no way inferior to the *Rabies Theologorum* at home. These differences were not of great interest to the Chinese. They regarded the matter as a whole, and mutually tolerated individual peculiarities. Many a problem which had caused discussion in Europe and had been dragged along as an historical burden, disappeared into the air; and thus a homogeneous Chinese church has been formed, which boldly ignores the differences among the missionaries. The feeling of the community of the Christian faith is overcoming the points of difference even between Protestants and Catholics.

So far, I have attempted to state, as objectively as possible, the facts concerning missionary activities in so far as I experienced them; which means that in the nature of things, the field of my vision was chiefly confined to the Protestant mission. The question remains of the justification of missions and they must be judged from the ultimate point of view of the evolution of culture.

The missions are phenomena which have the same significance in modern times as the crusades had in the Middle Ages. The crusades were undertaken in the conviction that God desired them. Our attitude to the problem is quite different from that of the enthusiastic crusaders of the Middle Ages. We regard the crusade as an historical fact; as a bubbling over of the desire for expansion; as a progressive effort of culture. We know that its results differed altogether from those which were intended. The Holy Land did not become a permanent Christian possession, Islam was not annihilated and Turkish dominion was not destroyed. To this extent, therefore, the crusades were not desired by God; and yet they had important effects. The rise of Gothic, the highest and most mature achievement of mediaeval culture, would not have been possible without the benefits which the Western mind derived from its contact with the Near East and the experiences of the new impressions derived from witnessing the aspirations of other distant worlds. A peaceful influence was also exercised upon Islam. We see, therefore, in the crusades an historical necessity which sprang from the profound unconsciousness of the mediaeval European soil, which needed a new conception to bring forth the highest of which it was capable. The position with regard to the missions is exactly the same. The missions were sent in the conviction that God wanted them. Just as the crusades to Palestine, the missions in China reached a standstill in so far as it cannot be assumed that China, as a whole, will ever belong to a Christian church. The clerical expression of the teaching of Jesus possesses only a limited power of penetration. There are other religions such as Judaism, Islamism, Hinduism, Buddhism, Confucianism, in the face of which the strength of Christianity as a clerical institution is insufficient; whereas the vital forces and great thoughts involved in Jesus have a far wider effective range than the churches which bear his name today.

As to the case of the crusades, a host of valuable cultural stimuli flowed unconsciously through the channel of the missions back to Europe, at any rate, in so far as intelligent people were concerned in it. The Jesuit fathers, who came to China during the period of Baroque, were for the most part men of large calibre. They were effective not through the mass, but through the quality of their personality. The name of every one of them is known in China even today. They brought not only missionary sermons, but the best of European knowledge in mathematics and astronomy. They re-established the Chinese calendar, and the astronomical theory of Tycho Brahe which they disseminated remained for a time the basis of astronomical calculations in China. They brought with them the fruit of European art and skill. They built palaces for the Emperor; they painted pictures for him; they cast cannons; they perpetuated his actions in engravings. In fact, they brought the forms of European culture of those days to China, and were met by the outstretched hand of a number of Chinese; China thus received valuable stimuli of a cultural kind. The last emperor of the Ming Dynasty had already become a Christian and the Emperor of the Manchus who reigned under the K'ang Hsi ensign was already very favourable to Christianity. One step further and China would have become Catholic. Europe, too, was influenced by Chinese culture. The final stage of Baroque, Rococo, the age of enlightenment, was not only influenced by China in the architecture of gardens and houses, in the minor arts such as porcelain and interior decoration, but also in matters of philosophy and morality. The Jesuits made considerable portions of Chinese literature available through translations. It was no less a man than Leibniz who saw the immense possibilities which would materialize from a mutual, mental fructification of China and Europe. The physiocrats, the founders of the science of economics, took their principal ideas from the suggestions which came from China. A rich life began to develop as a result of the contact of these two different but equivalent cultures.

In those days the movement was interrupted. The Jesuits were disturbed in their activity by the various orders—orders who came after them and who did not possess the same far-sightedness. Quarrels arose about the description of God, about the significance of ancestral worship and about the methods of conversion. Europe interfered. The Chinese rulers turned their backs; a persecution of Christians began which ruined all the work that had been done.

Wisdom and religion, culture and science were no longer the treasures which Europe brought and took back in fruitful exchange. Money was wanted and goods were bought. There came the time of the opium war by which China was forced to accept European merchandise against her will. English opium ships carried the first Protestant missionaries to China. There then followed long discords of the saddest mutual misunderstanding. Instead of the broad and free spirit of the Jesuit fathers, a narrow, violent spirit of material expansion and clerical zeal for proselytes manifested itself. Europe fought with cannons. China made a desperate attempt to shut herself off, deeply hurt by the ruthless destruction of, and disregard for, all which had been regarded as holy for a thousand years. China was compelled, step by step and by brute force, not only to give way, but also to make new concessions again and again, to the missions. In this way arose the Chinese animosity to the foreigners and the rejection of what the importunate visitors brought as philosophy, because, according to Chinese ideas, a religion which produced such fruits of violence could not possibly be good. So a distorted picture was painted of an ossified, immobile and worm-eaten China, which was presented as a mixture of grotesque foolishness and perverse cruelty. The missions have contributed to the creation of this image. It is really surprising how unproductive the later missions were in the matter of bringing cultural influences with them, compared with the valuable and extensive contributions made in the old Catholic period. The situation is due to some extent to the fact that the recent missionaries who have penetrated from the outside only come into contact with the uneducated portion of the Chinese population; whereas the Jesuit fathers were received with honours at the Imperial Court when they came and met the very pick of the scholars and artists.

When two forms of culture meet, an intellectual and spiritual contact and exchange is inevitable in the long run, and this process has begun today. The evolution of Chinese history has always presented the picture of the high level of its culture, rooted in its own nature, disturbed little by the barbarians in the vicinity or by importunate missionaries, assimilating external influences which its own power transformed into new blossoms. Such marriages of culture, if the expression may be permitted, were always the cause of a new birth, within the Chinese spirit, which proceeded to assimilate and co-ordinate the external influences. The ancient culture of the Tchou period may be traced to the invasion of patriarchal Western races into Chinese territory which was, at that time, predominantly matriarchal. The establishment of this contact created the basis of all the later periods and found its expression in Confucianism and Taoism. The contact between the northern Chinese culture of the Huang Ho with the southern autochthonous culture of the Yang Tse, resulted in a new and incredible harvest in the fifth to the third centuries B.C. Then came Buddhism which preoccupied the best minds for a long time, until it had been assimilated and resulted in the exquisiteness and beauty of the Tang and the Sung periods. The Mongol invasion created the Ming culture. The influence of the Jesuits in combination with the Northern race of the Manchus which had acquired predominance developed into that particular culture, unfortunately so insufficiently known in Europe, of the three best centuries. This development shows clear and independent characteristics and is by no means the mere phenomenon of ossification and decay as is stated again and again *ad nauseam* in European textbooks, owing to the complete ignorance of the facts.

Now comes the contact between the East and the West. This event is perhaps the last and the most important development which the history of the world has to offer. It is the synthesis, not merely of two directly opposed cultivated spheres, but also perhaps of two different periods of the history of humanity. At present, we cannot foresee what the fusion will bring for the East and for the West; but that it will be something of exceptional magnitude is already suggested by the tension and the distance which separates the two contrasted forms and which are to be converted into a synthesis in the process of mutual completion.

THE MAGIC GARDENS

North of the Lonely Hill Temple, west of the Old Tower
On the waveless waters of Ch'ien-t'ang clouds dangle their feet.
The mango-birds in many woods battle for the warmest tree;
A new swallow (from whose house?) pecks at the spring mud.
Though a blinding riot of spring flowers dances in the travel-
    ler's eye
The shallow grass can barely yet drown his horse's hoof.
But best I love the eastern shore, and walking never tire
Where under the green willow-shade is a bank of white sand.

PO CHÜ-I

I

"ABOVE there is the Hall of Heaven and below there is Suchou and Hangchou." This proverb expresses the magical charm which the districts near the mouth of the Yang-tse have exercised at all times in China. Every country has its fairy gardens, where its sagas and its fairy tales are at home, where the stones are alive and the waters speak and where every inch of the soil can tell a story. The mention of the name recalls a thousand memories and moods out of the subconsciousness and dreamily envelops the mind as with a melody. In this way, the Rhine is the home of the German sagas and Naples the goal of Italian aspiration. In China the names of Suchou and Hangchou exercise the same effect upon the senses. At their mention a mellow atmosphere embalms the thoughts; poems, myths and fairy tales are remembered and periods of the most exquisite and the highest florescence are called to mind. The most beautiful women come from there. Here the earth is neither sparing nor severe. Gently it provides plentiful nourishment and life is free from the struggle for the daily bread. The shepherd boy lies dreaming on the broad back of the water buffalo while, from a distance, the tones of a flute float from the reed-covered shore of a lovely lake. I shall

never forget with what emotion the Chinese poet returning
from Europe greeted the small hill of rocks which rises above
the rice-fields of his native village and how at the sight of the
fields in the green of spring he burst out: "This is where I was
born, this is the earth and the water of which my body is made
and which unite me with the past generations of my fathers!"
A Chinaman from the north would not have spoken thus. Here
dwells the spirit of Chuangtse who once dreamt the famous
dream of the butterflies.

Old stories tell of the origin of music: eastern music was
born from the plaint of a tragic fate, western music was born
of home-sickness, and that of the north from the song of a
girl to the swallow which flew away; but the music of the south
began with the first love-song which the girl of Tushan, wooed
by the great Yu, sang as she waited for her lover while he
achieved his great work of directing the waters of the earth
into their courses. This love-song is significant of the exquisite
and tender atmosphere which seems to hover over this district
and its inhabitants. This is the region in which the mighty
images of a powerful fantasy were poured into Chinese poetry,
breaking the severity of its form and overflowing in dithy-
rambic rhythms. Here is the land of the priest and high mysticism, of the union of heaven and earth, but also of the radical
thinkers who do not fear to draw all the consequences of their
thought in all its ramifications. People here are more cheerful,
more gay and more friendly than in the north, but perhaps less
earnest and firm. Here Nature gives her flowers and fruit,
and beauty and affluence are at home.

II

THE WESTERN LAKE OF HANGCHOU

In July

It is really a terrible idea to place an ugly hotel in the
Shanghai barrack style on the shores of the western lake. It is
not even the only one. These excrescences of modern foreign
industry are all the more offensive to good taste because they
are confronted here by the traces of a high culture. It has,

however, been the fate of the town on the Ts'ient'ang River that many storms have scoured it. First the storm of the Mongols which put an end to the fairy splendour of the Sung, then the Manchu storm, which stationed here a garrison of the foreign conquerors, then the T'aip'ing revolution, which caused such terrible damage by fire, then the revolution of 1911 which brought the Manchu city to its end and replaced it with modern trade settlements with wide and modern streets, with industrial exhibitions, cinematographs and associations for young men, which called into life hotel companies and built vulgar brick houses on the sea-shore like the "most modern hotel" at which the rickshaws have set us down after an hour's journey in the rain. It is a second-class hotel in which we are served with that pseudo-European food customary in the East and in which cleanliness is at war with a certain simpleness of bad taste. Is this the western lake, this paradise of all myths and fairy tales? It is horrible. The chimneys of the factories in the background are no more beautiful than the chimneys on the shore of the Rhine which now mirror themselves in its stream instead of the old castles.

When you are able to see through the incrustation, then the real Hangchou and the real western lake shimmer through none the less, and you find yourself bathed in an atmosphere which flits about the hills and tells of the days of yore. Small rowing-boats glide over the lake, roofs of sails are spread above them. You sit at a small table eating melon-seeds and drinking tea while the boatman plies the oars, drawing them rhythmically through the flat water. This place was created by two poets: Po Chu J, who discovered its charm in the Tang period, and an enthusiastic admirer of Po Chu J, who gave shape to the lake by the construction of an embankment and made it accessible. From that day on painters and poets have again and again spent their time here. Monasteries and pavilions, pagodas and gardens surround the lake, and its islands with stone inscriptions from all periods sing its praise.

The lake has stations like a place of pilgrimage. Each station of contemplation offers new beauties and all the seasons of the year participate in weaving the garment of eight pictures for the holy lake. Later on, more pictures were added to these eight:

The first picture. In spring when the tall willow trees unfold their shy greenness, the yellow auricula comes and sings of hope and beauty. The breath of a wind moves the branches of the willows and gives a ripple to the waters of the spring.

The second picture. The flowers throng in gay chaos about a quiet bay. A pavilion is built at the edge of the lake. Men sit and talk over a jug of hot wine, for this is China's wine country; you look down into the water and see the fishes play.

The third picture. The long dam which the poet Su Tung P'o has built, is drawn across the lake. The spring morning beckons. Dawn still hovers over the lake when you walk towards the day along that dam between the waters.

The fourth picture. Evening approaches. Near the south wall a monastery is hidden among the rocks. The single strokes of the great temple bell sound peacefully over the lake, calling the soul from eternity to eternity.

The fifth picture. Now the hot summer approaches, brooding over the yellow waters out of whose mud the lotus flowers rise, slender and pure. A gentle evening breeze bears the strong pure scent. The lotus blooms are not soiled in their chaste purity by the mud from which they emanate. They suffer no approach, but they exhale their beauty far and wide. They are the picture of the noble who remain distinguished, even when they give.

The sixth picture. The charms of autumn hang in the air, the lake is a mirror, the colours of autumn stand up together gaily and excite the emotions connected with the stillness of the departing year, the calm of the lake, the surrounding view into the distance.

The seventh picture. The mountains stretch from the shores of the lake up into the country. Two crests lie on the horizon, towering steeply and joined by a path in the middle. When the clouds come, they are caught here in the pass and they clutch the rocks, holding them fast, condemned to smouldering and change.

The eighth picture. You must have experienced the moonlit night of autumn in these mild southern places, when the full moon glides, in improbable radiance, dreamily, quietly through the stillness. In front of the islands of Su Tung P'o stand three small pagodas like stone lanterns in the water. Between them, as if attracted by the power of magic, the silver seal of the moon has been impressed upon the dusky surface.

The ninth picture. At the back, near the hilly shore, rises the Thunder Mountain beyond the monastery. A defiant pagoda stood there for many centuries. Its tiles were burnt red by the fire which was to destroy them. Undergrowth and trees grow on top of it and birds of prey hover over the place; but the pagoda stood there as a protection. The evening sunset blazed from the sky and the red pagoda glowed once more.

The tenth picture. Winter comes. He is not severe in this region. The clouds of snow which have gathered during the night, shedding their white flakes, have dissolved before the dawn. On the short bridge which was once covered by a pavilion, a few delicate remnants of snow have outlasted the night and dissolved luminously in the returning sun.

These pictures of the western lake have been painted again and again by artists and they occur in thousands of songs. It seems as though in them, landscape itself, with its changing life of light and seasons, had come down upon earth. Man has nowhere discovered nature, independent of human beings, as early as he did in China, and he has filled the atmosphere with a powerful life, which every one feels who can forget his own ego and listen to the great harmony of heaven and earth.

The building of the western lake was followed by other lakes and places with pictures of their own. This attitude to nature wandered from China to Japan, where Lake Biwa also received its eight pictures and the thirty-eight or fifty-three views of the famous road, leading through Japan, which were cut in wood by masters like Hokusai and Hiroshige.

There were also other poets who lived near the lake. The

Sung poet, Lin P'u, lived as a hermit on the hill near the lake. He did not marry, for the plum-blossoms were his beloved and the cranes who thronged about here were his children. Regardless of his fame, he entrusted his poems to the chance of the wind once he had made them. His friends caught many of them. Here is one of them to his beloved, the winter plum-blossom:

"All lovely things are trodden and mauled, only you in your
    pride
Possess this small garden, that is ugly and cold.
You slant thin shadows upon the clear and dwindling waters,
Your dark scent, floating, stirs the moonlit dusk.
How shall the prying bird, frost on wing, dare dip upon you?
And the butterfly—were this his time, how soon would his
    heart break!
But I who to your homage bring
No cup nor cymbal,
No golden glitter, with this soft song will woo you."

I was taken on a boat past the little island which is called the heart of the lake. A deserted temple is hidden there beneath thickly planted trees. I landed near the lotus garden of Su Tung P'o. Stone bridges lead to a pretty pavilion. The dew-drops still linger on the leaves like glistening pearls. Three small pagodas on the lake seem to wait for the reflection of the moon, which flushes up amidst them in the autumn night. On the far shore in a dense grove is hidden the Buddhist monastery, from which the road leads up through the quiet hills to the ruins of the Thunder Mountain pagoda. Many myths cling to this defiant edifice. An evil fairy, the white snake, lies beneath it, where she is banned and cannot harm men as long as the holy stone holds her a prisoner. In former days, a watchtower stood on the pagoda, overtopping the heights round about and commanding a free view of the sea. From there, the approach of the sea-rovers could be seen from afar, as they steered towards the coast from Japan. The population was warned of the approaching robbers by signals. The robbers

hated the pagoda and decided to destroy it. Under cover of
fog, they heaped up faggots against it and threw a burning
torch into the piled-up wood. Flames shot up and hissed. The
fire lasted day and night. The grey tiles of the pagoda became
red from the heat, but the pagoda resisted the fire. It burnt
out; but the red ruins stood up in defiance. Though the building has recently collapsed, ancient manuscripts and prints have
been extricated from the wreckage.

In the evening, when the sun was setting, I returned. Su
Tung P'o orides seemed to twitter and shed their yellow radiance among the dark branches. A breeze rippled the surface
of the lake and fireflies sped through the air. From the other
shore, the electric lights of Hangchou could be seen and the
stars stood in the high sky, mirrored in the lake.

Next morning, I drove to the town and from there to the
Ts'ient'ang River. The river is famous for its great spring-
tide, which comes up from the sea like a steep wall, several
yards high, at the time of the equinox. Thousands of people
assemble every year on the banks to see this marvellous spectacle. The Ts'ient'ang is a wide river, rich in water, such as
cannot be found in the north. Beyond the far shore rises a
chain of beautiful hills. Boats and junks glide over the wide,
smooth surface. Upstream you come to a large, red, painted
pagoda which stands on a hillock; from here a wonderful view
is afforded of the Ts'ient'ang and the sailing boats upon it,
which melt into the distance. Farther upstream the Wu Yun
Shan mountains rise from the banks. Firs and willow trees
and bamboos form a thick undergrowth on both sides of the
way. Tea is planted upon the red earth of the hillock. You do
not know what tea is until you have tasted it when prepared
with the water of the dragon spring, Lung Tsing, up here in
the heat of the summer, at the season of the tea harvest. Lung
Tsing is as famous in China as Rhine wine is in Germany. In
China you drink tea made of green leaves which have merely
been dried. Its taste is more delicate and less bitter than the
so-called red tea which is exported to Europe and which under-
goes a kind of fermentation before it is dried.

Near the Thunder Mountain pagoda you pass the valley which leads back to the lake. We were rowed to the so-called Emperor Island. This is an island on which Imperial gardens and summer palaces still exist. The library contains one of the few copies of the complete collection of the masterpieces of Chinese literature of all times, which was brought together by the Manchu Dynasty. The garden rises steeply by means of steps and paths of rock. On the top there is a pavilion to afford a view. There we took tea and read Chinese poetry, which seems to be more alive here in its own home and to resound with different tones than when, far from here, its cadence seems to reach us, from this spot. Night fell and we got into our boat. We passed a fishing smack in which a man wept bitterly. His wife had just died and lay dead before him. Our little vessel moved over the sea through clouds beneath the stars, and passed through many dusky shadows, which looked up from the depth of the water. A horse neighed, and a dog, somewhere on the shore, barked. All these sounds were only the intervals between the great stillness which stretched over the lake and which was made audible by the deep tone of the monastery bell, whose single sound reverberated at long intervals over the water. Bells in China are not rung, but struck. No chaotic confusion of warring sounds, each different in its nature, disturbs the ear here. Our European ringing of the church bells, whose confused waves exalt us, strike an Eastern ear as aggressive and inconsiderate. The evening bell of the mountain monastery has nothing persistent or threatening in it; it sends its deep rich sound through the evening. This sound is the revelation that behind all appearance, behind all variety, behind all suffering, there dwells the one great silence. This tone is like a gate into another world. Whoso chooses can enter, and whosoever does not so choose, passes by. It is there, that is all. The sound dies away, and then the great silence remains.

Next morning I went with Erwin Lang, the painter, to the Emperor Island. He wanted to draw there. Ladies soon appeared, who wanted to look on. They belonged to the family of a rich Parsee who had a summer villa on the island. The girls had been walking along the shore and were surprised to see foreign visitors. They watched the painter with curiosity and showed a keen desire to be painted by him. A few of the younger ones were as inquisitive as fishes, the older ones were cunning. They giggled a little and approached as soon as they noticed that they could speak Chinese with the foreigners.

I left the painter with his nymphs and went alone over to the heart of the lake. There is just enough room for a small temple pavilion between the closely-set trees. There the king of the dragons and the princess of the water of the Western lake are honoured. A barking dog stands guard. He made way for me, however, when he noticed that I knew something about Chinese fairy tales. A few fishermen sat on the shore fishing with a line. Not far away, there is another small island on which there is nothing but willow trees. The island is ghostly, even in the light of day. It is surrounded by a belt of morasses on which sand-pipers are digging. The lord of the island is an eagle who has two jays as messengers. When I landed, one of the jays announced me with loud shrieks. For a moment I looked about me, and all round me I heard hissing and bubbling in the morass. The deaf and dumb boatman gave me to understand, through signs and inarticulate noises, that I must proceed quickly. The ground was already beginning to sway. A few steps made of earth led into the small circle of willows in the interior of the island. There was nothing in the middle except a broken memorial stone of ancient days. There were a lot of chrysanthemums round about each group, planted between three roof tiles, and they stood about as if they were men under a magic spell. A few large vessels with all kinds of manure stood on the edge, from which they are fed regularly.

The temple of Yuo Fe, which stands at his grave, also belongs to the memories of the Western lake. Yuo Fe was a faithful general of the Sung Dynasty who wanted to protect his country against the increasing attacks of the hordes of the Kin-Tartars. But no matter how bravely he fought, plots were hatched against him by the wicked Ts'in Kui and his wife called *Long Tongue*. They were so secret with their black plans that they did not dare to talk, they merely wrote signs in the ashes with their chopsticks and immediately wiped them out. Through their treachery the brave hero Yuo Fe came to be killed, but retribution did not fail to come. A temple was erected to this hero in which he enjoys honours today no less than the honours of Kuanti, the god of war. Especially since the revolution he is honoured more than ever, as the national deliverer from the oppression of the Tartars. Iron pictures of Ts'in Kui are chained in front of his temple, and the scorn of centuries have been their lot. It was not until the recent re-building of the temple that tablets have been fixed which are destined to preserve them from injury. It is a curious coincidence that some of the victims of the struggles for liberation which led to the fall of the Manchus have halls of honour erected to them in the Western lake. Between all these blood-curdling heroes of ancient times and recent days it is touching to find the grave of the little Su Siao Siao, an exquisite singer of the day of the great poet Su Tung P'o.

The town of Hangchou honours the memory of the great Yu, who came here when regulating the course of the rivers in the Empire. But the town cannot look back upon so great an age as other cities. Its brightest period is crowded into a few brief centuries. It is the town of silk and tea. In its narrow streets there are also a few specially famous shops for fans. The mosque is an ancient building, referred to in a number of fairy tales. You enter through a gaily-coloured porch into the dark rooms which originally must have created a strange impression upon the Chinese. Old tablets with Chinese characters hang from the walls under the high and dark beams of the roof: "All roads lead to the same goal," "I am the only true one, there is no second beside me."

At present the adjoining rooms are used for school purposes, and boys and girls in modern clothes play about in the hidden courtyards and no longer allow the twilight of fairyland to persist.

The Acropolis was situated on a hill near the end of the present town. A large number of temples are in a state of decay. They reveal the elegant forms of the Sung period, but time has been victorious in its gentle fight of destruction against the work of men. There is no modern organized protection for monuments. The Chinese do not repair their old buildings year after year until you no longer know what is old and what is new, but they are built strongly and substantially; time is then accorded its rights until a new generation builds new temples, as, for instance, the Yuo Fe temple which has been created afresh in recent years out of the ruins of the old. From the top of it there is a fine view over the wide plain in which the town lies, and its many old trees give it the pleasant aspect of gardens. You can see from here the Ts'ient'ang River, which flows into the sea in a number of openings. On the other side you are greeted again by the hills of the Western lake.

III

SUCHOU,
May

The sky above the plain was heavily laden with humidity; but the yellow fields of rape-seed shone among the fresh greenery like bright sunshine. The district near Suchou is hilly. We descended from the train and went at first to the Tiger Hill along a narrow paved road. Life on these roads is conducted much more in the public gaze than in the reticent north where walls prevent the view from penetrating into the courtyards. The population also is of a different type. Physically they are much more delicate and the women have soft rounded features. The practice of binding up the feet, which still exists in the provinces in northern China, has never been popular here, though, like the pigtail, it has become the tradition of backward peasants. In these parts you meet women in charge of boats, and even as sedan chair bearers, which would be quite unheard of in the north of China. Li T'ai Po already admired the girls of Yu, their snow-white feet and their seductive coquetry. Life is gay and cheerful here, in fact, this is the gay district of China. The great harmony of life gives its share even to the poor and makes it possible for them to enjoy the fleeting moment without having to think with a worried expression of the future or to cast envious glances at rich neighbours. This cheerfulness, one discovers suddenly, makes life not so hard and serious and shows that the soft wind that smooths the wrinkles from man's brow is irresistible. A troop of soldiers accompanied by bugles passed us by. Their uniforms were not indeed quite uniform, nor did they march perfectly in step, but their enthusiasm was evident, and the false notes of the bugles at the head of the column spurred on the small sixteen- or seventeen-year-old recruits who marched in the ranks at the back. There are also policemen at the street corners with large white placards of cloth on their chest, on which the place they came from, where they serve, their number and their district are inscribed in the form of an official edict. But they are not disturbing. A country in which the policemen are not disturbing is always a happy country. This requires great wisdom. And here the traffic proceeds on its quiet course, considerate and cheerful as it was in earlier days. The policemen stand there because they are indispensable as the sign of the culture of a country. Occasionally they interfere to help, but inconspicuously and gently.

The people in the streets sit at their work. They may indeed cast a passing glance at a stranger, but not aggressively or disagreeably; and then their attention returns to their work. Only once one of my friends who was with us caused a sensation. He happened to be so extraordinarily tall that he could look in at the windows of the upper story of the little low houses. A cobbler, who was sitting at his work, fell from his stool from fright as he suddenly saw the face of a stranger before him. When he realized that he was confronted by a kindly creature, he calmed down and laughed at his sudden shock. The intercourse of the people amongst each other is harmless and friendly. A shopkeeper was sitting in his shop amongst his gaily-coloured wares: a neighbour approached him, he had bought a fish and a few vegetables at the market. He avoided the puddles in the street carefully, clinging close to the parts of the railing which separates the open room from the street, and began a conversation. People talk a little and continue to work, or they may light one of those long thin pipes which have enough tobacco in their small metal bowl for two or three pulls. The children played at a corner: no one tramples on them or runs them down. Even the little dog can bring the remnant of their food, which he has found in some corner, into safety.

In Suchou you still meet with the traces of the old culture of the Sung Dynasty. At that time the intellectual life of China had the tender exquisiteness of Gothic. Buddhism, which had softened the Chinese intellectual life and had fructified it in preceding centuries, had been assimilated. It had penetrated into the Chinese soul like the air which one breathes, and had made it soft and sensitive. Perhaps too soft, for the good days did not last very long. The wild Tartars thronged from the north and the house of the ruler had to be transferred from Suchou to the neighbouring Hangchou. This happened in the year 1127.

The Tiger Hill can still show the foundations of an Imperial castle which stood here in those days. On top of the hill there is a large flat expanse of rock surrounded by a circular mound. Another steep rock is joined at the top by a boldly curved bridge. Down below there is a green water pond known as the Sword Pond. A knight once found in this pond a sword, with which he fought victoriously the tiger which was devastating the region. That is why the hill is still called after the tiger.

Today, the ruins of a half broken-down pagoda cover the famous spot. Next to it there is a temple dedicated to Kuanyin and another to the Ruler Jade, the Lord of Heaven, a goal for pilgrims and friends of nature who come from near and far. In front of the temple of the Lord of Heaven there is a terrace from which a wonderful view opens up over this old country. The plain with its fields and groves spreads below like a garden. Silver rivulets of water run through the landscape in all directions. You see the Imperial canal of Hang-chou, which connects this district with distant Peking far in the north. A lively traffic of boats animates a hundred water-ways, which here almost entirely take the place of roads. The roofs of Suchou are huddled together closely and above them towers the seven-storied pagoda, the emblem of Suchou.

All the hills round about have, every one of them, a history and a name. The volcanic cone which rises steeply from the plain is the Lion Head; the long, drawn-out chain of hills in the distance, on whose back ancient funeral mounds rise, like the graves of the Huns, is the mountain of the Seven Sons. A little farther along the horizon there is the mountain of the Vault of Heaven, which is the goal of our journey. The hills are partly covered with vegetation and possess their pagodas. Everything is quaint and fantastic. The roofs are more alive, as it were, than in the north, their corners swing in steep arches upwards, while the north Chinese buildings do not know any such extravagant additions on the end of their gables. We tried to get into conversation with the priests of the temple of the Lord of Heaven. The conversation was somewhat one-sided because, though they understand everything that we say, they speak their own dialect, which differs very considerably from High-Chinese and can be understood only with the greatest effort.

On our return to Suchou, we went to one of the canals, where our servants had rented a house-boat. These house-boats are large, flat-bottomed vessels with a superstructure of several rooms in which a few friends or a family can dwell for a certain time. As the canals are almost all devoid of a current—the tide of the sea into which they run may at most just make itself felt—it is easy to move the boats by having them drawn from the towpath. Occasionally you can have your house-boat towed by a little steamer. It is impossible to lead a more de-lightful, lazier or more dreamy life, than to pass along these quiet canals in such a house-boat in good company, that is to say, either alone or in company of sympathetic friends.

Even the foreign merchants from Shanghai know this, and

for this reason they often spend their week-ends during the good season of the year on house-boats. But its real life is known to them only by hearsay. Even here, they cannot get away from themselves. Instead of drinking their whisky at the bar of their club, they drink it on the house-boat. They bring their *North China Daily News* with them and study the exchange from boredom. The "boy" is of course present and prepares the food with his habitual punctuality, the man's wife lies in a chair and sleeps, the children quarrel, the husband yawns secretly behind his paper, unless by way of diversion he can get excited about something, or beat a coolie who has annoyed him for some reason. Ku Hung Ming used to call his friends of this variety "momentarily satiated beasts of prey." The Chinese boatman, who is easily distinguished by his national flag, likes to avoid this kind of visitor.

Our journey along the canal was particularly delightful. The sun had come out, a fresh breeze filled our sails, and a cheerful Chinese company was on board. So we proceeded on our way through the country, beneath highly arched bridges between the spring green of the trees which lined the banks. Every now and again we would come to a hill, which was overshadowed by a quiet temple grove, or we would pass a busy market-place, whose surrounding houses stand on the edge of the water. Rowing boats glide along the canal for fishing purposes. On the edge of these boats there are rows of cormorants. They are trained to fish, and wear a ring round their neck which prevents them from swallowing the fish they have caught. They return with their booty, which the fisherman takes away from them. In the end, after the ring has been removed, they get their share to keep them cheerful and industrious. The people also fish with nets, some with very large ones which occupy the full width of the canal. Other boats met and passed us. As they could not travel in their direction by the aid of the wind, they were pulled from the banks, which usually have high dams. Two or three pulled the boat by ropes while a woman at the helm steered the vessel.

When evening fell, we made fast near the K'iung Lung

Chain (the mountain of the Vault of Heaven). We were met
by a number of laughing and chattering bearers, both men and
women, who wanted to carry us in their mountain palanquins
to the monastery. It happened to be at the time of the pilgrimage and the bearers had just returned from the mountain
monastery whither they had carried rich pilgrims. Their heavy
work did not weigh down upon their soul. They offered their
services with a laugh. We declined, but they went with us for
a while, always laughing and joking, in case one of us should
regret his early decision. When they noticed that we were
determined, they parted cheerfully from us and returned into
the village.

A steep paved footpath led up to the mountain. We
climbed up between thickets and low trees; places for rest
and stone tablets with inscriptions are found along the path.
You enter the domain of the temple on the summit through a
gateway which has partially collapsed. The sun was sinking
low in the sky. We climbed to the top of a round, grassy
hillock which rises a few hundred feet behind the temple, in
order to watch the sunset. The entire slopes of the quiet hills
are covered with blossoms, chiefly of red azaleas. On the top
of the mountain there is a structure of walls, which was probably originally a tomb, but the walls have now collapsed. In
the days of the setting sun, the T'ai Hu, one of the largest of
the Chinese lakes, with its islands and bays seemed to stretch
out into the infinity before us.

Darkness had set in when we returned to the temple. The
monastery is inhabited by some twenty Taoist monks. It is a
huge mass of buildings and courtyards. The pilgrims who come
here in the spring from far away usually spend the night out
on the mountain. When we came there were over seven
hundred other visitors and there was still plenty of room
left. A monk awaited us at the gate. He led us through long
passages and steep stairs past dark and ghostly dwellings of
the gods, and along wide halls full of cheerful pilgrims seated
at their meal, into a quiet out-of-the-way room. A fire was
burning on the floor which was made of stone slabs. A servant

of the temple heated water for us; a few candles burned on the little table, but their weak light fought in vain against the dusk of the ample room. We washed and set about preparing our meal. The news of our arrival had spread in the meantime among the pilgrims. They came in a close throng to watch us. The monks also displayed great interest in the foreign visitors. We tried to get into conversation, but could not get very far. They told us that the temple was dedicated to the Lord of Jade, who was the Master of Heaven. Pious practices and meditation were not customary here. The temple belonged rather to those in which Chinese service is performed according to a fixed ritual, and, apart from this, the temple served as a place of rest for the pilgrims. At last the abbot came. He was most advanced and showed the greatest interest for the brandy and the cigars we happened to have with us. A real European always has a surprise for a poor old Chinaman. One of us had an electric pocket lamp. He took it out of his pocket mysteriously and let it flash in the dark room. The pilgrims were amazed and even the abbot was full of admiration. It was then that we explained to him in detail how such an object had to be manipulated. At last he was allowed to switch it on a few times. The battery gradually began to give out and the lamp ceased to be as impressive as it was before. The abbot then took his leave and, in the calmest manner in the world, drew an excellent pocket lamp out of his sleeve. The pilgrims moved shyly to one side before its blinding radiance and the abbot disappeared into his cell with a friendly greeting along the illuminated passages.

My travelling companion was furious and wanted to rush after the abbot for having stolen his pocket lamp. I restrained him with difficulty and, behold, there was the lamp. The abbot had had his own with him, which was far brighter, and we had pretended to miracles by the aid of our modest little lamp! We must have seemed to him like the negroes who brag with their top hats. The abbot had also gained the day as far as the pilgrims were concerned. They gradually retired and silence imposed itself upon the large room.

We then set about finding a resting-place. We had brought bedding with us. In the hall there was only one bed on which we had spread our cooking implements; in the back wall there was a hidden little door leading into a mysterious back passage. A steep staircase led upwards. We went upstairs and found a row of empty chambers side by side, and in them there was some old rubbish and also some bedsteads. The darkness prevented us from getting a proper idea of this chaos of rooms and closets which seemed to lie about as in a confused dream. We selected a few of the best rooms and as we were tired we soon fell asleep. I had not slept for long when my dreams led me back to the dark hall. Two priests were seated in their wide garments at our table, drinking. One of them cut a round disk from a sheet of paper and stuck it on the wall. The other asked: "Where are the strangers with the pocket lamp?" My friend rose proudly and said in a military tone: "Here!"—"Then switch on the light." He turned on his lamp, which soon went out. Then the white disk began to shine and it was perceived that it was the moon which hung in the room. You could see the marble castle and the cassia tree beside it quite clearly. Laughter was heard and the moon fairy appeared. She was made to dance and all the pilgrims were merry and took delight in her beauty. Then the moon floated up to the sky once more. My friend, who wore a khaki suit and a tropical helmet, grew longer and longer until he out-topped the mountains and reached the moon. The priests and his companion climbed up upon him as on a ladder, went towards the castle in the moon and disappeared into its room with the moon fairy. My friend began to yell, so that the pilgrims dispersed terror-stricken, and I—awoke. He was, in fact, snoring loudly next door.

Next morning the chill before sunrise penetrated the thin walls made of boards noticeably, and in the pale light of dawn we gained an idea of the position of the rooms in which we had slept. We looked out over the roofs of the temple buildings far into the country. After breakfast we looked at the walls of the temple. The priests, most of whom were opium smokers, were still asleep. We left a suitable sum for our night's hospitality and went on.

At the bottom of the mountain there was a little old man standing in front of a table on which he had built up a little carved image and a few sacrificial vessels. He could tell people their future. The image of the god no longer had any legs and was considerably worm-eaten for the rest, but the carving was not bad. I wanted to buy it and asked the man what the little piece of sculpture would cost. "At least two dollars," was the reply. He had probably named a fabulously high sum intentionally. When, however, he saw the two dollars lying on the table, in front of him, he was alarmed and a hard but brief struggle raged in his breast. "No," he did not want to sell the god after all. Then he breathed a sigh, relieved by his decision. The poor old man knew things which were, after all, more important to him than the money.

The return to Suchou was rapid. We passed a few police junks, large picturesque house-boats, usually fitted in front with a small gun, which was more effective as a deterrent than for purposes of hitting a mark. Moreover, complete peace and order reigned on the canal. We disembarked by the new bridge in Suchou.

A stroll through the bee-like activity of the streets offered sights which are not uncommon in Chinese towns and yet we had a few experiences which revealed traces of the fine old Sung period. The shops are only separated in the daytime from the streets by a railing; at the entrance there are two wooden posts which culminate usually in a gilt carved ornament of a lion. Only one rather small shop had on top of the posts, instead of the lions, a pair of human figures crouching comfortably and grinning kindly at those who entered. It was a charming little work of art, no taller than the length of one's hand. The owner of the shop knew well how to appreciate this inheritance. He patted the pieces lovingly when we spoke about them and told us that they had been there for several generations.

Suchou is also a home of music. The singers of Suchou

are famous throughout China. The violins here have a gentle viol-like tone, not the shrill nasal sound one hears so often elsewhere. Near the pagoda in Suchou, I had the experience with the blind man which I have already related. The evening was beginning to fall and the crowd busily thronged the narrow street near the pagoda. Sedan chairs were carried past at a rapid pace. Elegant ladies with their servants tripped shyly along the path and, like flowers, they filled the air with sweet scent. Business people with set faces, still reckoning up figures, workmen discussing their daily wage—every one went his way. The cookshops let out smoke and the odour of oil and were surrounded by hungry customers. Wooden shutters were fixed in front of the doors and windows of the shops. Two friends sat on a bench smoking their thin pipes. Up above, birds circled about in the sunlit dust over the tufts of grass which grow on the edges of the roof of the pagoda. The wind gently swayed the little bells at the corners of the pagoda. It was the moment in which the day seems to stir once more before it sinks into the twilight. The spring seemed to ring through the remnant of the day. There was a sound: a thin sweet sound in the midst of the chaos of the street. A few pricked up their ears for a moment, whilst others hurried on. The sounds of spring approached. It penetrated the noise of the street quite clearly like a shimmering golden thread; a melody was heard with that sweet sad strain which makes you suspect autumn in spring. It was almost painfully beautiful. A blind man was playing soft notes upon a Chinese violin. Wherever he passed men ceased to speak of money, the children stopped their games and the tired wanderer stood still for a moment. The song of spring flowed like magic from the violin of the blind man. His vision was turned inwards.

He accepted no gifts. He played and passed on. His melody vanished slowly in the distance. In the meantime night had fallen and the world with its bustling people and dusky houses was there once more, and only high above persisted the sound of the little bells of the pagoda.

In the town there is a garden: one of those magical Chinese

gardens where you wander in a labyrinth amidst ponds, rocks, pavilions and groves, where every step presents a new picture to the eye. Formerly the garden was hedged in by solitude. It lay beyond the gates of the town. Today, the railway station and ugly inns for passing visitors are situated in its vicinity. After we had derived an idea of the beauty of China, all the ugliness of Europe grinned at us once more. People sometimes speak of the animosity of the Chinese to aliens. The Chinese are not at all hostile to foreigners. They merely defend themselves against being dragged into the mire which emanating from the West threatens to choke the world. How well we could understand it if the Chinese were resentful of the foreigners! When one returns from seeing something of the old China to the ugly noise of the town where the Sikh policemen in English service stand there, stern and haughty, like horrible machines, and hold the thraldom of the Chinese before their eyes; when they beat a poor rickshaw coolie with their sticks or kick a gasping carrier, so that the motor-car of a rich foreigner may rush past without slowing down, one is sometimes seized by a deep anger, not against the poor black Sikhs, who are also slaves, but against the human machine of that monster which avails itself of man to destroy mankind.

But China will not die. It possesses the power to save itself from the "White Peril," and there are men who have the faculty of understanding the nature of European culture, of distinguishing it from those expressions of what is ugly in it. In Shanghai an invitation to a Chinese restaurant awaited me. It was an insignificant building in an out-of-the-way street. No noise, no bustling, penetrated here. On the walls there were sayings on red scrolls, poems by regular guests who had passed pleasant hours in the familiar circle of their friends. There were good names among the artists who had left their traces behind them. A small group of artists and scholars met to partake of a choice meal. An old gentleman spoke of the incomprehensibility of modern European art. The painter Ch'en Chu Ts'ung, the leader of the modern Chinese painters (he has died in the meantime, and his pictures and drawings have become very much sought after in China by collectors), gave in a few sentences a survey of the modern artistic movements and tendencies, and really hit the nail on the head, in his quiet and matter-of-fact way. He himself has expressed some of this new spirit in Chinese art: not by means of the superficial imitation of the language of form, nor by vain attempts at a half-understood technique of oil painting. He has assimilated in a perfectly free manner, on the basis of the Chinese technique of ink drawing, the stimulus supplied by French artists, and he has created from it a new national Chinese art, which, because it is art, is universally comprehensible. This conversation in a quiet corner of Shanghai shows that even in the modern hubbub of the world there are, as it were, islands of refuge where quietly and strongly the good taste of the Sung period still finds expression today.

PEKING

C ITIES have their day, their periods of growth and of decay. There is no town—not even the Eternal City—which had a significance of its own at all times. Differences, however, exist. There are those which are merely the product of special circumstances to which they owe their greatness and efflorescence. All the buildings, streets and squares are then eloquent of the greatness of this period. Other times come in which the stream of the world hollows out a new bed. The town decays and becomes a ruin. There are towns in the desert which have been definitely untouched by the history of the world and there are others which are visited, as it were, by different ages. Troy is one of these places, in which the succeeding centuries have erected one story after another upon the ruins of the past. There are towns which have been dormant for centuries. They show gaps. Various epochs touch above these gaps just as the geological strata of certain places seem to have skipped individual periods and in them what is new takes direct contact with the oldest foundations.

Peking is a town of many epochs. These periods followed one another and what they have created there has grown into a homogeneous whole which is still alive today, even though it is undergoing a new change. Peking means the northern capital. The political situation of any period in China was always indicated by the locality of the capital. The Chou people conquered the Empire from the west a thousand years before our era. The capital lay in the western part of China and their chief endeavour was directed towards securing the frontiers of their culture against the western barbarians. The dynasty grew feeble, the barbarians advanced and the capital was moved into the centre of the China of those days. That was the beginning of the end of the old feudal state. The western state of the Ts'in, which penetrated into the former territory of the Chou, acquired the supremacy in the course of time. Later on the north, whither the Huns, the Mongols and the Manchus aimed, became predominant. The Huns were kept off by the erection of the great wall. A thousand years later the Mongols penetrated into China. The Sung Dynasty moved its capital farther and farther south. At last it was swept aside. The Mongolian Khan became the ruler of China. He turned his camp, which lay in the centre between Mongolia and China, into his capital. Marco Polo visited the Mongolian Khan in Cambaluc. This was the first Peking. It lay somewhat farther to the north than the present town. The belfry and the Drum Tower, which lie today at the northern circumference, formed its centre in those days. They are still used today. In one of them hangs the great bell whose dull sound rings out over the town at the hour of the night watches. Nothing is more imposing than when at midnight the sound of this bell awakens. The bell is surrounded by myths. It was not possible to cast the bell properly before the little daughter of the man who made it had banned the evil forces which wanted to prevent its casting by the sacrifice of her life. Even today an exquisite voice can be heard moaning in the metal when the large wooden rafter strikes the bell. The big drum in the Drum Tower gives the time when the gates of the city are closed. It announces the night. A steep staircase leads upwards to a dark tunnel. Round the tower galleries, whose balustrades have fallen down, descend at an angle. Up aloft in the woodwork the doves coo, and there is a far view over the roofs and trees of Peking into the plain which is surrounded in the north and in the west by the frontier hills. There the great wall winds over the crests of the mountains and through the abysses of the valleys.

The Mongols were driven away by a former monk when their hour had struck. The new capital was founded in the heart of China, near the Yangtse, in Nanking. It did not remain there for long. The third ruler of the Ming Dynasty, Yunglo, was an unconscientious individual who robbed his nephew of his throne and his life. He was a man of strong calibre. He saw the position with great foresight. He knew that the power of the Ming would soon be over if they re-

mained in the south far from the frontier walls, which had to
be rebuilt once more against the continual onslaught of the
northern hordes. Accordingly he moved the capital again to
the north, to the neighbourhood of the old Mongol camp.
That was the second Peking. The construction of most of the
palaces, castles and walls of the so-called inner northern town
dates from this period. In those days people built for eternity.
How marvellous are the walls which surround the town in a
square! They are built of gigantic bricks, and they are so wide
that three coaches could comfortably drive side by side on top
of them. They are carefully paved along their whole extent
and fitted with pinnacles and emplacements from which the
inhabitants could shoot. It takes a whole day to walk round
the wall on foot. The achievement which the construction of
this wall represents can be judged by the fact that when recently a small piece of a far more moderate wall fell down, it
took months to repair it. It was hardly possible to utilize the
material of stones and bricks, and finally the process of pulling
down the wall had to be stopped because it was too complicated and too expensive. What then must have been the work
of construction! It may safely be asserted that in spite of all
modern methods of science, it would be impossible to find even
the financial means to erect such gigantic constructions as rose
from the ground in those days.

Even the Ming Dynasty, like so many of its predecessors,
decayed owing to the luxuriousness and the unscrupulousness
of the men who occupied the throne. Internal rebellion raised
its head. The disturbances which came about in this way were
used as an opportunity by the Mongolian tribe of the Manchus
to interfere in the internal struggles of China. When the last
unfortunate ruler of the Ming had hanged himself behind his
palace on the so-called Coal Hill on a "tree of life," after
fleeing before the invasion of the rebels, the Manchurian hordes
arrived and revenged the expiring Ming Dynasty upon the
rebels. They were exiled and killed, and the leaders of the
Manchus mounted the dragon throne. Peking remained the
capital. The new dynasty, which called itself the "Great Pure"

(Ta Ts'ing), assumed the position of the legal successor of the "Great Clear" (Ta Ming). For this reason the altars of the former dynasty were not destroyed. The tombs in the north of Peking were not desecrated, and even the last ruler found, in the company of his faithful eunuch who had died with him, a tomb in the vicinity of his ancestors. The Emperor K'ien Lung had a large stone tablet erected, in honour of the past dynasty, in the middle of the street of the spirits which leads to the tombs. Upon this tablet he bemoaned their destiny, while four dogs placed upon pillars round about it cry out to heaven in despair. The palaces and their treasures were taken over by the conqueror. Everything was renovated and improved. The Imperial city of the Ming was reserved for the warriors of the new dynasty. The Chinese had to leave and they settled down farther south, outside the town, in the so-called outer or Chinese town. This town was surrounded by a wall, which was, of course, far more modest, though it embraced wide stretches of tilled fields beside the district in which the Chinese lived. This was the third Peking. This Peking became a factor in the world and not merely the capital of the Chinese. This was the place in which power was exercised over the invaders as well as over the Chinese. The two peoples remained separate. Even though the Chinese had to adopt the pigtail of the conquerors and their costumes, no intermarriage took place. The Manchus, whose garrisons were dotted round about in the country, refrained from commerce and agriculture. They remained warriors and lived upon the tribute money which their lord and master, whose slaves they were, distributed among them. The Chinese, the productive part of the population, were governed by Imperial officials whose highest authorities had their seat in Peking.

It always suited the Manchus to encourage Confucianism. In the north of the town expands the marvellous Temple of Confucius in its sober imageless severity. Near by there is Kuo Ts'i Kien, the Hall of the Classics, a square room in a round pond (symbolizing the circle and the right angle), in which the great emperors personally proclaimed the doctrine.

The Mongols were also represented. They were secured
by the adoption of their religion. There is a whole series of
temples of Lamaism, such as the Yellow temple (Huang Si)
and the temple of Harmony and Concord (Yung So Kung),
which stand in Peking and have formed a bridge leading into
Mongolia and towards Tibet. More than one living Buddha
or Great Lama has visited Peking and some of them even died
here, and their story is told on beautiful marble sculptured
pagodas in these temples. These Lamaistic sanctuaries often
perturb visitors to Peking. Lamaism is a form of Buddhism
which is full of magic and terrible occultism. The powers of
nature are embodied by divinities whose ruthless cruelty is
appalling. The long trumpets which extend through the whole
courtyard have a horrible sound. Drums and triangles and
special kinds of horns can be heard in their monotonous songs
emanating from a closed room. Imagination is left free scope
to picture for itself what terrible things go on behind those
walls. In reality mass is merely being celebrated. The human
skulls are used in this cult. The blood-scented ikons, in animal
shape, which often carry their feminine Shakti with them as
the symbol of their creative activity, are terrible to look at.
The demons' dance with the great terrifying masks, the devil
who is first beaten and then burnt at new year—all these
uncanny secrets display a form of desert magic which does not
seem compatible with the mild, noble and kind Buddhism of
which they form a sect. The foreigners, however, who look
at these things without understanding them, are surprised
when these great, strongly built Mongols in their gaily coloured garments fall reverently upon the floor in front of these
ghostly figures, whilst the incense rises above them. The
foreigners, with a delight in lascivious horrors, have the little
curtains removed from the divine couples whose intimate productive activity is hidden from the gaze of the uninitiated, and
if particularly religious, they are scandalized by the horror of
Chinese paganism and attempt to procure for themselves, on
the quiet, out of pure scientific interest, an imitation of these
terribly piquant things. In reality we are not concerned here

with Chinese religion. The Chinaman is as alien to these cults as the European. It was merely the statesmanship of the rulers of the Manchus, who themselves were supporters of the purer form of Mahayana Buddhism, which made them build these temples for the faith of the desert and mountain tribes of the Gobi desert and of Tibet, who therefore were attached to them. Just as Charlemagne protected the Pope in order to secure the loyalty of the priests, so did these rulers foster the cult of these tribes in order to maintain the connection between the mysterious districts of central Asia with their own dominions. These temples in Peking were for many centuries far more effective bulwarks against the sons of the desert than the great wall had been.

The Mohammedans—for the most part they are Turkish tribes from the western districts who settled formerly in the country as warriors—have had their temples and sanctuaries here. Opposite the Red Wall of the forbidden city of the Imperial palaces there used to stand a high two-storied gate. Originally it had been covered with marble sculptures, but they have fallen down long ago, so that the decayed brick wall looks out from underneath. Behind this gateway there was a mysterious confusion of trees and thickets, from which large worm-eaten rafters, formerly part of a building now in ruin, stuck up into the air. Upon closer inspection you find among the ruins a marble table surrounded by gorgeous dragon ornaments, upon which in Turkish, Mongolian, Manchurian and Chinese characters, was written the deed of foundation of the Emperor K'ien Lung, who had built the mosque for the local Moslems. Beyond the street there rises a hill over the Red Wall of the forbidden city. On it there is a small pavilion serving as a look-out with a view to the west. Here the beloved wife of the Emperor, who was called the "fragrant spouse" (Hsiang Fe), used to live. She had been brought home as the most precious piece of booty from an expedition against an insubordinate tribe of Mohammedans. She was always homesick for her home in the far West. But the Emperor loved her. And he built for her the mosque and this pavilion. Her portrait was painted, representing her in a romantic knightly armour, by the Imperial Court painter Lang Shih Ning, who in reality was called Castilhone and was an Italian. The picture was painted in oils, and can be seen today in the Imperial Museum in Peking. Her fate was tragic. All the love of the Emperor could not protect her against the fatal net of Court intrigue which surrounded her. One day, when the Emperor had gone into the southern suburb to perform the sacrifice upon the Altar of Heaven, for which purpose he stayed there, fasting and praying, for several days, she was accused of having killed the Emperor. When the lord of the world and the son of heaven returned, he found his beloved wife dead: because her enemies had taken care that the punishment for the horrible murder of which she had been accused was executed immediately. Today the small mosque and its secrets have disappeared. A broad asphalt street winds along the walls. Here is the entrance to the presidential palace and on top of the old hill flutters the five-coloured banner of the Chinese Republic. Where the temple used to stand is now a police station built of red bricks in a modern style. The Mohammedans are to be found for the most part in the "Street of the Oxen," in a part of the town where they lead a pretty meagre existence.

Other tribes have occasionally appeared in Peking. Inscriptions in stone have been found in the neighbourhood which no one can read today. The Europeans, who live at present in the south-eastern corner of the Manchu town, from the Hatamen (the Eastern Gate of the southern wall) to the Ts'ien Men (the "front," that is to say Central Southern Gateway), which constitutes the Embassy quarter, are careful that in the fourth Peking, the republican city, diversity of tribes is not lacking. When, to the accompaniment of a jazz band, the foreigners perform on hot summer nights their negro dances on the airy roof of the Hotel de Peking, there is not a very great difference from the cult dances in the Yung Ho Kung Temple in the north of the town, according to Chinese ideas. There the Mongols dance in the winter and their Lamas are wrapped up and are masked, so that almost nothing of their original appearance can be seen and the horn and skull-drums beat the rhythm to it. Here, in the summer, the Europeans dance and their ladies are so *décolletées* that almost nothing of their original figure can be seen, and the negro saxophones and wooden rattles beat the rhythm. Of course their gods are different. There they are the mysterious and magic creatures beyond time or space, and here it is the plain and sober divinity of Mammon holding the dollar in his hand. There is, however, another difference. The old China has never participated in the dances of the Lamas. Young China is beginning partly to take delight in foxtrots and onesteps, and the slender Chinese gentlemen with their delicate hands and the exquisite, though at present still for the most part decently dressed, Chinese ladies with an Eton crop can well afford to show themselves by the side of their European and American friends.

All this is merely on the surface. There are other things which are of decisive significance for the fourth Peking. So many generations in the past in China have had connections with the ocean and towards the south. There lay colonial land. Even today colonial exchange takes place between the east and the south. It was from the sea that the men came who founded the foreign colonies along the coast of China which are today the grief and the shame of every patriotic Chinaman, because they go hand in hand with political oppression and the personal arrogance of the colonists. England and Japan, the countries of Imperialism, are the representatives of this colonization. A different form of colonization, however, is travelling over the sea and this emanates from China. It is beginning to infiltrate quietly and peacefully into the English, Dutch and American possessions in the south-east of Asia. Today already the Chinese merchants and workmen are indispensable there. These problems will in the course of time raise quite new questions for humanity; for here too the old China has found of its own accord the new way. Peking, the capital of the north, seems more remote from these events. Here is the place where an understanding is reached with the mainland, the north and the west. As long as this understanding is necessary and possible, so long will Peking continue to exist. At the beginning of the revolution, when everything pointed towards America, it looked for a moment as if Peking would sink back into a period of sleep and decay. This moment has passed today. It is, of course, no longer the Mongols and the Manchus who count; today Russia has taken the place of these powers—Russia supports and encourages China in its fight for independence. For this reason Peking will gain a new significance as one of the centres in which the politics of the world are made. It is easy to get excited about Bolshevism and it is also superficial. We are faced here by world problems: the vivification and advance of the continental masses against oceanic aggression. Who knows how to see here can cast his gaze into the future of humanity.

Before we look more closely at the modern Peking in which the past and the future are interwoven, we will return once more to the Peking of the past whose ruins are more accessible today than they were in their former seclusion. This accessibility, of course, brings it about that just as the grey of dawn, in a sense, forms part of the moonlit night, so does the new era constitute a part of the remnants of what has gone by.

How much has there not been written about the Altar of Heaven in the extremity of the southern town! It is now open to visitors, not as it used to be in the days of the Emperor when it was only in the middle of the New Year's night that the great secret of the sacrifice to heaven was performed here at the central point of the world, in the midst of the ancient sacred trees of the grove, upon the marble pediment of the three steps of the terrace, while the big red lamps glimmered on top of three tall masts and the fire from the sacrifice burnt up towards heaven. The altar was covered with carpets and lanterns. The tablets upon which the names of the heavenly and Imperial relatives, who in their capacity of holy family encircled the highest God, and also the tablets with the names of the heavenly and earthly powers honoured in turn by the princes and ministers had been fetched out from beneath the blue roof of the Northern Temple. In the night which followed the sacred fasting the Emperor cast himself reverently upon the ground; he, the Son of Heaven, otherwise always seated, upon his throne, with his face towards the south, looked on this occasion northwards in honour of the venerable ancestor, the Father of Heaven, of the Earth and of Men, from whom he had received his position and his office.

Everything about this altar is abstract. The circular form is the symbol of heaven, there are three cloisters approached by thrice nine steps, and the round stone in the middle surrounded by nine stone slabs covers the entire surface. The gates which lead outwards to the four corners of the wind from the altar precincts are decorated with cloud formations made of stone. The red wall which surrounds the innermost circle is covered with blue tiles, and round it there is another wall whose plan is square, also covered with blue tiles. There is only one straight line in the chaos of walls and gates, of marble steps and slabs: it is the thin straight line which points between the brickwork of the slabs and steps from the very centre towards the north. It is only a gap in the wall, a direction, a tendency. It is this direction which indicates the proper position to the Emperor, which contains the whole secret of the veneration of the heavenly and incomprehensible power which rules over all.

The temple in the north with the three steps and the blue glazed roof tiles is situated on this line. It is known as the Temple of Heaven and has become the emblem of Peking. It is the temple in which the ruler prayed for the blessing of the harvest. The rich symbolism of the structure suggests the intermingling of heaven and earth, which makes all growth and evolution possible. There is a similar sequence of circular steps within a quadrangular wall as in the case of the altar and its form signifies what is earthly; for the earth is square and the heavens are round. The galleries are decorated at the bottom with clouds, higher up with phenixes (the earth), and above them with dragons (the heavens). The rafters of the temple are also ornamented with dragons and phenixes. The colour of heaven is blue, the colour of the earth is green; the intimate union of heaven and earth is suggested by the dragons floating in the green and the phenixes in the blue fields, and also by the fact that the dragons are depicted below and the phenixes above. Heaven has subordinated itself to the earth. Since the motion of what is heavenly and creative rises upwards and what is earthly and receptive downwards, their forces take contact and unite. The same interplay can be seen inside the round hall. The round roof is supported by a square structure of rafters reposing upon four large pillars whose position symbolizes the four seasons. Round about are the twelve pillars of the twelve months. The thrones upon which the tablets of the divinities were placed during the performance of sacrifice are disposed in a circle. If one considers the meaning of these symbols, which go back to the oldest antiquity, one sees, as it were, the forces of nature before one's eyes and one understands why Confucius once said: "Whoever understands the meaning of the great sacrifices will find it as easy to govern the world as if it lay in the palm of his hand."

All this belongs to the past today. Yan Shih K'ai made once more a feeble attempt to vitalize the old customs artificially. The effort brought him no good, and since that day the blue sky broods above the vast field, the clouds draw past, the rain falls, the snow tumbles in flakes, and the wind blows. Time passes quietly and gently and breaks off gently and quietly the remnants of the past, until one day they will collapse when their hour is done. The temple is a national monument today. The place is kept up by the entrance money which the foreign visitors pay. Cypresses are planted by the young men in the wide space, on the occasion of the feast of the trees in the spring, and as they grow, they will gradually fill the plain. In the south the masts of the wireless stations loom up and the whistle of the railway resounds from a distance. Busy officials collect money in order to inaugurate before long an international exhibition upon the soil of the Altar of Heaven.

Whereas the Altar of Heaven and its surroundings continue to inspire reverence in the soul of every sensitive human being, the Temple of the Tilling of the Soil, across the road, is entirely left over to decay. It was the field where the Emperor, to the accompaniment of sacred flute music, drew the plough through the furrows with his own hands, and his ministers followed him in this most fundamental and sacred of actions. Beneath the black glazed tiles of the roof there used to be the Temple of the Great Year, of the Star of Jupiter and of all the heavenly images in which time is revealed to man, that time which is so important for the tilling of the soil. Today there is a garrison in the buildings of the temple. The holy grove in which the grasses and the herbs used to grow undisturbed beneath tall *trees of life*, as was pleasing to Mother Earth, has now become a public pleasure park. The beds of grasses have been torn up upon the square terrace on which sacrifices used to be offered to the clouds and to the mountains, to the rain and to the wind who dreamed there in mysterious stillness beneath curiously shaped pine trees. Shanties made of matting have been erected and on summr afternoons families visit them and drink poor coffee and soda-water upon these altars. The desire for popular festivities has killed the sacred place.

The altars upon which the great cosmic forces were honoured used to be situated in the outer districts of the "four corners of the wind" of Peking. In the south the heavens were honoured upon a round altar, in the north the earth upon a square altar, in the east the god of the sun, and in the west the goddess of the moon. All this is the most ancient heritage and dates from a period preceding the Chou Dynasty, because in those days the sun was feminine and stood in the south and the moon was masculine and stood in the north, while in the east there was thunder (masculine) and in the west the sea (feminine). Today all these altars have decayed. The altar of the sun shaded by dense trees lies dreamily in a quiet district, and when you wander along the town wall, towards the gateway of the rising sun, you see it in the plain, quiet and apart, as though it were upon a dead planet. The buildings of the two other sanctuaries (the altar of the earth and of the moon) have been transformed into barracks.

The spirits of the "young blade of corn" and of millet belong to the terrestrial divinities. Their altar used to stand near the palace. Because the *young blade of corn and millet* (Së Tsi) were the divinities of the country and of society. Whoever possessed them owned the country. Five different coloured kinds of earth were piled up upon its terrace; in the centre yellow, in the east blue, in the south red, in the west white, in the north black. In the old days the feudal princes used to receive a piece of this sacred earth for their altars. If a ruler fell, the conqueror walled up the altar of the vanquished in order to exclude the light of heaven from it. Flowers blossom today round the altar of the *young blade of corn and millet*. The most ancient trees grow in front of its walls and the cry of strange birds is heard in them. A pond separates the sacred place from the Imperial Palace with its red walls and battlements and its golden yellow glimmering roofs which are reflected in the still waters. The youths of Peking throng the walks between the cypresses. The students of both sexes, whole families with their sons and daughters are there, and the little singing ladies are not missing. There are all kinds of small hills and ponds, and near the ponds there are small harbours in which people celebrate their little festivities. Birds populate the ponds, cranes stalk about the shore, and red-flecked geese are heard cackling. In one of these harbours there is an aquarium with all kinds of goldfish; many different types of vessels stand there side by side in which strange fantastic animals with round protruding eyes and long veil-like tails swim about. Photographers abound, and different kinds of amusements and restaurants beckon to the visitor. People come and go, they take their rest and chat and while away the afternoon or meet their friends, and frequently exhibitions and mass meetings or scientific societies or groups of actresses meet here. At the entrance there is the former Ketteler archway with its inscription whose meaning has already been superseded by the passage of time.[1] The students wish to erect a monument to Lenin. It will be seen that the gay activity of life is in progress near the altar to the *young*

[1] Compare Chapter II.

blade of corn and millet. The old times have been forgotten here altogether. It has become a kind of central park.

Now the time has come for us to turn to the Imperial Palace and its surroundings. In Europe there are magnificent castles and palaces which, for instance, command a wide area, or whose generous formation is so conceived that it harmonizes with its surroundings. In Peking the palace does not command a square or a similar area; it is a town in itself, and the entire city of Peking with its million inhabitants is, as it were, subordinated to the plan of this palace town. Three districts precede the palace: the Chinese town in the south and, separated by a broad wall, the Manchu town. Again, surrounded by another wall, there is the Imperial town in which the officials and courtiers live, and finally, safeguarded from the entrance of those who have no business there by a moat, there is the holy forbidden town of the palaces themselves. Any one who wishes to understand the magnificence of this composition and its relation in terms of space to the whole of the rest of the city, must mentally, at any rate, wander southwards to the southern gate of the Chinese town. From there there is, as it were, an axle running directly northwards for more than a mile. In the haze of the distance and at the end of the street, you barely see the contours of the southern gate of the Manchu town. The road leaves the Altar of Heaven on the right and the Altar of the Tilling of the Soil on the left. The empty spaces which line the road are covered with tents made of matting and tea is sold in some, while others serve for theatrical entertainment or market booths. A busy activity is unfolded here every day throughout the year. As you proceed, the solid buildings become more frequent. As soon as you have passed the Bridge of Heaven, where before break of day a market is held, in which many a piece of the booty of thefts committed overnight is offered for sale, the suburb of wooden houses becomes more and more the town of the merchants. You can observe the gilt lettering of the ensigns which hang vertically on the outside of one-storied shops, and at night their gay splendour is illuminated by thousands of electric lamps. The tumult increases as one approaches the Manchu town. Motor-cars, rickshaws, horse carriages of a Chinese kind and the somewhat old-fashioned glass coaches of the officials begin to jostle each other. Among them you can see the men who pour large buckets of water upon the streets, so that the dust which is continually whirled about in the air settles at any rate to some extent. People move in close throngs along the sides of the streets. All along the footpath, at intervals of a few paces, there are the flying booths belonging to all kinds of small traders. The whole throng, which is sometimes so close that the carriages are brought to a standstill for a quarter of an hour at a time before they can proceed on their journey, carries out its business quietly and without any quarrelling. Soldiers and policemen are posted in the middle of the streets in order to regulate the traffic. One then approaches the districts where at right angles you find the fashionable shops. On the left there is the Tashalan which contains the tall golden silk shop, then the street of the jewellers who offer, besides jade, pearls and precious stones, all kinds of genuine and fraudulent works of art. Beyond that there is the street of the lanterns where the pretty Chinese painted lanterns and fans can be bought. To the west the road leads to the Liu Li Ch'ang (the workshops of the glass blowers), in which there is also a big gathering of art dealers.

Let us, however, for the present leave all this district and drive through the gaily painted wooden passage to the place where the road divides into two streets which to the right and the left run around the Ch'ien Men or the Cheng Yang Men (the front gate or the main southern gate). These bulwarks used to be connected with the main entrance by protective walls. They had, however, to be removed owing to the great increase in the traffic at this place. The main gateway with its gaily coloured structure has become an ensign which looks far into the country and, as it were, salutes the other gateway structures which stand at intervals along the high road of the wall. To the right and to the left of the gateway there are the two little temples in honour of Kuanyin and of Kuanti who protect the

city, whereas farther along buildings form guard and lean
against the wall of the city. The central gateway is always
closed. It was reserved for the emperors. The traffic proceeds
through two double gateways, to the right and to the left,
which have been cut in the wall.

The southern gate may be regarded as the entrance to the
city of the palaces, because from here there is a continuation
of the axle that has been spoken of running from north to
south, which is a street which here continues northwards and
is paved with marble. A little farther on there is a red passage
beneath a gaily painted roof of rafters covered by a yellow
glazed roof, and thus the district surrounded by a wall is
reached. After that you come to the great marble bridge in
front of which two dragons stand guard over a mighty building
crowned with battlements. The corners of this building are
secured by substantial square towers and the way leads from
courtyard to courtyard, from hall to hall, ever farther northwards. The height and immensity of the buildings of the
palace is less noticeable. They have been placed within these
enormous empty spaces and are effective without being surprising. The district seems to grow continually in impressiveness
and sanctity, and it seems more and more secluded, until eventually in the far north a moat, behind the hidden labyrinthine
chaos of the courtyards and halls of the Imperial residence
brings the whole plan to its conclusion. The entire scene is out-
topped by the crest of the Coal Hill, whose cleft-tree corpses
and the pavilions in ruin seem to be abandoned to the decay of
time.

The time which is required to traverse all these courtyards
of marble and these luminous coloured halls has the effect of
creating an entirely new sense of volume and distance, to which
the strongest contrast that can be suggested is perhaps the
Gothic spire with its narrow formation shooting straight up to
a height which is overwhelming at the very first glance. In
the Gothic spire we perceive striving motion, superfluity of
height, narrowness, the absence of volume, unrest leading ever
more steeply upwards to dizzy heights, away from the earth
into the empty blue of the abstract, into the beyond. Here in

the Chinese palace we perceive consciousness of the earth, calm, infinite room in terms of width and depth, a perception of time in the form of volume, the great noble ability to wait, comfortable reality, solidly based upon the secure earth, yellow and luminous in its colour, and above it all, and lending it significance, there arches the immense, noble and blue sky. It suggests the unity of the sky and the earth. Concrete eternity is manifested in time and the dignity of this world is revealed.

This concept of the world—ultimately the concept of the plain—has indeed passed away today. We no longer wish to perceive the wealth of space in the width of the road or in length of time. We wish to save time, we wish to overcome space, everything has become a stepping-stone, a means to an end, and every end itself has become the means for something else. This explains why this vital efficient reality excites so many people who see it. They no longer have time for it. As a result the great error was made of cutting streets and laying down tram lines throughout Peking. In Peking you have to have time and you must not go hunting sensations. If you have no time you may go to Shanghai and there the devil himself will teach you what goes to make up a large city in the way of vehicles and all the turmoil, struggle and going and coming of a disturbed ant heap. In Peking there are other demons. Mephistopheles would be bored here and feel as little at home as he is at the classical feast of the summer solstice.

One does not realize the whole immensity of this town of palaces until one reflects what has grown out of its various parts since the revolution. Two of its buildings have provided large public museums in which works of art and the specimens of arts and crafts, collected in the course of centuries, are exhibited; the central park, the palace of the president on the "Middle Lake," apartments and offices for the Cabinet Ministers on the "Southern Lake," the great park with its halls and libraries, the round town, the great marble pagoda and all the temples of the "Northern Lake," the countless number of offices and the accommodation for all kinds of local authorities, the halls and courtyards which are used for Parliament, the rooms in which the foreign visitors are received, and, besides all this, the enormous expanse of buildings in which thousands of courtiers, eunuchs, ladies-in-waiting, servants, empresses with their entire suites of domestics, had to be accommodated; the halls which in the course of the last years have fallen a prey to outbreaks of fire and many, many rooms which are still available. All this shows the extent of this immense system of buildings, the like of which cannot be found anywhere else upon earth.

The palace forms the heart of the town. A system of streets encircles it, and it is only since the revolution that the communication of the eastern town with the western town has been facilitated in one or two places by the fact that streets have been cut right through the district of the palaces. The long period of seclusion has brought it about that the two parts of the town, the east and the west, have each acquired a totally different character. The eastern town is divided from south to north by the great Hatamen Street; the street itself is lined for the most part with shops and business offices, but on the right and on the left there are streets which contain the most curious chaos of men and animals. Small self-contained courtyards with their surrounding buildings are occasionally rented by Europeans, who settle down in them very comfortably in a more or less Chinese manner. If, at night in the early summer, you meet a few good friends in these flower-scented courtyards of such a Chinese property, when those present wear wreaths of flowers in their hair and sit about, drinking a bottle of good wine, it is wonderfully easy and pleasant to talk of the life outside. The moon shines upon it all over the top of the roof. From outside you hear the various cries of the traders, the laughter of children and the dull noise in the distance. The night finally grows silent and only occasionally a dog barks at the moon or at an early thief.

There is an ancient tradition about the nights of Peking. Something of the desert and of infinity looks down upon them when the candles of heaven shine with all their might. Ghosts creep along the black shadows which crawl about the stone floors of the courtyard, after the paper lanterns have flickered out and the moon alone twists the houses and their shadows into queer shapes by its gentle light. The ghosts, however, are not very evil; perhaps a fox who wished to warm himself a little at the soul of a man and who has for this reason transformed himself into a pretty girl, or else it may be a corpse which has not been dead long enough and emits its phosphorous reflections into the dark. Or else they are perhaps only the glow-worms which play about the roof, and that strange sigh in the far corner in the shadow of a tree is perhaps only a wayward breath of wind dreaming of autumn when it may go forth to furrow in the dust of the streets. The ghosts are not very evil provided one does not disturb them.

Peking is a good town even if just as much evil is done there in secret and in public as in other cities, but the place itself is good. If you put a twig into the earth, it brings forth leaves and blossoms because the soil is so fruitful. There is plenty of dirt. The hygiene of these modern days has not yet set out upon its chase against the bacilli in every corner. The fear of bacilli is after all only the modern form of the older belief in spooks. In Peking real ghosts still run about and therefore people do not chase the bacilli as yet. It is almost incredible what a chance of development they have. For hundreds of years, almost everything was allowed in the streets—permitted not only to man, but also to beast. You could throw out dirty water or remnants; dogs and cats, if they could not help themselves might die there—in short, the street welcomed everything and every one in its kindness and covered everything which was disagreeable in its dust. (It is only the odours which are sometimes difficult to conceal.) When moreover you consider the waywardness of the wind who mixes all these things together from time to time and throws the damp dust into the eyes, ears and nose of the traveller it would theoretically not be possible for any one to remain alive in the face of the millions and millions of bacilli; but Peking is a good town, the sun shines, year in year out, and its rays vanquish also the evil spirit of the bacilli.

We will not fail, however, to refer also to the shadowy side of life. Near the four gateways in the east (Tung Si T'ai Lou), which stand at a street crossing, there is the Monastery of Blessing and Good-Fortune (Lung Fu Si). Every ten days a market is held there. Peking holds a large number of these markets, and it is most instructive and amusing to wander about in the tumult. The market of Lung Fu Si has been "discovered" by Europeans, and the Chinese merchants, for their part, have also discovered this fact. Accordingly one of the courtyards of the temple is now always filled with cups, vases, little boxes, dishes, snuff bottles, statues of saints, objects in jade, and a thousand other valuable and worthless articles. The prices are sometimes purely imaginary, the vague wishes of the merchant, a mere indication of the figure which perhaps he would like to have for his object, but the people are open to argument. A struggle begins about the price which delights the initiated on both sides. It is a battle like the drinking game. You do not fix the figure which the object is worth to you and beyond which you do not propose to go, but a figure which is far inferior. The object of trading is to agree to some figure somewhere between the two extremes. This is a test of nerves, of the inner power of an imposing personality. The merchant displays all the art of primitive magic in order to let his wares appear as attractive and as valuable as possible. He sometimes has the most remarkable success. Frequently forgeries, pieces with obvious faults which have been broken or are damaged are not noticed by the purchaser, who is subsequently unable to explain to himself how such an oversight has been possible. As a general rule, one must keep as calm as possible, one must not desire an object at all cost—it is only when the buyer is inwardly free that he is able to bargain properly, and above all one must not desire to cheat the merchant. If a European returns home with the elated feeling of having done down a dealer thoroughly he will generally have an opportunity, in the course of time, of regretting this mistake. Here again there are no rules without exceptions. I have known buyers who have simply departed with the goods they have purchased without paying for them—these foreigners were by no means the kind usually described as thieves, but on the other hand one cannot affirm that every antique that has been honourably acquired is really genuine.

Near this market there is another one where pigs are sold from time to time. This indeed is a perfect purgatory. People with any sensitiveness often prefer to make a wide detour rather than witness the tortures of the poor animals who are helplessly tied up and lying about on the floor, nor do they wish to hear the terrible cries when they are pushed, beaten and killed. This is a hell for animals which does not differ from the other hell outside the eastern gate, which is the temple of the God of Death. The dogs in the streets have a bad time of it too. It is rare that they are cared for, they run about often ill and diseased wherever they can find food, until at last they die in some corner.

In these quarters you sometimes meet with a camel transport. These animals have a thick woolly coat in the winter which is tattered in the course of the spring and in the late summer they are completely naked, whereupon new wool grows again for the winter. This process of moulting often makes these animals look like the most grotesque caricatures. They have a discontented, haughty and contemptuous expression about their mouths. Some of them bite and you can see by the look of any one of them that they are not loving creatures. They have to put up with a great deal and do so in silence for the most part; only when they have been loaded and are to get up do they resist. They are drawn by the ring through their nose and then they scream horribly, they also express their complaints audibly when leather soles are sown to their feet, which is done in the desert if they begin to get sore feet. Otherwise they go about their wretched existence quietly and malignantly.

People have often asked whether the Chinese people are cruel. Such a question really presupposes a mistake. There is no people which as a whole is cruel, just as there is no people which is mild and good. At most it may be said that certain customs and practices have established definite traditions. Here in China the boundary line between kindness and inconsiderateness is indeed drawn in quite a different way than in Europe. The Chinaman considers European family life heartless and loveless. Even the sons of brothers are comparative strangers and there are children who do not look after their parents. All this is quite different in China. Here the feeling towards parents and relatives is so hearty and genuine that it is a common subject for lyric poetry, but that readiness for public assistance which helps a total stranger in the street is not as highly developed in China as in Europe—precisely because of the high development of the feeling for the family.

Moreover, where cruel punishments are practised, manners and customs become coarse, as can best be seen from the example of the Great War amongst the most civilized people. In this way the former cruel punishments in China resulted in a blunting of the feeling for suffering in others. In the course of the last years, however, since these punishments have been abolished, a decided improvement may be observed.

The man in the street in China is not cruel but thoughtless as far as animals are concerned. Of course he loves and cares for the animals with which he lives and which serve him as domestic animals. These beasts are on the whole treated very well, although without any sentimentality. The gentle consideration which elderly ladies show for their dogs in Europe is not as a rule to be seen in China. Animals are regarded by the Chinese as more imperfect and lower beings than men, and accordingly less attention is paid to them. In this respect Buddhism exercises a softening effect by virtue of its compassion for everything which lives; not indeed the drawing-room Buddhism which on feast days goes to the market to purchase doves in order to liberate them while the dealers catch them on the nearest roof in order to sell them once more. Buddhism, however, exercises deeper and profounder stimuli, and the revival of a profoundly spiritual form of Buddhism will undoubtedly have a good effect on the customs and manners of the people. The fact that the Chinese are richly endowed with feelings, that is to say, that they are not cruel, can be seen best in their relation to children. You can see almost everywhere that children are treated with kindness and gentleness. A people who loves children and can laugh and play with them is good in the depth of its soul. In turn, the children are for this reason innocent, kindly, often importunate but not impertinent. If they become too importunate, they are calmed down by having a thousand beautiful things promised to them. The nurses in particular are experts in this practice. The children do not take these promises seriously, but they are delighted to listen and in the course of listening they become quiet.

My road led me every day along the wall of the Imperial city, towards the north. Inside these walls there is a moat in which water flows slowly and lazily towards the south. Closely set willow trees stand on the edge. You pass old temples whose gods have died and serve worldly purposes today. A stone lion whose head has been knocked off stands somewhere in a corner. A doctor, with many tablets in his honour, which have been presented to him by patients he has cured, has taken up his abode by the canal. A busy life is manifested along the green dull water.

Near the Coal Hill in the eastern city there is the Government University, where I had to give lectures. I recall with great joy the memory of my Chinese colleagues with whom I had many an interesting conversation during the intervals, and also of the students, who, for the most part, listened to what was proffered to them with enthusiasm and sympathetic intelligence. The university is an insignificant-looking building, a bare dark red-brick building (other portions of the university lie farther south and west and are more agreeable in their exterior). In the twenty-five years of its existence this university was a mental power in the public life in China such as probably no other university enjoyed to a similar degree. This power made itself felt in the free manifestation of life, in social and political reform and in the reconstruction of the entire Chinese spirit. The financial circumstances of the professors are meagre. Most of them are compelled to earn a living by writing in their free time because their salaries are paid very irregularly on account of the wretched state of Government finances. The lecturers are imbued by a high idealism and therefore remain faithful to their calling, and every one of them regards it as an honour to belong to this institution.

There is a road near the Coal Hill which leads from the eastern to the western city. It passes through one of the gateways of the old palace town and leads over an arched bridge made of marble, which is divided into two sections lengthways by a tall wall. The southern half belongs to the garden of the palace of the president; the northern half is devoted to public traffic. From here a view is afforded of the Northern Gate (Te Ai), overgrown with lotus flowers and surrounded by buildings and little hills of the shore, and the view is finally shut in by the great Pagoda Hill. Beyond the top of it looms the marble Thibetan pagoda which has become the emblem of the north of Peking.

The character and aspect of the western town are quite different from those of the eastern city. Curiously enough, Peking also belongs to those capitals in which the west is the most fashionable district. Even outside the Shung Chih Men, the south-western gate of the northern town, there is a fashionable quarter in which many of the favourite restaurants are to be found. The street of the art dealers, Liu Li Ch'ang, extends as far as this and the educational and medical faculty of the university have their headquarters here. The women's university is in the street of the "Princely Husband of Stone." I have lectured at all three universities and had the most satisfactory experience in all of them. I found the women students in particular intelligent and interested in their work and entirely familiar with scientific research. Some of these women students—just as the men students—are poetically somewhat radical, but this is a prerogative of youth in progressive nations. It is a peculiar fact that, whereas the women students have the right to visit all the universities for men, the women's university does not admit male students. Consequently, at any rate

in this respect, the so-called equality of the sexes gives preference, if anything, to the women in Peking. The women's question was solved in China very easily. The young women have
found their way to freedom and mental activity from dependence and from the tradition of patriarchal marriage and family institutions far more easily than has been the case in our
modern Western states. Here too the old proverb has turned
out to be correct: "And the last shall be first."

In the western city very ancient gardens are hidden behind
walls in the seclusion of out-of-the-way streets. The branches
of the trees in these gardens form a roof by joining their
branches above the adjoining courtyards and houses, so that
a shady coolness is maintained even during the greatest heat
of the summer. Passing over mossy steps you reach quiet
courtyards and apartments filled with green twilight, the
shadow of the trees. Not many people forgather there. Only
a few familiar friends are found there in quiet conversation.
They look at pictures, discuss a new poem, examine an old
bronze or pass a beautiful old piece from hand to hand and
drink a bowl of tea meanwhile. Such conversations were the
origin of the Japanese tea ceremony, but in Japan everything
is styled more severely and has been ossified into rigid formality. In China such conversations are still alive. They assume a special form according to the people who are present,
according to the day which preceded, according to the weather,
and according to the mood. China has succeeded in keeping
its customs so alive that they are garments which it wears. In
Japan the customs are more severe, more fettered; politeness
is not set the limits of inner freedom, and for this reason
Japanese politeness often seems puppet-like, and therefore
the Japanese are often considered false. Such an opinion does
them a great injustice. Their severity, their self-control, commands them to grin when their heart is bleeding, for the centre
of their being lies outside their own personality; it is the state,
the Ruler of Heaven. The Chinaman, however, if he is a normal
Chinaman, has his centre of gravity within himself. Custom
must serve him to bring about the harmonious expression of

his nature and the individual must not serve custom for the presentation of the iron law of form. This kind of freedom is perhaps the most exquisite and the highest form; it is the politeness of the heart, and the reason why one is bound to love the Chinese as soon as one knows them. A Chinaman is as courteous as a Frenchman, but he is devoid of those obstacles which prevent the Frenchman's character from being rooted in his being. The Chinaman does not know fanaticism. The Chinaman is more childlike than the Frenchman, who is perhaps too old.[1]

The road leads out of the western town into the open country. It leads to the Temple of the White Cloud. This is a Taoist sanctuary. Here you feel that Taoism still possesses vitality. Here Laotse is not the magic god; but the men of a later age have dwelt here who have managed to attain an inner life by mystic self-contemplation. The monastery possesses many halls devoted to meditation, and a garden in quiet seclusion upon whose artificial little mounds people may sit and look out into the far plain in which dark funeral groves, orchards and pagodas are strewn at random much as one looks out from the quiet harbour into the far sea upon which small sailing vessels float. In the presence of so many mysterious powers as live in this monastery, it is marvellous that there are halls in this temple in which Lü Tüng Pin prophesied the future, while there are others in which women shyly take the image of a child made of clay from one of the altars so that their secret wishes should come to be realized.

The western hills stretch out their distant beauty along the horizon. They are animated by temples and castles. Their outrunners used to be transformed into the summer palaces of the Emperor. A canal leads from the Imperial Palace in the capital right out to the pagoda of the Marble Spring near the hills in which the translucent source is situated from which all the water of the many ponds at the foot of the mountain is filled. It must have been an extraordinary splendour of gar-

[1] There is also a young France to which no reference is made here, which is pregnant with the future and with hope.

dens, towers, castles, and palaces. There is also a French baroque palace among them. Fairy gardens, fairy castles lay behind strong walls along the slope. Today only remnants remain. Englishmen and Frenchmen have put an end to all this glory by their "punitive expeditions" in the 'sixties. The temples are in decay, the hills are covered by ruins, wild shrubs flourish in the gardens among the gay tiles of porcelain and along marble ponds with their boldly arched bridges.

Here and there some little portions have been rebuilt, for instance, the summer palace of the late Dowager-Empress in which she spent her holidays and desired to pass the evening of her life. The most extraordinary mixture of European bad taste and evidence of decadence appear here side by side with real old beauty. Another palace is occupied by the Ts'inghua university where a limited number of students is prepared for a future visit to America. There are also other foreign schools which are erected here upon the ruins of a bygone pomp. A general has erected a garden for himself near by. Modern Chinese structures and pretty gardens with thatched huts and artificial springs alternate with places devoted to gymnastics and skittle alleys. I will never forget the gracefulness with which the wife of the general in her blue tussore dress performed on the horizontal bar. The foreign visitors took their fill of amazement and not one the European ladies was able to imitate the performance of the youthful wife of the general.

Other hidden groves with little huts for students suitable for study and meditation are to be found here and there in the tree-covered district. Everywhere the greater past looms up into a lesser present. The present today brings forth a good many things in Peking and its surroundings which point beyond our day. Most of these things belong to a mental realm and have not yet found visible or external expression.

Peking is a town of mysterious freedom. Men come and go and every one finds a circle of friends who offer him what he desires. Every man who lives here finds suitable surroundings for the work he has determined to do. The air which breathes over Peking is good and free. Whoever comes here may be a hermit or a sociable fellow, he may wish to cast the cares of life away from him by indulging in steaming wine or strive for eternity in severe castigation. Every one can do the bidding of his own will. There is here no pressure of custom sufficiently strong to limit any one's personality. This divine freedom is the profoundest factor in Peking and fills the heart with gratitude.

OCCULTISM AND RELIGIOUS MOVEMENTS

THE present extent of occult revivals and religious movements is quite a new phenomenon in China. In the course of the last decade, there have also been signs among the people of religious tendencies which have led to the formation of secret sects. To this category belongs, for instance, the Christian movement of the so-called T'aip'ings or the anti-Christian one of the Boxers. These movements, however, were semiconscious outbreaks of a volcanic kind on the part of repressed elements who thus obtained an irrational expression. Even if there were a few officials in the Boxer movement, notably among the little-educated and primitive Manchus who believed in the movement, it was nevertheless on the whole a manifestation confined to a small locality. Profound layers of the soul were not touched. This fact also explains the rapid decrease of the movement and rendered the present reaction against it possible.

Educated circles in China have always been very enlightened and sober. It was the form of religious custom which had gained the victory over the emotions. Most of these people possessed a somewhat sterile agnosticism. They would occasionally converse about ghost stories and no one would deny the possibility of occult manifestations which are far too numerous in the East to be ignored, especially since deception as a means of livelihood does not enter into the question in this domain. People just accepted things as they were. They assumed that just as the body does not disappear suddenly after death, but is heir to a slow process of decay, so does the psychic portion of man survive death for a period, also to decay in the course of time, and that at most where the spiritual strength holds the elements of the soul together a personality might be able to maintain itself in an ethereal form with the possibility of materializing in various ways at the expense of living plasma. Such creatures were gods and demons who might prolong their existence through many centuries in so far as they found convenient points of support in living human beings. These views strike the European observer as contradicting the doctrines of Karma of reincarnation, as well as being opposed to the doctrines of the various hells and heavens in which the departed souls remain, and finally inconsistent with the veneration of ancestors which evidently presupposes the continuation of life after death. These contradictions are only superficial. This attitude is in all probability to be traced to various origins, as, for instance, the doctrine of the beyond goes back to Western Asiatic, the Karma teaching to Indian concepts; the worship of ancestors is based upon a Confucian idea, but life passes over such contradictions and easily combines even more striking oppositions.

According to the Chinese view the process of being human is only one form of existence among many others. A man is composed just as much of various bodily as of various psychic elements. If these various elements are held together after death by a strong power, the personality continues upon a higher, because a materially superior, level of existence. It becomes a genius. These genii constitute the Taoist pantheon and reveal themselves according to their power to those who revere them for a longer or a shorter period. Taoist tradition recognizes in particular eight such genii which, belonging to different periods, constitute a sublime company. There is also a lady among them who, in the absence of her husband, partook of the cup of immortality and thereupon immediately became one of the genii. It is important to observe that these genii are always conceived in a more or less bodily form. They can appear and disappear and have a transfigured body. Ghosts constitute their counterpart. In this case the material is unclean and is a torture to them and others. They are the unredeemed spirits. Some of them have to find a representative in order to be relieved of their unhappy earthly and unearthly situation. Especially the spirits of those who have been drowned or hanged are dangerous, and therefore people avoid the places where spooks of this kind appear, because it happens frequently that as a result of fright or cunning a poor human being is persuaded to hang himself in the very place in which some one else has previously committed suicide. These unhappy ghosts, who cannot liberate themselves from their earthly life, torture and frighten human beings because they are unable to produce anything else but misery.

In China, as elsewhere, frequent conversations are held as to whether such ghosts do or do not exist. The following occurrence excited a great deal of attention for a while. A Chinese steamer had gone down during a storm in the winter near Shanghai and the majority of the passengers and the crew had been drowned. A merchant who had been drowned with his wife appeared to his son one night, and he said that he and his wife could find no rest until their corpses which were still in the cabins of the steamer had been brought to safety and buried. He also related how terrible the event of the disaster had been and described the place exactly where the corpses could be found. In evidence of his story he offered the following proof. His son was to spread a sheet of white linen in front of the pavilion in the garden and to have this sheet photographed precisely at twelve o'clock in the course of the next night. The son did as he was bidden, and on the photographic plate the contours of a feminine and a male figure could be distinguished which looked on the photograph like dark shadows on a pale background. It is also said that the corpses were found in exactly the place which had been described.

When I heard of this story, I decided in the company of one or two Chinese friends to go into the matter. We obtained a print of the spiritist photograph. It was a photographic print upon which one could really distinguish the contours of shadows, which, however, could not be regarded as offering proof. We were told that against payment of a higher sum it was possible to obtain an unchallengeable and direct photograph. The photograph came and was indeed very curious. The picture was very dark and it was only when held against the sunlight on one side that we saw, as in the case of the old daguerreotypes, only much weaker, the traits of an elderly Chinese gentleman which, as those present remarked, really resembled those of the deceased. An excited discussion arose as to the possibilities of such an occurrence. I requested one of the younger gentlemen to investigate the facts carefully, when it appeared that we had simply been given a photograph after an old photograph of the deceased which before being rephotographed had been covered over with a special ink. Thus this notable case, which preoccupied even the Press for a certain period, turned out to be a swindle. We did not examine if the first unclear photograph was genuine and whether only the second had been manufactured in order to add a further proof over and above what was true.

Apart from these spirits and demons which are always ready to exercise their effect upon men and among whom there are also creatures of animal instead of human origin, a good deal of importance must be ascribed to the conception of the beyond. On the one hand, man unites within him several psychic beings which were originally some sort of formation resembling the shadowy soul of the body according to the Greek tradition. On the other hand, the beyond in its present conception is only conceived as a traditional stage. It is not a bodily condition, but merely a state of consciousness. "Heaven and hell lie in the consciousness of men." This is a phrase which occurs again and again in the Chinese doctrine of the next world. For this reason it can also happen that a man may pass through heaven and hell in the course of his lifetime. If his presence in heaven has "exhausted" his treasure of good work, or if he has done penance in hell for his sins, the soul in its innermost being comes to be clothed again with a body. The souls are brought to the great wheel of life where they drink the yellow water of oblivion. Then they are pushed into the wheel which turns with a creak. They lose consciousness and find themselves born once more upon earth. Just as it is possible for the body of the child to develop in the body of its mother, while the soul tarries in the beyond, it is conceivable, on the other hand, that in the early stages of life in the next world, so long as the soul still looks outwards, that it may appear to those whom it has left behind, while it wanders already in the next world. One of the first distant halting-places is the terrace from which the parting souls are allowed to look back once more upon their home before they have to cross the river. The fact that one does not remember one's former life is simply due to the occasion on which one drinks from the yellow waters. It is given to some people, however, suddenly to pass back into their former stages of existence.

One day in the Taoist monastery of the Laoshan I heard a story of this kind, in the twilight beneath the mysterious camellia tree in which a flowered fairy dwelt. The abbot allowed the sound of his cithara to die away and a bright sky peeped through the dusky branches of the peonies, while beyond the rocks of the mountain-top beckoned to him and a crackling fire sent its smoke towards heaven. The priest began: A little while ago a man was here who knew about his earlier existence. He had got into hell on account of evil conduct and had been compelled to pass several centuries there. At last the period of his torture had come to an end. He was brought to the wheel of life. There he had been given a coat of dark velvet, which pleased him particularly. He had put it on and after that he was pushed into the wheel. He turned—and he found himself upon earth once more. His little brothers and sisters were small and blind and drank greedily at the breast of their mother. He too had joined them. They lay upon dung. Flies buzzed about and sat upon their eyelids. All the dirt and the smell of which he was conscious did not strike him as being in any way unpleasant. He rolled about, delighted, in the soft substance. After a little while he saw a pretty dusky maiden coming round the corner. After sniffing him briefly she had promised him marriage. In the course of time she begat children, in fact, quite a litter at once. He now noticed that his wife and his children were pigs, but even this discovery was not disagreeable to him. With blinking satisfaction, he devoured some of these delicate and charming babies, whereupon his wife made him a scene. He thought: "Yes, women are really strange, and, in addition, this one is a pig:

why should I bother about her any more?" Thereupon he deserted her and directed his attention to other things. In the course of time he came to recognize that he himself was nothing better than a pig. In itself he found it fairly easy to make his peace with this discovery because every being possesses above all a love of life and is content to be whatever it is. A deep sorrow, however, took possession of him when he noticed that the human beings in his surroundings, to whom he had hitherto paid hardly any attention, cast an eye upon him. "Now he is fat enough!" they said one day, and he was tied hand and foot. They put a hook in his ear and lifted him by his ears and his tail upon a cart. No amount of screaming and resistance were of any avail. Then a period of sorrow came upon him. Thrown together with a large number of companions in woe, he had to experience the tortures of hunger and thirst and the misery of being rattled about while held by hateful fetters in the course of a long journey. The market was horrible with all its miserable screams of the other unhappy creatures who were torn away from wife and child and hurried to a death of torture. Eventually it was his turn. He received a stunning blow upon the head, a stab, and he felt his blood run. It was only after that, however, that the worst happened to him. The heat of boiling water into which he was thrown, the extraction of his hairs, entrails, and the process of cutting him to pieces. He felt and experienced all these humiliating sensations to the full. Then he was taken to the market and every pound of flesh which was cut from off him was a new pain and torture to him. Finally at sundown an old woman had laid the last remnant of his flesh into a basket and then he lost consciousness. When he came to himself again he heard the voice of a judge that he had now done enough penance and would be allowed to return to earth. A herd of devils grinning wildly immediately seized him and dragged him away. In the meantime he had acquired his old form again. They wanted to take his black velvet jacket away from him, but he did not wish them to have it. Eventually they began to pinch him and to tear the garment to pieces on his body. The more he resisted the more did they torment him. Finally there was nothing left but one of the sleeves, which he thereupon seized with his fingers above the edge of the sleeve, and said: "I will not part with my coat." He had, however, already been pushed into the wheel, which turned round, and thus he was born as a human being once more into the world. One hand, however, showed a few fingers which looked like the claws of a pig. They had forgotten to give him to drink of the water of oblivion and for this reason he remembered all these occurrences. He could never relate them without tears and shudders, and he has devoted the whole of his life to piety and to sanctity.

As for ancestral worship, it relates to quite a different domain. The funeral practices in their modern form contain much which is due to the outlook described above. In Chinese culture so very many different elements meet that this fact is not surprising, but on the whole the practices of mourning and those of ancestral worship as evolved by Confucianism are a thoroughly patriarchal institution. It is worth while noting that in the old days the representative of the deceased ancestor on the occasion of the sacrificial feast, the so-called death boy, was, as a rule, the grandson of the departed. This fact allows us to conclude that ancestral worship originally did not assume a continuation of life on the part of the ancestor in the next world, but counted upon a reincarnation as a rule in the next generation but one. In the higher sections of society exceptions were made. The proper execution of ancestral worship lent power to them, as it were, just as it was able to bless those who were left behind so that a greater personal continuity became possible. Even the Imperial ancestral tablets were removed after a certain number of generations, and only the founder of a clan and particularly meritorious fathers of later days were honoured continually as Tsu (founder of the family) or as Tsung (founder of the clan). Confucius, for the most part, recognized the old traditions, which he accepted and arranged into a system. His object was to develop the fundamental duty of reverence in a child so as to make it an absolute duty quite independent of the fact whether the parents, the recipients of such reverence, were alive or not. As far as concepts of the beyond were concerned, he practised a noteworthy resistance. "You do not yet know life, how can you then hope to understand death?" he replied to a disciple who asked him about the next world. He also refrained from any positive statement as regards the length or duration of the personality of the ancestors. "If I say that they have consciousness, pious sons will sacrifice anything in order to serve the dead. If I say they have no consciousness, inconsiderate sons will cease to bother about their dead altogether." For these reasons uncertainty in such matters was the state of the soul which seemed to the master the most desirable, because in this way people did their duty independently of external motives and merely for the sake of duty alone.

In the later stages of Confucianism we meet with a pronounced disbelief in these things, but custom has developed in such a way as fosters a regular form of auto-suggestion. Fasting and meditating upon the life of the deceased by concentrating upon his appearance, his voice, his habits, his expressions excite the emotion of the son to so great an extent that he often merely sees visions and hears voices. All that happens is always, as it were, preceded by "as if." In no circumstances whatever is a real appearance postulated. The vital conception that you are in the presence of the departed is sufficient for purposes of performing the sacrifices with the necessary devoutness. This religion of the "as if" signifies in the tersest manner the profoundest nature of Confucian ancestral worship.

It is, of course, obvious that this latent freedom of attitude is not destined for the mass of the people. In that case much more solid conceptions have predominated and the upper sections fostered these myths. Where divine power was manifested and showed its activity in the interest of society, it found public recognition. The new god was admitted to the list of public sacrifices. It was sufficient if this myth was penetrated by the perception of the leaders as though it were a transparent veil. The mass of the people did not feel at ease upon the icy summits of recognition.

The population was, of course, not satisfied merely to pray to the gods who had thus met with the approval of the state. An attempt was made to get a closer personal contact. Here begins the domain of the secret sects and occult movements which have manifested themselves here and there, especially in restless times. These organizations often possessed a strongly political background, and in that case they were pursued with severity as being dangerous to the state. Often they were the place of refuge of a quiet element in the land and then they were suffered kindly. It is one of the privileges of Christian Europe and her Western Asiatic relatives not to go to war about matters of religion, perhaps because people regarded religion too stolidly and did not want to know anything of the sublime spiritual freedom of thought which has always manifested itself in the East.

In the course of the last generation various movements of a religious kind have manifested themselves among the people and excited men for a certain while, eventually to return in a harmless manner to the normal activity of life. One of these movements sought its headquarters chiefly in Manchuria and from there jumped, as it were, to Shantung which is in constant contact with Manchuria. It was probably owing to Japanese influences that the worship of the Fox-God became popular. The fox had been regarded for a long time as a curious intermediary being. It is possible, by means of Yoga exercises, for the fox to assume human form. Moreover, all foxes are by no manner of means good creatures. They change for preference into beautiful girls and overwhelm the men whom they have chosen for their victims. It does no one any good to have dealings with such foxes in women's form because while the fox imbibes higher forces through his intercourse with human beings, men are dragged down and weakened and their souls become impoverished. In the end men become the toy of these intermediary beings which enter into them to utter all kinds of blasphemies by their command. The new aspect of this fox movement was that there were sections among the people who honoured this "third Father Fox" as a divinity who showed itself, every now and again, as able to heal diseases and to help in all the needs of life. It can truly be said of the "third Father Fox" that he was a strange saint, but he did his duty towards his faithful supporters who in turn honoured him accordingly. Nor is he directly called "fox." He might not like this, and therefore he is described by the family name of "Hu," which corresponds with the character "Hu" = fox in pronunciation, but is written in a different way.

Another movement which met with a considerable popularity, especially among the lower section of the people, is the Tsai Li sect. Tsai Li really means "within the order of reason." They revered Kuanyin and they abjured by her help all alcoholic and narcotic stimulants. They are permitted neither tobacco nor opium and they avoid wine in all its forms. This society has helped many a poor fellow to liberate himself from the power of corrupting influences by virtue of religious faith.

The misery of the age has recently prepared the soil in which a new revival of religious instincts was made possible. Lately, especially in the western province of Szechuan, a most extraordinary revival of religious sensibility has taken place, which has suddenly burst from the narrow confines of isolated sects to which it used to be limited and has drawn wide masses of people under its influence. You feel yourself transported to bygone days because even the religious practices are being called to a new life. It is curious that this movement jumped over, as it were, the individual religious communities. There are religious unions of the five religions. Christianity, Islam, Buddhism, Taoism, Confucianism, or of the seven religions, in which case Christianity is divided into Protestantism and Catholicism, and not infrequently the faith of the Jews is also accepted. The methods well known in the history of religion, such as meditation, ecstasy with visions and voices, oracles, clairvoyants and hypnotic and spiritualistic manifestations, serve as the means to bring about a contact with the divine. A procedure which for a time caused a considerable excitement was the dissemination of a prophecy which was published on the first day of the seventh month, that is to say on the 12th of

August, 1923, by the general union of all the world religions in Peking. A great universal catastrophe was prophesied for the fifteenth day of the eighth month which was to be recognized by the following phenomena: an enormously powerful earthquake, five days' disappearance of the sun and the moon so that a great darkness would rule upon earth, thunder, shooting stars, floods, storms, and snow, ice and hail and great cold. The consequence of this catastrophe would be the destruction of one-third of mankind. This prophecy emanated from Szechuan, the western province of China. The tenor of the message was that of genuine horror and the prophetic warning to save whatever might be saved. Sixteen rules were given to enable people to escape the catastrophe, all of which amounted to advising people on the one hand to provide themselves with drink as a protection to the lack of water which would occur as the result of the earthquake, and on the other with food and warm clothing against the consequences of cold and hunger. This advice is no longer a direct portion of the prophecy, but results from reasonable considerations of the impending events. The prophecy with its mixture of an ecstatic prophetic call and its friendly advice caused an immense impression. Printed notices were distributed everywhere, but fear was spread abroad like an epidemic, and when on the first of September the earthquake occurred in Japan with all its unspeakable horrors the people seemed to be absolutely convinced that the end of the world was at hand. Other religious institutions profited by the expectancy in the air, and thus one prophecy has succeeded upon another. A printed sheet was disseminated on which a prophecy was printed which was said to have been found in Shansi upon a stone on the first day of the year. According to this publication great misery in the last three months of the current year were announced and ten plagues were enumerated which were to visit the world. The first plague is that confusion will reign throughout the world. The second plague is that in the East and in the West men will die of hunger. The third plague is that great poverty will occur in the valley of the Yangtse. The fourth plague is that robbers will appear in all the provinces. The fifth plague is that peace will be taken away from men. The sixth plague is that poverty and disease will oppress mankind. The seventh plague is that while there will be food there will no longer be men to eat it. The eighth plague is that while there will be clothes there will be no one to wear them. The ninth plague is that the bones of the dead will lie about while there will no longer be any one to bury them. The tenth plague is that it will be difficult to outlive the year of the pig and the rat. The years of the pig and the rat were the years 1923 and 1924. "It is further mentioned that on the twenty-third day of the tenth month (30th of November) there will be a day of misery and that wild animals will appear upon earth to oppress men. When the new year arrives, all men will laugh and when they are asked why they laugh, they will say: 'The true lord is here and we go to meet him.' Then will come the great period of salvation and the faithful will live to see it. The unfaithful, however, and those who do evil will know great misery. He who does good will save his life."

Another prophecy which was spread abroad mentioned that in Nanking a stone had fallen to earth amidst a great thunderstorm and upon it was found the promise of a great period of misery. This prophecy was said to be the word of Buddha. It also contained an announcement of ten great plagues, which differ in various respects from those enumerated above. Magical signs were indicated, three of which were to be placed upon the door of the house and three upon the incense burner, whereas the three last were to be worn upon the body.

An older prophecy from the year 1890 was spread abroad which also emanates from Szechuan and contained the warning of the military god Kuanti, who had for this purpose personally descended upon earth.

These publications were distributed in great quantities in the streets of Peking. In the temples incense was burnt all day long and the faithful hurried thither in order to obtain the assistance of the gods whom they feared. In particular, wealthy old ladies distributed considerable sums of money for the printing and dissemination of these prophecies. Food was purchased, and the story goes that even Europeans supplied themselves on the quiet with tins of milk as advised by the prophecy to protect themselves against the lack of water. Eventually the matter developed to such an extent that the police had to interefere. A decree enlightening people was distributed and also a dissertation by the observatory. What contributed most to calm men's minds was the fact that the fatal day passed without anything peculiar happening. The day was dull at first and dusky, but the weather improved, and in the evening the full moon appeared in all its splendour surrounded by a rainbow-like halo and full justice was done to the feast of the autumn equinox.

If we ask how these prophecies come about, we shall receive the best impression of the matter if we examine a little more closely into the activity of such a religious society. For this purpose I will choose the Tao Yuan Co. "The academy of the world law," in which the five religions are combined. It is incidentally curious that St. John is revered as the representative of Christianity. This company numbers many former officials, and its statutes have been elaborated with truly bureaucratic accuracy. The will of the gods is here ascertained in two ways: one by means of the planchette and the other by meditation, and phenomena of materialization also occur. Revelations by means of the planchette are made in the following way. Four people participate: two who handle the planchette, one who reads and one who writes down the words. Before the action begins incense is burnt in honour of the saint from whom one desires advice. The participants kneel down in a row and burn a piece of yellow paper, which is thrown into a pot from which the ash after it is burnt, still glowing gently, is suddenly whirled up in a spiral motion right up to the top of the ceiling of the room. This raising of the burnt paper, which causes a curious impression, is regarded as the sign that the spirit has approached. On the altar there is a large flat vessel which is filled with fine sand. The two people who are to write with the planchette now each seize with one hand a smooth twig in the middle of which a smaller twig protrudes downwards. The god then proceeds to write his monogram. In the case which I watched it consisted in a very regular spiral being drawn over the entire surface and when it reached one extremity it was inverted and went backwards. There are all kinds of monograms of this kind. The highest god, for instance, has a Latin G. After the god has given evidence of his presence the writing begins. The signs, as it were, write themselves, and the definite impression is created that it is not a conscious process on the part of the participants. Indeed it would not be easy for two men, each of them holding a branch in one hand, to be so skilful as to write sometimes very complicated signs. Conscious deceit is all the more impossible as we are not here concerned with a performance for the public, and as a rule it is precisely the pupils who have recently joined the company who are employed for these purposes. The signs are written without any interval between them. Every sign is read aloud by the reader and after that its correctness is verified. If, as happens sometimes, a sign is not properly recognized, it is struck out by the invisible hand which guides the planchette and the sign writes itself new. If the sign is confirmed, it is written down on a sheet of paper by a bystanding writer. Thereupon the sand is smoothed and they proceed to the next sign.

On the whole it may be said that the spirits are rather talkative, but that the content of their revelation is usually confined to somewhat vague exhortations, although sometimes individual events are predicted. As an instance, our arrival is said to have been known before we came. The actual procedure of spiritual writing can frequently be seen depicted in old woodcuts. The god floats through the air on top of a cloud of incense. The goddess Kuanyin, the divinity of charity, for instance, makes her revelations through the intermediation of the magician Lu Tsu. He directs the little twig of the planchette by the magic power of his wand which is made of horsehair. Kuanyin has a girl and boy in her service, who do her bidding as she dispenses her blessings with a reed of willow while the boy holds a bowl containing holy water. The magician Lu Tsu, to be distinguished by the magical sword which he wears on his back, is waited upon by the spirit of the willow tree, who is his own particular servitor. The present-day procedure is much the same as that described above and delineated upon old woodcuts.

We were also invited to see the other room. It was the room of Lu Tsu. We met various of his followers whom we found in an embryo-like position, that is to say squatting with their arms and legs drawn closely about them, practising auto-suggestion and meditation. They were so preoccupied that they did not even notice our presence. Behind the altar there was a number of life-size photographs. We were told that these pictures were the result of an order given by the gods to expose a negative at night in a certain place. When the plate comes to be developed the pictures which we saw resulted from this procedure. The impression which these photographs made is by no means divine, but they reveal the peculiarly rigid, almost terrifying facial expression which is sometimes found upon spiritualistic materializations in Europe.

Spirits frequently manifest themselves not only through the writing of the planchette, but also by the aid of mediums. The medium in question loses consciousness and talks with a strange voice of which it has no recollection when the individual in question comes back to his senses. These performances seem at times to be extraordinarily impressive. A scholar with a thorough historical training once declared himself completely sceptical as to the possibility of these revelations by spirits. When I saw him again a few weeks later he told me that he was now nevertheless inclined to recognize the possibility of such manifestations. He had experienced such a case in the person of a female member of his family after the death of his mother in so impressive a manner that he had derived the absolute impression of having been in contact with his deceased mother. Not only her voice and her facial expression but also the entire nature of her communication had been so intimate that he alone was able to understand the full extent of its meaning. In this case, of course, conscious deception was quite out of the question. In fact all these manifestations take place, as it were, in a more natural manner in China than in Europe, where there is frequently a secret struggle between the medium and the man who makes use of her, which of course falsifies the whole situation from the beginning.

The institution in question maintains a certain intellectual level and also carries out charitable work—at the command of the highest god—that is to say, they founded the institution of the Red Swastika.[1]

Apart from the many more or less superstitious societies which have sprung up lately like mushrooms from the earth, there is also a society which concerns itself in a scientific manner with the many problems connected with the principle of life and has for its object the systematic care of the inner life as well as the sane formation of the social community of mankind. The founder is a man born in very humble circumstances in Szechuan. He was not a scholar or an official, but gained a deep insight into the mentality of man by virtue of his highly developed inner experiences. In order to show the views of this group which bring a profound understanding to every form of religion, we will give below a section of their fundamental doctrines of the triple ego. It is most remarkable to what a great extent these views coincide with what is profoundest in all the various idealistic philosophies. Echoes of the mysticism of St. Paul and St. John and the deepest principles of Buddhism, no less than those of Taoism and Confucianism, are confirmed in their attitude.

THE DOCTRINE OF THE TRIPLE EGO

The first ego is an unreal ego, the second ego is the real ego, and the third ego is the divine ego within the real ego. According to nature the first ego is the mortal body. The second ego

[1] The hooked cross or Swastika was used already in the early days of Buddhism as a symbol. This symbol was chosen in order to stress simultaneously the similarity with Christianity and the difference from the Red Cross.

is the soul, the third ego is the true spiritual being, or expressed more precisely, the first ego is a combination of the four elements (water, earth, fire, and air); the second ego is the first beginning, the third ego is the transcendental primary cause which is common to all creatures. When man finds that ego which is at the bottom and common to all creatures then, and only then, does he become the great ego. Of this great ego it is said: The heavens may pass away yet I will not pass away, the earth may be destroyed and yet I will not be destroyed. The Highest God says in reference to this ego: In the beginning there was my spirit, then the heaven came into existence. Because Sakya Muni was able to proclaim his doctrine of the third ego he became the teacher of God and men. K'ungtse proclaimed his teaching by virtue of this third ego. For this reason he has proved to be the model and master of countless generations. If a man who seeks the truth does not find this third ego he not only fails to achieve his work in this life, but he will not achieve it in the course of a thousand lives throughout all the periods of history. If therefore a man is truly concerned for his salvation he must endeavour to find and understand this third ego.

All the so-called heroes and great statesmen in the history of the world, no matter how great their achievements may have been, and even though their flame has filled the whole world, have not got beyond the unreal ego and have understood nothing of the true ego. The faithful and the supporters of the various religions have indeed recognized the real ego, but they have perceived only imperfectly the all-embracing divine ego within the real ego. These saints have not yet reached the stage in which they can say of themselves that they are so great that nothing can envelop them and so small that nothing can divide them. If this heaven- and earth-embracing divine ego is hidden and inaccessible even from the saints, where is it to be found? Master K'ung said: "He who directs men by the power of this inner being is like the north star which is stationary while all the other stars encircle it." This north star, encircled by all the others, is the ever-present divine ego, which does nothing and yet leaves nothing undone; it is the true lord of the world and of men.

In the Great Learning it is written that it consists of the purification of the original impure being: that is the work performed upon the unreal ego in order to evolve the real from the unreal. When love to one's fellow-men is referred to, it is the work performed upon the real ego which seeks to destroy selfishness and to recognize all creatures as belonging to one great body. To aim at the highest good signifies the work upon the ever-present divine ego. For that reason it is called "The highest good."

All the works of the saints and the sages which outlive the centuries are based upon this third ego and harmonize with it, just as works of art which men are able to create contain this third ego in secret.

Whence comes then the unreal, real, and that divine ego which stands above the real and the unreal ego? This is one of the mysteries of the world. The unreal ego is born of the flesh and blood of the parents, the real ego is the issue of the monads which were formed when the heavens and the earth appeared. The great ever-present ego exists without beginning, is born of itself and lives eternally. It is the great secret of which the Highest says that it lived before the beginning of the world and that it will not be old after its decay, nor can it be named and it may only be roughly described as principle. This principle is so mysterious that it is not attainable by thought. The name of this principle, that is to say, its revelation, has emanated from the great all-embracing ego. In the very beginning the two opposing forces of light and shade were created which have developed into the idea containing the seed of all things. The process of the evolution of light and shade has constituted the heavens and the earth, the sun, the moon and all the stars, and thus the monads of all creatures are endowed with the powers of light and shade in heaven and upon earth, and the power to bring the seed to blossom is bestowed by the sun and the moon. The pure and the good constitute the monads of the divine spirit, the impure and the mixed constitute the monads of the terrestrial spirit. All these monads, when they enter the maternal body, are confined within the power of earthly strength and darkened by their desire for external things so that they are not able to escape the laws of the empirical world with their five conditions of change and laws of destiny whereupon they enter upon the cycle of birth.

In this realm of destiny, even the monads of the heavenly spirit, if they do not form and preserve themselves, run the risk of being turned into terrestrial spirits, whereas, inversely, the spirits who come from below, if they hear the truth and gain consciousness, are able to develop into heavenly spirits. It is only the highest of human beings, monads from the highest spheres of heaven, who recognize ten things immediately when they behold one, who perceive the heart and the nature of all things—they alone are externally secure from falling into the depths.

If the truth is proclaimed it is not easy to persuade men to hear and to understand it. Today, however, the time has come when the great principle of life is revealed and heavenly and earthly nature is given the opportunity to return to the great primeval beginning and to save itself upon the shore of principle from the sea of folly. It is, of course, exceedingly difficult for the earthly monads, because every original monad has its own peculiar primordial constitutions; if, therefore, the earthly monads who come from below wish to attain to the understanding of the great principle, they must be broken and polished in the course of a thousand experiences to be able to change this primordial constitution, and without this process it is impossible for them to attain to the perception of the great principle. This primordial constitution is not easily changed since the original monad is the real active being and to sacrifice this real active being is exceedingly difficult. It is really hardly necessary to refer to this real innermost being because even the least external possession which we do not bring with us when we are born and which we do not take away with us when we die is difficult to sacrifice. How much more difficult is it then to change the primordial constitution so that a spiritual body evolves from the flesh!

But today a new era has come in which all beings have the possibility of salvation. That which was not possible some time ago for the greatest saints—because even all the secret magical forces do not lead away from the sphere of the second ego and consequently out of the dominion of the powers of destiny—is today made accessible to him who has recognized the third ego. Whatever dwells in us which is beyond birth and decay is the third ego. The heavens and the earth will pass away, but I shall not pass away: this refers to the third ego. And therefore the noble in spirit is so great that the whole world cannot seize him, and on the other hand he is so small that nothing in the world can divide him: and this too refers to the third ego.

THE WEB OF LIFE

IN China life is not arbitrary. In spite of all its freedom firm threads are woven into it which support and regulate it and form an harmonious texture out of light and shade, happiness and misfortune. Life unfolds like the web upon the loom. The shuttle of experience carries the thread backwards and forwards. But the warp lies firm, giving to everything direction and form from whose shape that significance derives with which the chaos of life is bound up.

The year is divided by its seasons, and experiences are regulated by custom. China has no divisions into weeks, and the regular rest of Sundays is only beginning to be adopted throughout the country by the modern school. For this reason the festivals were particularly important in the old China. They decorated life with the flowers of joy. The first of these festivals was the new year which occurs at the beginning of the returning spring. It is usually celebrated in the course of February. In spite of the official introduction of the Gregorian calendar, China has in secret kept up its good old moon calendar. This moon calendar is close to man and leads him directly into the connection between life and cosmic events. The months are real moons, they begin with the new moon, and on the fifteenth day there is full moon. You need only cast a glance into the clear sky in order to read the calendar. Apart from the moon, the sun also receives his due in the Chinese calendar. Twenty-four terms of the sun are divided into fortnightly sections independent of the date of the moon and they form the point at which the time of the sun and of the moon cross. They serve as a guide for agriculture, and their names are for the most part related to the various conditions of sowing. Spring begins on the 5th of February, on the 19th comes the rain, followed by the awakening of those who sleep in winter, then the spring equinox, then pure clarity, then the rain of the corn, the beginning of summer, then the little fullness, then the acorn, then the summer solstice, then the small

heat, the great heat, the beginning of autumn, the end of the
heat, the white dew, the autumn equinox, cold dew, the coming of the frost, the beginning of winter, the small snow, the
great snow, the winter solstice, small cold, and the great cold;
these periods are definitely fixed according to the sun calendar,
but since the months are regulated by the moon, these periods
do not always coincide with the same Chinese day of the
month. The months have twenty-nine or thirty days. The
missing days are, so to speak, collected, to form a leap month
which is added every few years so that the moon and the sun
remain in harmony. This procedure was an important function
and every new dynasty had to adjust it to the period in which
the earth provides her gifts. This astronomical arrangement of
life also contributed to the fact that according to the position
of the sun or the stars, astrological periods were indicated
which are particularly favourable for the different kinds of enterprises. Even today the Chinese calendar shows days which
are favourable for weddings or funerals, for the beginning of
schools, the erection of buildings, visits to friends, bathing, hair-
cutting, and all the daily labours. There are also some days
which are not favourable to anything. On these days the best
thing to do is to stay at home following some regular occupation
without beginning anything new. It is not merely the days
which have their special significance, but even the years have a
character of their own. The years possess a great cycle of twelve
signs, whose daily cycle corresponds to double hours. Every one
of these signs is placed beneath an animal image and receives its
peculiarities from the character of the animal. In this way midnight and the beginning of the cycle of the year belong to the
mouse, then come the ox, the tiger, the hare, the dragon, the
serpent, the horse, the ram, the monkey, the cock, the dog, and
the pig. These cyclic signs must not be mistaken for the signs
of the zodiac. There exists still the very ancient cycle of ten
which combined with the cycle of twelve forms the great cycle
of sixty years, which corresponds with our centuries in China.
This relationship of the division of time to all that happens
lends a special significance to life. The days are not the cold

meaningless numbers that they are with us, but each one has its peculiar nature, its special gifts and possibilities. The changing hours thus give significance to life.

The new year is a period of general rejoicing. The old year with its sins and its debts is over. The outstanding accounts have been collected in so far as the debtors have not escaped. Now people proceed to procure festive decorations for their houses and good food for the common meal. Any one who is able to do so returns about this time to his home. New year is the feast of the family. The parents and the children reunite. Sons come from a distance and bring with them the money and gifts which they have been able to save during their activities in the outside world. The newly married daughters sometimes return to their family and tell their parents and sisters of their experiences in the new house and new family to which they now belong. Contact is also taken with the divinities. The god of the hearth, whose picture was hung throughout the year over the hearth and who has watched dumbly all that has been of good and evil deeds during the year, has departed on the twenty-fourth day of the twelfth month to heaven to make his report to the Father of Heaven. He was accompanied by fireworks and shooting, but not before his mouth had been covered with a sweet glue so that nothing displeasing could pass his lips. After the new year he will return. Therefore a new image must be hung up over the hearth where he takes up his place again. Contact is also taken at this period of the year with the ancestors. Their pictures are hung up. They are invited to accept their sacrificial share of the family feast. Behind closed doors, which are protected both by the genii of the doors and by red signs against the evil spirits, people watch the approach of midnight while eschewing most carefully the use of all words which signify misfortune.

Before the new year's feast, all the streets are decorated gaily, preparatory for the coming event. Lanterns in the queerest and the most romantic shapes are offered for sale: for instance, there are lamps like gold fish, who look out from red eyes, and lamps of the slim virgin transfigured by the pale illumination, and all forms and colours are represented. Paper dragons await the day when they will populate the air as soon as the south wind has awoken and the wide plains, relieved from the pressure of winter, allow the south wind to rise up comfortably from the ancient dust. Along the walls gay pictures are put up for sale. They mostly represent round, well-fed children, or else the familiar saints of the home and the hearth: Kuanti, the protective god with his faithful red face, Kuanyin the goddess of charity with her falcon, who brings the unending chain of earthly prayers which rise up to her and the vase with its blessed branches, her waitress and the gay boy who has since the penetration of the Catholic missions in the Ming period been placed upon her lap, thus completing her similarity to the Virgin Mary, although the significance of the picture— Kuanyin dispenses the blessing of sons—is quite different. The god of wealth is also present in reproductions. He is not missing from any shop throughout the whole country. In fact, frequently there are two of them surrounded with treasures and bars of silver. The old mother of the T'aishan is also offered for sale, so that she may join the company of household gods.

It is not only the pictures of pious faith and old customs which can be bought. Swiss snow mountains and wild Indian tigers hang next to pictures of fops and little ladies who in their short modern dresses attempt to smile like European ladies. All these images are painted in gay colours and crude blue, violet and green are particularly in favour.

Apart from these pictures you can see artificial flowers and objects cut out with a pair of scissors in paper, in dainty patterns for embroidery on white sheets which are pasted upon the shoes as a pattern for the embroidery to be added on top of them, delicate red lace curtains which are usually hung up above the gateway on new year's day to keep the demons away. A rich imaginative life throbs in these graceful objects cut out with a pair of scissors. In another booth you can see silhouettes, all kinds of figures which are cut out of transparent coloured donkey's skin and are manipulated from behind like the illuminated paper screens of shadow-marionettes. These silhouettes are used to perform entire plays and they are a specialty of the district of Peking.

Of course there are also all kinds of materials, household objects, incense, toys for children made of wood, clay and paper offered for sale in the greatest profusion and variety. It is most amusing to observe the difference between the modern Chinaman who sells motor-cars and railway trains made of tin and the old man, across the street, who still continues to offer his solid wooden travelling carts. In another place they sell soles for shoes. Of late years these are made of leather because it is stronger than the paper or the felt which they used to employ. The rest of the shoe is made by the female members of the family. The claims of the moment are also attended to. Travelling kitchens announced by their odours the glories which await the visitor who needs to rest at these fairs.

In some corner a teller of tales can be found who recites a story to the rhythmic accompaniment of a drum. There are also peep-shows in which changing pictures can be inspected.

The temples are visited, especially the temple of the T'aishan in front of the eastern gate. This divinity rules over the beginning and the end of all things. Round about the new year crowds of people can be seen there who offer their sacrifices when the change of the seasons makes men's thoughts turn to the change of all earthly things. All day long incense candles are burnt here and the faithful cast themselves down in prayer before the images of the gods.

Considerable activity also proceeds in the other temples in Peking and the surroundings in the period of the new year, for the new year in China is not a day, but half a month. The day of full moon is the lantern feast and the time in between is taken up with vacations and amusements of all kinds. In the temple of the fire god, who is called upon like a saint Florian so that the harmful fire which is in his control shall be kept away from the household gods, the great jewelry market

takes place in the first week in the year. The courtyards of
the temple are covered with mats and an unending turmoil of
human beings threads its way through all the treasures there
exposed. You learn to understand the colour of the fairy tales
of a Thousand and One Nights after you have gone through
here once. The things which stand about have all kinds of
shapes: statues made of lapis lazuli or topaz or out of pale waxy
jade, vases of amethysts and chrysoprase, bowls of agate with
duskily flowing veins, bowls of mountain crystal in whose
bright depth the future condenses itself into dull clouds, pen-
dants made of amber or carnelian and chains of pearls and
painted porcelain beads. Rings can be seen there in which sap-
phires sparkle and rubies burn. Above all, there are the snuff-
boxes! They are shaped like small vases or bottles and made in
all kinds of patterns and of all sorts of materials: ivory and
jade and green moss agate with red stripes. The most curious
object amongst all these things was a snuff-box from Mongolia
made out of pale white human bone and inlaid with silver and
turquoise! The merchants stand there calmly with interlocked
sleeves. You say a few words to them, take up a little pot, ask
them in passing what the price is and you put the object back
again. Perhaps you return and make a counter offer and finally
you agree about the price.

Tea houses are erected near the temple of the White Cloud.
Crowds of pilgrims come from afar to do reverence here, but
the entertainment of the people is also provided for. There
are horse-races, and gay lanterns give a cheerful brilliance to
the activity at night. There is another market near the Yellow
temple in front of the northern gate, where there are also
horse-races and the famous masked dances in the course of
which a devil and evil spirits are chased away. The Lamas
come from far away to display their magical powers. The
greatest number of people, however, are attracted by the great
masked dances which take place near the Lama temple, Yung
Ho Kung. Wild dances performed behind ghastly masks sway
to the deafening sound of shell-horns and to the accompaniment of drums. The whole square in front of the temple is

thickly sown with people. They talk and laugh and jostle each other. Some climb on top of trees and walls, and the large stones lying in front of the gate are always covered with riders, all of whom wish to get a better view from above, although they frequently slide down into the human chaos, where they are received amidst laughter. Priests with long whips beat the invisible devil, but human beings who stand near by retire as the crack of the whip approaches them. Policemen are there to regulate the proceedings. Every one tries to get a good view, for now the procession approaches. All the wild animals and human masks appear to the accompaniment of the cracking whip, amidst endless noise, and the devil, a bony creature with a pointed malicious-looking bony head, is driven out. On the occasion of another dance, on the following day, he is burnt. Then the world is rid of this horror for some time. At night the air is filled with showers of fireworks, rockets and exploding frogs are heard and seen at all corners. Then the great fireworks take place. A basket is pulled up on to a high scaffolding and the quick-match is set alight. Then all kinds of formations fall from within the basket. Flowers, pagodas, pavilions, trees, human beings, and wolves. Thin contours of a kind of scaffolding made of string are seen, which are illuminated from top to bottom with manifold colours by the fireworks. One pattern after another falls from the basket and hangs for a time in the air. Some twist fantastically, while others seem to remain stationary in their quiet radiance. At last it seems as if an explosion had occurred, after the last fire picture has faded away, when a dull kind of explosion indicates that the whole performance has come to an end. The crowd disperses and the moon eventually hangs alone in the sky like a round paper lantern, and long after everything has grown quiet she continues to pour her grey velvet light over the sleeping sea of roofs.

When the lantern feast is over, work is resumed and life proceeds upon its ordinary course. In particular in the country the return to the work of the fields is marked by the feast of the beginning of spring. When the Emperor used to plough on the slope in front of the town, a similar ceremony took place in the rest of the country. The officials went outside the town and performed the ceremony of ploughing with an ox made of paper. The colour of the ox differed in accordance with the various years. After the act of ploughing the paper ox was divided in friendly battle by the multitude, and any one who was so fortunate as to secure a horn or a leg carried it triumphantly to his home in the certain knowledge that in the coming year it would bring him good fortune. Such popular customs are of course dying out more and more. They have fled into the country and they are developing into local idiosyncrasies. These practices become petrified or else they are discarded. Such is the course of time.

The sacrifice to Confucius which used to be offered in the spring and in the autumn has, for instance, disappeared altogether from the public consciousness. Formerly it was a very festive affair, when the Emperor in person did reverence to the representative of the highest spiritual ideas. In those days, the holy dances were performed to the accompaniment of flute music and pageants decorated with pheasant feathers and axes and shields. The old music was performed when the sacrifices of silk, wine, fruit and food, the bull, the pig and the sheep were spread out before the master and his four faithful followers. At first the spirits of the revered were received. The burning of the incense, the sound of the kettledrum to the accompaniment of singing and dancing were the signs of their approach which was saluted by a deep bow. Then came the most sacred portion of the ceremony: the actual offering of the sacrifices and their appropriation by the spirits. In the end the spirits were accompanied and the sacrificial gifts cleared away. The silk and the sacrificial prayer written out for the occasion were burnt, while the rest of the gifts were divided among those who assisted in the sacrifice. The service of Confucius was devoid of any divine image. Nothing but a tablet indicated by an inscription the place in which the saint was placed in thought during the sacrifice.

This sacrificial service, which is after all only a particularly solemn kind of temple service in general, gives many a clue to matters which strike foreign visitors to Chinese temples. People enter a temple full of horrible or friendly looking divinities. The guide explains everything, remains perfectly frigid, touches the images, and sometimes even participates in the more or less witty comments of the visitors. People have concluded from these facts that the Chinaman is irreligious and laughs at his own gods. This, however, is not the case; these pictures are not gods at all. They are merely places which they enter if they are called upon in the right way. When the god is there then the presence in his image is a stern and holy matter. When he is not there, then his image is a piece of wood or clay. It is very interesting to consider how the presence of the divinity is brought about. The gods must after all be somewhere in the neighbourhood so that they approach when the sound of the kettledrum and the bell is heard and the smoke of incense rises up. The answer is: Everything depends upon the heart of the faithful. If he who prays has true contact in his heart with the name of the god, then the god is there. And whatever he asks for in this contact with this super-personal deity he will receive, in fact, he already has it in the moment in which he asks. For this reason you find so often in temples tablets with the inscription: "He who asks will surely be heard," or similar words. The service of Confucius was moreover never a divine worship in which petitions were made, but merely a demonstration of the reverence for the master. For this reason Confucius does not play any part in the Pantheon of the people. He is there. He is revered, but people ask nothing of him. Especially at present, since the organization of the state has adopted other methods this sacrifice to Confucius in the early morning, in which only a limited number of invited guests may participate, has become almost an historical ceremony, confined exclusively to academic circles.

On the other hand, the spring festival of "pure clarity" (Ts'ing Ming) is popular throughout China and corresponds more or less to our Easter festivities, and also frequently takes place about the same time of the year. Originally it was undoubtedly some kind of an agricultural feast. The day before people had to fast and they were not allowed to eat any boiled food nor to light a fire. On the feast day itself, curiously enough, people eat boiled painted eggs. This feast is today surrounded by all kinds of myths, by means of which the customs connected with it are explained. When Prince Wen Tsin, in the year 635 B.C., had to fly from his home, Kia Chih T'ui was also among his few faithful servitors who followed him into misery. One day when they had no more food, he cut a piece of meat out of his leg in order to offer it to his master to eat. Yet when the Prince returned and mounted his throne, he forgot him on the occasion of the distribution of honours. Thereupon Kia Chih T'ui retired with his mother into a close mountain forest. When the Prince was reminded, too late, of his ingratitude, he sent out some one in order to have his faithful servant fetched, but in vain, he was not to be found. Thereupon the forest was set fire to, in order to make the smoke drive him out, but he stood firm and perished, together with his mother, in the flames. The Prince, seized by profound contrition, issued an edict to the effect that never again on this day should any fire be lit.

This feast of the return of life is simultaneously dedicated to the memory of the departed, for resurrection after all presupposes death. Therefore the tombs of the deceased are cleansed of weeds, the funeral mounds are piled up and a new layer of earth is placed upon them on which a piece of paper, to represent a sacrificial plate, is weighted down by a stone. If it is at all possible, each family returns home in order to celebrate the spring festival in the company of their clan.

This festival has maintained itself under the republic. It is celebrated as the feast of trees in all the schools, and it has developed the custom that the pupils make an excursion and plant trees in an open place.

Just as Whitsun follows upon Easter so does the Ts'ing-Sing festival follow upon that of Tuan-Wu, on which occasion the height of the year, the beginning of the early harvest, is celebrated. It takes place on the fifth day of the fifth month. The bright power of the sun is at its height, but precisely for this reason, the dark demons lie in waiting. Illnesses crawl about, evil influences in the seedlings are to be feared, and for this reason people protect themselves against evil influences by hanging up talismans on the outside of doors and windows. Usually strongly scented herbs such as artemisia or calamus are used. They are hung up in branches or bundles in front of the openings through which the evil spirits might enter. They also cut serpents, toads or tortoises and all sorts of worms out of red paper and hang them up in front of entrances.

This festival is a feast of the sun. It is celebrated in particular in the district of the Yangtse. There it is called the feast of the dragon boat. Gay junks festively decorated with figures of dragons row about on the river. On the boats all kinds of tricks and dances are performed. The dragon is the symbol of light, of male power, and the ships are to remind people of the old days in which this sacred cult came from across the sea. Here, too, the joy of light is connected with the protection against the demons. In the sea and the river there are so many souls of those who have been drowned and who can therefore not benefit by the sacrifices offered to them by their successors. Something has therefore to be given to them. People prepare dumplings of rice wrapped in reeds and they are thrown into the water for the benefit of the spirits below. The living, however, also eat these dumplings wrapped up in reeds on the occasion of this festival. This ceremony too has its legend. The poet K'u Yüan, the founder of the lyrical rhapsodies of the south, took a stone in his arms and cast himself into the water of the river when his royal master had expelled him and despair at the destiny of his country made life impossible for him. The rice dumplings are thrown into the water primarily for his sake.

The feast of the young girls is the "Seveneve," the seventh day of the seventh month. In the radiance of the slender sickle of the moon sacrificial gifts are piled before the divine lady who weaves. The girls practise threading a needle in the uncertain light of the moon. If they are successful it means that the goddess will give the happy girls skill in all handi-work. On this day people sit together and tell stories of the cowherd and his lady love who was a weaver. They are two stars in the sky. The weaving lady was originally the seventh of the nine daughters of the Father of Heaven. She was surprised by the cowherd, a human being, with the help of his wonderful cow when she was bathing, and she had to marry him, because the old willow tree, whom she asked, said:

"It is seveneve to night
The cowherd woos the lady right."

After they had been married for seven days, she had to return to heaven in order to weave the silk of the clouds. When the cowherd wanted to follow her, she drew a line with her hand right across the sky. This became the Milky Way. Since then these two have been so close and yet so far from one another. Only once a year may they visit each other. On Seveneve all the crows upon earth fly together and form a bridge upon which the weaving lady can come across to her beloved. On Seveneve there is often a fine rainfall. The women, and especially the old ones, then say to each other: "Those are the tears that the cowherd and his weaving lady shed on parting." And that is why Seveneve is a feast of rain.

Apart from the new year festival, the most beautiful feast of the year is probably the feast of the autumn equinox on the fifteenth day of the eighth month. At that time you get the round moon cakes which are painted red and filled with sweet-meats. The feast of the equinox is a moon feast and the moon of the autumn is particularly distinguished by a radiant bril-liance. The full moon hangs in the sky the whole night and pours its bright resplendent silver light over everything. The sacrifice to the moon takes place beneath the open sky. The fruits which are offered up all have a symbolical meaning. The melon means that all the members of the family are to remain united, the pomegranate indicates the blessing of children, and the apples signify peace. The pastries have the round form of the full moon.

The feast of the moon is in the autumn, for the moon represents the Yin principle as the sun corresponds to that of the Yang. The Yin principle is everything dark, shady, cool, feminine, and this power commences its predominance in the autumn. Since the autumn, however, is simultaneously beneath the sign of the harvest rejoicings, the moon festival, in spite of its thoughts connected with the dying year, is yet a festival of joy. The women in particular delight to celebrate the moon festival, for the fairy of the moon, who lives in the castle in the moon, where floating in the dark sky alone above the sea she has found the secret of immortality, is the representative of the feminine sex. Near the castle in the moon there is an acacia tree, for about the middle of autumn the acacia tree puts forth its sweetly scented small gold-yellow blossoms. The acacia tree in the moon grows and grows and covers the entire light of the moon with its shadow until from time to time it is cut down. There is also a hare in the moon—just as there is a crow in the sun; this hare prepares in a mortar the herbs of eternal life. For this reason hares made of clay are given as presents to children during the moon festival. The hare of the moon is white and has beautiful red eyes. You often see pictures of the fairy of the moon with a disk of the moon, while the hare of the moon is seated cosily next to her. The moon is the principle of the heavenly water which can be fetched down by means of a convex mirror, just as the heavenly fire can be brought down from the sun by means of a concave glass.

The moon, however, is not only feminine. There is a mysterious old man, the old man of the moon, who pursues his business up there. He crawls about secretly at night and ties up the little legs of new-born boys and girls with an invisible magic thread. This invisible thread is so strong that no one can resist it. When the boy and the girl have grown up, they are drawn together, without knowing anything about it themselves, by a powerful fetter, and woe to them if their paths in life cross, because in that case they cannot get out of it without marrying.

Women in China take a special delight in arranging marriages. There are some who make a regular profession of it, but also the others like to assist when it is a question of bringing a suitable pair together. Without the assistance of others, no one can make a marriage in China, because it is not those immediately concerned who marry each other according to their preference, but it is a family matter. This old man in the moon takes a special delight in making marriages in heaven. Perhaps that is why the women honour him so.

The feast of the autumn equinox takes place in the most beautiful time of the year, and it is far removed from the three hot periods of the "dog days" as from the three cold periods of the late winter; moreover the autumn in China is far more beautiful than the spring, for the spring has to struggle out of the fetters of winter through many storms and belated fits of cold. The continental high pressure with its north-westerly dusty wind broods for a long time over the Chinese plain. When the change occurs, it usually brings the summer with it at once. The autumn, on the other hand, is a mild dying down of the hot damp cloudy days of summer. The sky is of radiant purity for weeks together, the air is so clear that the contours of the horizon are silhouetted clearly and darkly as far as the eye can reach to the mountain range. No storm disturbs the quiet luminosity of these days. The lake is calm and the wailing tones of the flute float from the reeds through the air.

When these beautiful days are over, when the cold dews fall, then the fog of autumn comes out of the valleys. Those are dangerous periods of pestilence. For this reason, people go to the heights in order to enjoy the autumn once more and to drink wine where they are secure from the fogs of the evening. This happens on the ninth day of the ninth month, the double Yang (Tch'ung Yang), for nine is the number of the Yang principle and the doubling of this number dedicated to light is recalled on this occasion by the festival of the sinking year. The light fights here with darkness. While the year externally slips away into the arms of cold and winter and the crickets of autumn raise their pitiful voices, the first seeds of the new year are formed in secret in the depths of the earth and they are so delicate and fine that they are not visible to the human eye.

Now comes the period of the chrysanthemums, and their pure blossoms are the last greetings of the passing year. In Japan a chrysanthemum festival is celebrated, and on these occasions there are exhibitions of magnificent flowers. The blossoms are cultivated to be as large as possible, and it is not rare to see thirty or forty blossoms on one plant. It is quite different in China. The chrysanthemums are not like the peonies which decorate the early spring, flowers of magnificence and proud display. In China they rarely cultivate more than three or five blossoms on one plant, but the blossoms have to be perfect and of a chosen peculiarity, and the leaves have to be strong and green and they must cover the whole stalk down to the ground. The great friend of chrysanthemums was the poet T'ao Yüan Ming. He has made many a verse in which he has given expression to his love for them:

"All dabbled with dew
  Chrysanthemums, lovely in their autumn colours; I plucked
    a flower
  To float its petals in the tide that brimmed my cup,
  The magic flood that washes grief away.
  I was alone;
  Yet no more brooding on my deep quarrel with life,
  I filled my own cup, tilting that jug towards me often and
    again,
  Till the last bird was home and every creature in the fields
    at rest,
  Then wildly chanting sat in the eastern porch
  And felt like one who has died, and lives again."

Just as the cycle of the year is arranged by the sequel of its festivals, so the life of the individual is surrounded by a wealth of firm habits which thus include him in the great social cohesion.

The child is born. It is dressed already on the first day in a little shift of festive red colour. Nine red eggs are sent to the parents of the mother in order to convey the news of the joyful event. The father, however, if the newly born baby is a boy, goes to the sanctuary of his ancestors, in order to report to them that the race is propagating itself. The spirits of the ancestors have less interest in girls because after their marriage they leave the family and contribute to the continuation of the line of another house. This habit has often been regarded as a want of affection for girls, but this is by no means the case. Chinamen do not kill newly born daughters as a stupid rumour claimed for a while in Europe, nor do they despise them. The family, however, is an organism which goes beyond matters of personal inclination. The growth and life of the family possesses pre-eminent interest, as opposed to that of the single individuals who belong to it, and in fact the family is built upon a thoroughly patriarchal base. The man is linked with his preceding ancestors and has the duty, in so far as he represents the line, to hand on the inheritance of the past to the future. The woman, however, is taken into the family as the helpmate of the man and it is her duty to help the family of the man, to provide him with successors and to fit into the paternal home of her husband, in which the mother rules and to whom the daughters-in-law are subordinated. For this purpose the woman must be separated from the ancestral tie of her father's house, and again, for this reason, the bridegroom fetches his wife, for the wedding, away from her own home and the marriage is celebrated in the house of the father of the bridegroom. The parents of the bride are compensated by money or presents. The separation from her family which awaits every girl is therefore the reason why the ancestors are not informed of her existence.

In other respects the customs also differ when a boy or a girl is born. When a boy is born, a bow made from a mulberry branch is hung up outside the door with four arrows made of zizyphus. On the third day the bow is taken down and the arrows are shot off to the four corners of the wind. When a girl is born, only a little handkerchief is hung up because the life of the girl is destined to be spent inside the house. A very special day is the hundredth day after the birth of the child and it corresponds more or less to our christening. Friends and relatives send presents. They provide little bracelets, little bells, necklaces with locks on which good wishes are engraved and which are to attach the child to life. Most of these objects are made of gilded silver. They are gifts which correspond roughly to our christening presents. The boy is placed upon a table on which books and swords, the insignia of office and money are piled up. He chooses his future calling by the objects which he seizes first. For the girl scissors and a yard-measure, powder and paint, diadems and money are put on the table. As a result they become either good housewives, or celebrated beauties, or they will have the good fortune of finding a distinguished or a rich husband. On this occasion children are given pet names, which are mostly very insignificant so as not to attract the attention of demons. Boys, for instance, are called "Little girl" or the name is chosen after any object which happens to be at hand or is seen at that particular moment. It is only on the occasion when the child enters school that he is given his real name.

The patriarchal attitude to the significance of children has once been expressed very prettily in the old book of songs from the first millennium B.C. In it the story is how a house was built for a ruler and how in the first night he had a dream promising good fortune, and the dream was interpreted by a magician (Shih King II, 4, 5).

"Firm, firm the river bank.
Dark, dark the Southern Hills.
With woods of bamboo round,
With forests of thick pine.
Brothers, young and old,
Love one another in this house,
Do not vex one another!

As grandfather and grandmother before us
So have we built this house;
To west and south its doors.
Here to dwell and be, here to laugh and talk!

Strong the battens of wood,
Hard-stamped the walls of mud.
No bird, no rat can enter;
But the master shall dwell in pride.

Like one who walks tip-toe,
Like an arrow in flight,
Like a bird in its new plumage,
Like a pheasant on the wing,
The master shall go up into his house.

Well-levelled is the courtyard,
High are the pillars,
With sunny spaces,
And deep nooks.

Mats of bamboo
Spread on mats of rush;
On these shall he lie in peace;
On these, awake.
And waking he will ask
The meaning of his dreams:
'Is it lucky to have dreamt
Of little bears and great bears,
Small snakes and serpents?'

And the reader of dreams shall answer:
'Great bears and little bears
Mean a boy shall be born;
Small snakes and serpents
Mean the birth of a girl.'

Then a boy is born,
Put to lie on a bed,
Robed in a gown
With jade tablets to finger.
And lusty he wails.
But one day in red knee-caps shall he walk,
Lord or prince, sprung from this house!

Then a girl shall be born,
Put to lie on the floor,
Robed in rags,
With a roof-tile to finger.
No bad thing shall she do,
Nor good thing either.
Enough if she can carry
Wine and plates of food
And give no trouble,
To her father and mother."

These old customs have been superseded. The women in China have long ago left all the fetters of old prejudices behind them. Young girls are far freer in China today than, for instance, in Japan, where the old knightly ideal is kept up to a greater extent. Even freedom in the choice of a husband is proclaimed more and more and in connection with this movement the women of young China are making energetic attacks upon the comfortable practice which used to allow the husband, for his own pleasure, to have a number of servants or concubines who were included in the family. The free choice of the husband naturally removes the main reason for the existence of the concubines, because every man has to ascribe it to himself if he should find that his wife is less satisfactory than he had hoped. The question of the male succession alone will continue to play its part in marriage problems as long as the patriarchal family continues to exist in China, and, as long as this is the case, the possibility will always remain, if the wife does not provide male issue, that the husband can

take a concubine, in case the marriage is not dissolved on that
account—and he marries a new wife, which is permitted according to Chinese law. These new Chinese laws are, as far as
divorce is concerned, far more free and easy than most of the
corresponding European laws. On the one hand they are not
burdened with considerations of the church, and on the other
hand the question of providing for the children and their education is easily solved in divorce cases in China, because marriage is only a connection within the larger family and the
children belong in any case rather to this family than to its
particular parents.

From what has been said, it is evident that marriage is not
so significant an epoch in the life of a man in China as it is in
Europe, because it is not necessarily connected with the beginning of their own household. If the bride, by entering a new
family and by her new social position, begins an entirely new
chapter in her life, the position of the young man within his
household remains more or less unchanged, for at most he is
given a special building within the general family property for
himself and his wife. The choice of his life-companion will
have been made long ago by his parents. The date of the
marriage is fixed, at a moment when, for instance, domestic
affairs make an additional worker desirable to the mother of
the youth. In that case the bridegroom, if he happens to live
away from his home, would return for a few days. If he happens to attend a school in a different locality, one week's holiday
suffices, whereupon the young husband comes back to the school
as heretofore. This practice brings it about that the husband,
as long as his parents are at the head of the household, is often
away from his home for years with the exception at short
intervals. His wife is looked after just as well as the children
of the family, and for this reason it used to be a more important problem for a young wife how she got on with her
mother-in-law than with her husband. She had to live continuously together with her mother-in-law, whose influence as
a mother upon her son would be so great that he would not be
in a position to protect his wife if serious discords should cloud

the relation between the two women. Such discords did indeed occur. Although the number of unhappy marriages appears to be far less than in the capitals of Europe, the struggle with the mother-in-law has always been a very serious matter (for the woman, since the husband had never anything to do with his mother-in-law) and sometimes suicide was the last resort of the tortured woman who could not find any escape from the hell of daily domestic strife. Such an event was always a very delicate matter for the mother-in-law, because, apart from the fact that it cast a very bad slight upon her as far as the public was concerned, she always had to reckon with being troubled by the ghost of the woman who had committed suicide.

Young China expects a great deal from its marriage reform, which, as has been said, is beginning to be applied. People wish to take the happiness of their marriage into their own hands and watch over it for themselves. It goes, of course, without saying that the old form of marriage can no longer be maintained now that personalities have become far more differentiated. The Chinese family, which used to pay very little attention to individuals, presupposed that individual personality submitted itself without any friction to the wider cohesion, which was, of course, possible only whilst people's characters and their peculiarities were less strongly developed and less self-conscious.

There is no doubt that in the country the old form of marriage will continue to exist, because, there, great old embracing connections and a patriarchal system, based upon the traditions of the soil, still continue. In the town, however, new circumstances will inevitably lead to new forms of marriage. The destruction of the large family which is inevitable for the inhabitants of the large towns, from economic considerations, produces a new form of marriage. The question is: What will this form be? Marriage presupposes always the superior cohesion of some kind of family connection. Isolated and proletarian beings experience real marriage only in exceptional cases. Young China is full of hope for the future. What kind of experiences will it bring home, and what will their marriage which the melting process of the present days is crystallizing eventually look like?

At the end of life there come finally the customs which deal with funerals. Here there is an end of the red colour. Colourless sacking is the mourning garb, and asceticism in external matters, from which every comfort is removed, corresponds to the heart-felt sorrow of those who are left behind. In spite of this mourning, which lasts twenty-seven months, death is not excluded from consideration whilst the parents live. The mortality of men is a fact that no one in China attempts to dissemble. When the period approaches in which repose beckons after the heat and burden of life, it is customary to put one's house in order in good time, and it is regarded as a tender consideration on the part of the children if they order the coffin and the funeral clothes for their aged parents while they are alive. The parents can then contemplate without worry the last dark journey by which they return to the soil.

Death and burial is of course surrounded by a rich wreath of customs. The doctrine of Confucius which made the reverence of the children the centre of popular morality was bound to stress the moment in which the faithful services of the living parents came to an end, and the reverence of the children had to change from the ethical to the religious form. Fasting, asceticism and mourning were prescribed. The Master cared more for the seriousness of the attitude than for the pomp of outer splendour. It used to be customary that the deceased was buried according to the rank which he occupied during his lifetime. The sacrifices, however, were performed according to the rank of the sons or grandchildren who remained behind. Nobility was not transferred to the children and grandchildren. Only the eldest son assumed his father's rank as the head of the family, while all the ancestors participated indirectly in the social distinction of their successors.

Apart from the customs associated with the dead, resulting from Confucianism, a whole series of customs have been established in the course of centuries which originate from quite different sources. The various forms of attendance upon the dead became in China a meeting point of all religions. Taoist priests make music at the house of the dead and the Buddhist monks read their masses. Alongside with the customs which relate to the veneration of the dead as more perfect and higher beings, there is a whole host of practices which see in the dead dangerous ghosts which have to be banished. Whereas people pray to and look up to what is transfigured and spiritual in the deceased, which is honoured and served by sacrifice, so the decayed bodily portions are an unfortunate human remnant which as an impersonal ghost is antagonistic to life.

In Peking, the funeral of a high state official took place not long ago. The funeral procession swayed through the streets for hours. Crackers were let off and great gongs were beaten in order to frighten away the spirits along the path of the corpse. Flags and the insignia of office were borne along and white twigs wrapped up in slips of paper were carried in the wake. At the head of the procession they carried a kind of honorary cupboard and a special sort of honorary umbrella. Then followed the gifts for the tomb. They are no longer made out of clay as they used to be and put into the tomb of the dead, but they are made of paper and are burnt by the side of the grave. Everything which belonged to the luxury of life, beginning with the villa and the motor-car down to the indispensable horses, servants and utensils were represented. More than a hundred huddled people carried the magnificently shrouded coffin beneath a canopy. Chopin's funeral march was played by a gaily dressed orchestra and alternated with the terrible bugle calls and the whimpering clarinet music and the drums and gongs. The son dressed in white, supported by servants and trailing a mourning staff after him, dragged himself along behind the coffin. Carriages and motor-cars without number, wreaths of flowers and honorary inscriptions accompanied the dead outside the town to the carefully walled-in family tomb.

In a small side street two workmen were carrying a meagre coffin barely shrouded by a dirty old bed-cover. The coffin had been fastened with ropes to a pole. It was perhaps the only bed-cover of the son, who walked behind the dead. Somewhere or other he had bought a white European hat made out of stuff for some child, so that he should also wear something white. The hat was dirty and many people laughed at the spectacle, but the son did not notice anything. He had to control himself so as to suppress his sighs. He had no time to lose and the bearers walked on steadily. The dead have to be buried before sundown and one moment later they had disappeared in the throng of the street.

As they shovelled away the earth they found a skull. Perhaps it was the same which had once appeared to Chuangtse in a dream and had said: "In death there are neither princes nor servants nor is there any change in time. We allow ourselves to be driven about and our springs and autumns are the motion of heaven and earth."

SOCIAL INTERCOURSE

Social life in China is carried on, as it used to be among all peoples organized on a patriarchal basis, exclusively among men, and this practice has extended right up to the present day. The women rule inside the home, they visit each other, exchange their views and experiences, but they do not appear in society in the company of their husbands or fathers. A breach of this custom only takes place when temples or theatres are visited, and it also happens occasionally that married women and girls show themselves with their servants at fairs; but even these exceptions are suffered rather than desired. Intimate friends often hardly know each other's wives and it is only among the Manchus that there is a greater liberty in this respect. The separation of the sexes has, of course, determined the character of public social life. On the whole this intercourse was free and easy, people let themselves go a little on occasion, for many a man felt relieved at escaping from the guiding hand of his wife, for in China, in spite of the predomination of patriarchal tradition, there were occasionally official relapses into a mild matriarchal form to which its victims were usually very sensitive although they concealed this fact externally. It may be said, however, that social life in educated circles is neither uncontrolled nor lacking in refinement. The rules of tradition control and guide it far too definitely and provide proper directives of an external kind for every situation in life without troublesome formalities.

It is also due to the circumstances described above that social intercourse takes place usually not in private houses but in rooms of a more or less public kind. There are in Peking, for instance, a number of clubs located usually in old princely palaces or other distinguished buildings with large halls and gardens which provide suitable opportunities for conversation. Owing to the great distances a custom has developed not to take the hour of invitation too meticulously, which again provides plenty of time before the meal for all manner of conversations. Rooms other than those in clubs are also used. People borrow the rooms of a friend who has suitable accommodation, or hire quiet pavilions in some public garden or rooms in one of the larger restaurants in the capital. You always find separate rooms situated in isolated courtyards, so that each company of guests is left undisturbed to itself. The public traffic of Europe where people sit about in large public rooms and where possibly two different groups are seated at one table would be regarded as coarse and disagreeable in China; people meet, after all, not merely to activate the process of nutrition in company, but a well-chosen company selected for the mutual suitability of the guests is supposed to be a small masterpiece of social communion. Hence the greatest care is taken to hit upon the harmonious choice of guests. Only such men are asked as fit in with one another and have something mutual to offer. Accordingly not too many must be present, as otherwise the conversation between individuals breaks up the company; and not too few, because in that case one or other of the guests may be isolated. The members of the company are usually kept in the vicinity of the number of the eight genii. The history of the Tang Dynasty tells of eight saints who are associated with the drinking of wine, a bibulous gathering of poets of the circle of La T'ai Po who were glorified by the poet Tu Fu.

Such a company forgathers gradually at the appointed place. Before the last guest has arrived you stand or walk about. A servant brings hot damp towels with which you wipe your face and hands, a practice which refreshes you in summer and warms you in winter. A cup of tea is placed before each guest. Melon and sunflower seeds are put about the room on small plates; you crack the shell and eat the kernels in the course of conversation. People smoke cigarettes and pass the time in light conversation about literary novelties, politics or art. There would not be time to engage in serious discussion, as the intermittent arrival of friends would continually interrupt one's thoughts. If the menu has not been fixed previously, the host hands a bill of fare to each guest who chooses one of the dishes which is to appear later at table. Eventually, when all the guests are present you proceed to the dinner table. In small country towns this procedure is always a difficulty almost similar to the occasion on which two Germans are to go through the same door. It often happens that individual guests maliciously sit down in an inferior position to make the unfortunate younger victim go up higher. The young members cannot permit this in any circumstances and consequently there are frequent battles of politeness based on mutual modesty. Such struggles are no longer customary in society in the big towns. As every one of the guests has a predestined place owing to his age and position the host either writes out cards bearing the name of his guest—and these cards are placed at each respective seat—or else he pours out wine into the bowls on the table in the sequence in which the guests are to be seated, and he calls out the name of the person concerned and bows after filling the guest's bowl. The guests respond to the invitation of their host with mild attempts at occupying less dignified places. The host then drinks to his guests and when they have replied to his greeting the meal begins.

Then the battle begins. Each guest is provided with a small plate for sauce, another little plate for sunflower seeds or apricot kernels, a spoon for soup, a pair of chopsticks and a bowl for wine. Paper with which the utensils are wiped is also supplied. The dishes are not handed round singly but are placed on large platters on the middle of the table. The host invites the company to help itself and each member takes with his chopsticks as much as he wishes. The food is of course cut up into small pieces so that it can be taken conveniently with the chopsticks, provided that you know how to manipulate them. Europeans are very rarely able to do this, and this fact usually provides them with a pleasant subject for conversation when they demonstrate their ignorance in word and deed before their Chinese neighbours.

In the course of the meal you act as you please. You drain your little bowl of wine, partake of a bite of the cold meat and vegetable dishes which are placed foremost on the table, then you put aside your chopsticks and talk, munching a few melon seeds or you drink again and then sample another dish. There is no hurry and you take your time. Foreigners usually make the mistake of setting to work upon the *hors-d' oeuvres* far too seriously from the very start. It frequently happens that they are at the end of their capacities when they come to the third or fourth course, or else they are condemned to over-eat themselves hopelessly by the aid of too much wine. A Chinese dinner is a lengthy and thorough business which requires to be appreciated with thought and consideration. The European habit of swallowing the dishes which are served without further consideration is alien to the Chinese. He knows what he eats and is not ashamed to honour a good dish.

The wine is usually brewed from rice and is not unlike sherry in colour and taste, although it is less alcoholic. Every Chinaman knows exactly how much of this beverage he can imbibe and arranges his meal accordingly. The best wine comes from Shaohsingfu district near Hangchou, but the finest and oldest vintages are rarely to be obtained there, because they are for the most part exported to the capital.

Among the hot and cold *hors-d' oeuvres,* you find bamboo shoots and larch-blossom, eggs, also called black eggs, which continue to be described in Europe as Methuselah eggs, although their colour and their somewhat cheese-like taste is due to their special preparation in chalk chaff, salt and clay, some of which penetrates the shell and discolours the albumen which contains sulphurous matter. The only food with which these eggs can be compared are ordinary eggs boiled in a strong solution of salt. Various special delicacies are then served as the chief dishes. Fashionable dinners begin with swallow-nests. These nests are made in the Indian Ocean by a particular sea-swallow which uses a special kind of seaweed for their construction. They are boiled in clear chicken broth and have a remarkably delicate taste, something like very good mushrooms. This is a very costly dish and therefore very often faked by the substitution of a particular variety of vegetable gelatine. Europeans generally bring to these delicacies, which presuppose a really artistic palate, astonishment rather than understanding.

A former Chinese Ambassador once provided swallow-nest soup at one of his dinners in Europe. A lady who was sitting next to him was curious to see such an object. He sent for a nest from the kitchen. It amused her and she wanted to take it away with her as a keepsake. The interest of the other guests was also roused and the whole company took such souvenirs with them without suspecting in the least that they were divesting their host of the value of many five-pound notes. After the swallow-nests the fins of sharks are served. These are boiled for a whole day in the broth of chickens or ducks, until the structure of the fins is reduced to a gelatinous substance which acquires in the process a remarkably strong though delicate flavour. They taste best when eaten with soy sauce. A proper Chinese dinner has thirty to forty courses. You only taste a bite or two of each, otherwise you would soon be incapacitated.

The habit of drinking is by no means forgotten during the meal. Drinking games are played; partly old ones, like the well-known finger game and partly new ones which have often a humorous side to them, such as the game of man and wife and concubine. The thumb is the husband, the index the wife and the little finger the concubine. The husband in the card sense of the word beats the wife, the wife beats the concubine and the concubine is victorious over the husband. Or else a flower is handed round while a servant beats a drum. Whoever holds the flower when the beats of the drum stop has to drink. There are many more or less amusing and witty games; the object of all of them is that the loser is condemned to drink.

In the meantime dish after dish appears. After each series a sweet is served such as Lotus seeds, boiled in sugar or sweet potatoes encased in sugar threads. You wash your spoon or chopstick before and after the sweet course! The sweet course is always followed by a new series. When the guests seem to have come to the end of their culinary capacities, the host proposes to proceed to the real dinner. Everything served so far is stigmatized as being merely somewhat elaborate *hors-d' oeuvres*, the real dinner then consists of rice or millet with a few meat and vegetable dishes. When you have eaten the rice you get up, rinse your mouth and smoke a cigarette while drinking a cup of some strong tea. You then exchange a few words more and quickly take your leave.

The individual meals do not really take a long time once they have started. It happens to busy people that they attend two or three dinners on the same evening. If they have been invited by various friends, they do not want to hurt any of them by refusing to come and they therefore arrange the sequence in which they will appear at the different dinners. They attend accordingly the first half of a dinner in one house and the second at another. It is a humane trait of these dinners that food is provided, not only for the guests, but also for the coachmen, chauffeurs or rickshaw coolies who have brought them. When the guests are united, a list is made of the servants outside and every one of them receives a small sum of money for his dinner and these expenses are added to the bill of the host.

These meals give rather the official side of the picture. There is a whole series of restaurants in Peking which are popular among Europeans, because their dishes are so well prepared that many foreigners wish to break their daily routine by eating a Chinese dinner.

The Chinese have been masters of the art of cooking since time immemorial. The most important statesman and the sages have not considered it beneath their dignity to occupy themselves with the contemplation of food and its preparation. Legends relate that in the first part of the second millennium before Christ, the famous statesman I Yin had brought the great King Tang to adopt his plans by entering the royal service as cook. This may be merely a myth, but we possess a dissertation dating from the middle of the third century B.C. about the conversations which were held in this connection. At that time, at any rate, thought must have turned to such considerations. Amongst other things it says: [1]

When King Tang had found I Yin, he put him into the

[1] Compare Lu Shih Ch'un Tsin.

temple of the ancestors. He placed him into the light of the holy fire and smeared him with the blood of the sacrificial pig. On the following day he gave an audience and received him. Then he spoke with Tang about the art of cooking: Tang said: "Can you prepare the finest dishes?" I Yin answered: "Your land is small and therefore every thing cannot be obtained. The man who is a great king can find everything." Then he began: "Of the animals of the three natural kingdoms those that live in the water have an oily flavour, those that eat meat have a wild flavour and those that eat grass have a rancid flavour. In spite of these flavours, it is possible to make them taste good. It depends upon their preparation. The basis of all cooking is above all water. There are five kinds of flavours, three materials, nine ways of boiling, nine ways of roasting food dependent upon the use of various kinds of fire. The fire must be sometimes fast and sometimes slow. The oily, wild or rancid flavour can be removed by the use of strong counteracting means, if you do not fail to use them in the right sequence. In making a mixture you must judge to a nicety what is sweet, sour, bitter, sharp and salt; you must know which has to be added first, later, and how much of each. This distribution is very complicated but it must be controlled in every detail by addition. The changes which take place in the food after it has been prepared in the dish are so delicate and mysterious that it is impossible to describe them in words. It is just like the most subtle tricks of shooting and the driving of chariots or like the mysterious processes of growth in the course of nature.

"Meat which has been kept must not be high, meat which is boiled must not be sodden, sweet dishes must not be sickly, sour food must not be astringent, salted food must not be oversalted, sharp dishes must not be burning, mild morsels must not be tasteless and fat nourishment must be served at once.

"The best meat dish is made from the lips of the orangoutang, from the tails of young swallows, the marrow of buffaloes and elephants. To the west of the wandering dunes of the red mountains there are phenix eggs which the people of Yu eat. The best fish is the turbot from the Tsung T'ung Lake and the sardines of the Western Sea. In the Necta Springs there lives a fish called Scarlet Turtle, it has six legs and pearls as if of green jade. In the deep sea there is a fish called the flying fish. It looks like a carp and has wings with which it can rise above the water. Among vegetables, the best are the seaweeds which grow near Mount K'unlun, they are the fruit of the tree of life. On the shores of the South Pole there is a vegetable called the tree of recognition, its colour is that of green jade. The best parsley comes from the Hua mountains and the best celery from the Yun Mong Lake. In Ts'in Yuan there is a herb which is called Earth Blossom. Among the spices the best are ginger from Yangpu, cinnamon from Chao Yao, mushrooms from Tuolo, sauce made from eels and pike and salt from Tahsia. Among the different kinds of grain the best wheat comes from the Black Mountain, millet from the Pu Chou Mountain, sorghum from the Yang Mountain, black millet from the South Sea. Among waters, the best are the dew on the Sanwe, the water from the fountain on the K'unlun Mountain and from the hills near the Yangtse which is called trembling water. Among fruits, the best are the ones from the apple tree. North of the Chao range there are all kinds of fruit which are eaten by the gods. In the South there are sweet oranges, mandarines and pumalos and steinohren from the River Wan. The fastest horses are required to fetch them.

"If you are a great king, you can obtain all these things, but even if you are a great king, they must not be obtained by force. First of all the truth must be recognized and truth does not lie about somewhere outside but it dwells within us. If we ourselves are complete, then the kingdom is complete also—if the kingdom is complete the finest dishes are all at our disposal."

While this statesman induced his ruler to tread the path of virtue by conversations about food, there was later on a cook called J Ya, who caused the ruin of his master, the Duke Huan of Ts'i. This cook butchered his own son, because his master wanted to taste human flesh. The minister Kuan Chung warned the duke against this man, who had thus offended against the most natural feeling of love for his son. The duke made his cook J Ya and his companions nevertheless into ministers who later on formed a conspiracy. They closed the palace gates and built a high wall around it, allowing no one to enter and they pretended that they were carrying out the order of the duke. One of the wives of the duke climbed over the wall and reached him. The duke said: "I want to have something to eat." The wife said: "I cannot obtain anything anywhere." The duke spoke again. "I want something to drink." The woman said, "I cannot obtain anything anywhere." The duke said "Why?" His wife thereupon told him of the conspiracy. Thereupon he hid his face behind his sleeve and breathed out his spirit in the palace of long life. After his death a quarrel arose among his successors and he lay there unburied for three months, so that in the end the worms crawled out at the front door.

Such stories show what a part for good and evil the art of cooking has already played in the course of Chinese history. There are scholars and statesmen to this day who occupy themselves with the preparation of new dishes. Connoisseurs only go quite exceptionally to large restaurants, because they have generally only definite dishes to offer. The choice is indeed very large, but they are always of the same type. There are the restaurants of the old Shantung type, which serve the famous dishes usually required for a festivity. The new Shantung restaurants provide rather the Tsinanfu type of cooking which has adopted many of the ways of the European cuisine, such as sauces made with milk, asparagus and various kinds of bread. There are also the Honan-Sechuan and Yangchou restaurants. Canton cooking is very different from the other Pekingese cooking and is not greatly appreciated in the north. A connoisseur can tell you on tasting the first morsel what kind of cooking he is eating. It is a curious fact that none of the restaurants in Peking are run by Pekingese. It is the same story as with the wine; everything is imported from other provinces, but the cooking is nowhere as good as in the capital.

Apart from the large restaurants, there are places supplying specialties and they are frequented by connoisseurs. In Peking, for instance, there is a small house in an out-of-the-way place. The owner kills a pig every day. The various parts of the meat are then prepared in the most cunning manner so that the greatest variety of different dishes appears on the menu. People throng to the place at an early hour so that frequently the whole pig has been eaten shortly after noon. The inn is then closed. Neither money nor persuasion can induce the innkeeper to depart from this habit. His ruthless method is of course the best propaganda. As soon as it is possible to make the enjoyment of any pleasure really difficult to the public, it comes in shoals in its pursuit, as though its eternal salvation were at stake. In this respect, the public in the capitals of the East resemble those of the West. In Pien Yi Tang there is a famous chick restaurant. Here the reputed duck of Peking is served, which is the crown of all dishes when its skin is well browned on the grill and appears on the table cut up in small pieces. It is served with a kind of pancake sprinkled with soy extract, the strips of duck being wrapped up in the pancake. Connoisseurs take leeks with it. The most variegated dishes are served; more than a hundred in number, all of which are made of Peking ducks. The restaurant is situated in an out-of-the-way district in the extreme south of the town. The rooms are dark and uncomfortable, but the narrow street in which it is situated is thronged in the evening with motor-cars, horse carriages and rickshaws, so that the street is almost blocked for a long stretch, because every one has to go at least once to the duck restaurant. Even the foreigners go, though the heaviness of the duck meat causes many of them subsequent trouble.

There is another place near the southern gate, rather less refined than original. If you enter the courtyard through the archway at night, you see flaming fires and glowing coals everywhere. Seated and standing, visitors throng around them to receive their roasted meat direct from the grill. This is the mutton restaurant. Mutton is here served hot, steamed, boiled, roasted and fried on dishes together with all kinds of vegetables which add to the flavour of mutton. Instead of the mild rice wine people usually drink the stronger corn brandy which is also served hot. In the winter, you can also order a "fire pot," that is, a copper kettle which is heated from below by charcoal or methylated spirit. It contains broth. Dishes with raw meat of all kinds, vegetables, chrysanthemum leaves and noodles are served. People sit round the pot and every one takes the pieces they fancy with their chopsticks and hold them into the bubbling broth until they are cooked. By this method you can have your food cooked to the exact degree which pleases you. This dish is very warming in its effect. By the time you have swallowed the corn brandy and mutton in this fashion you almost acquire the instincts of wild wolves and you can understand quite well that certain animals intoxicate themselves with hot blood.

The opposite extreme to this primitive inn, is a certain vegetarian restaurant. The proprietor has had the story of his conversion written out on sheets of paper which are hung up on the walls of the room. In a dream, the souls of all the animals which he had eaten appeared to him: there were the malicious-looking pigs, some grunting and some squealing sentimentally, then came the bleating sheep and goats with their protruding eyes. Half a deer crawled along and hordes of pheasants, ducks, hens, chickens, and even eggs cackled and quacked in wild confusion. The fish twisted about on the floor, crabs and octopods glowered out of their treacherous eyes and the small rice birds sat sadly, all plucked on the wires. They accused him of their murder, and in revenge they proposed to kill him. He pleaded for his life, and took an oath never again to kill an animal and to do everything he could for them. They let him go, and into the bargain they gave him some secret recipes to enable him to prepare specially good food. Since that day, you can get in that inn everything you want: roasted pig, kidneys, sharks' fins, swallow-nests, fish cutlets, and a hundred other things, all of which are excellent to eat, but they are prepared on a strictly vegetarian basis. The proprietor has the greatest skill in making the guests forget that they are being very holy and practising the asceticism of renouncing the eating of flesh.

There are a whole host of trivialities with which you can pass away the time. Apart from the permissible pastimes, those of an illicit variety are not altogether unknown. Occasionally friends come together in secret places to gamble. As a rule they play "Mah Jong" which in Chinese is called "Ma Ts'uo Pai." The story goes that a certain general Ma invented it during a campaign to provide his soldiers with a pastime. Like every other game of chance, this game is forbidden in China because it causes a great deal of domestic misery. Although the pretty and harmless dominoes are handled with perfect calm, they have a habit of exciting the passions of the players to the utmost, and it is not unusual that the whole night is spent in gambling and the loser adds up his losses when the dawn shines in at the window. The industry which manufactures these games has recently taken considerable extension on account of the incredible number of Mah Jong sets which were exported for a while particularly to America. The passion for this game was so great that the ladies bought special Mah Jong gowns from China. These garments, which were out of fashion, were discarded by their wearers who were prostitutes and their raiment thus found honour in the West. Later on, special antique Mah Jong gowns were manufactured which had the advantage of looking quite clean and new. The power of the passion for Mah Jong outside China is well illustrated by the story of a parlour-maid giving notice. When her mistress inquired into her reason, the maid said that she had nothing whatever to complain of in the house, but the master had gone out of his mind and this frightened her. When she entered the drawing-room first thing in the morning, the light was still burning and the master was cursing and crawling about the floor in an exhausted condition. When she inquired if he were looking for anything he had got up and said, giving her a terrible look: "I am looking for the East Wind." [1]

Opium smoking has by no means disappeared altogether, but it can be observed that it has declined considerably. People are afraid to practise it openly, not merely because it is forbidden by law, but because it has lost, as it were, its social status, especially in the educated circles of young China. The "Opium devils" are looked down upon with unconcealed contempt. Unfortunately a host of substances have been imported, chiefly from Japan, which under pretext of being medicaments for the cure of the opium habit, are really preparations containing morphia and other poisons. In fact, it is really revolting what foreign countries import and sell in the guise of medicine. By means of dreadful advertisements, things are sold which people should be ashamed of. At best they are worthless goods which are of no use, but frequently they create by this means the habit of assimilating all kinds of poisons. The whole country is disfigured by vulgar and importunate advertisements.

After a survey of the clubs and restaurants, we must throw a glance into the tea-houses. We have seen already that Chinese society is on the whole male society. This fact brings with it, as it did in ancient Greece, the custom of allowing little ladies who sing to appear while the men are united over their meal. Originally these girls were young artists, they had a knowledge of literature, they usually made verses themselves; they played the zithern and sang to its accompaniment. They were used to intercourse with men and whereas the society lady became dumb and blushed, or if there were two of them, giggled into her handkerchief when confronted by a strange man, these little ladies were free and *spirituelle* in their conversation at such cheerful gatherings of young men. They had the pride and tradition of their profession: "We sell our voices but not our person." For the protection of their virtue they were always accompanied by an old servant and usually by their music teacher, who accompanied the songs of his pupils

[1] East Wind is the name of one of the dominoes in the game.

on the lute or the violin. But as is often the case, this kind of free and intellectual companionship leads easily to erotic associations. The men found in their intercourse with these artists what was denied to them in their married lives, which was hardly ever preceded by a period of wild oats. Chinese lyric poetry is full of verses about these girls and tradition has handed down many stories of faithful love, the pangs of separation and of anguished longing which has ended in death; in fact, all the pathos and tragedy of love not protected and hallowed by social sanction existed in these relationships. In the course of time, this state of affairs did of course change somewhat. The houses in which the little artists live are mostly owned by brothel proprietors. The servants who are supposed to protect the virtue of these girls, usually have a financial interest in a form of conduct on the part of their charges far removed from innocence and purity. Appearances are nevertheless well preserved and the girls live in tea-houses where you can visit them and talk to them and form friendships. You drink a cup of tea, eat a few melon seeds or sweets, smoke a cigarette and pay a fixed sum, a quarter of which goes to the girl with whom you converse. Another quarter is received by her "aunt" —this is what the old ladies in whose care the girls are, are called—and the remaining half is the due of the owner of the place. The proceedings are conducted in a perfectly decent way. For instance, after dinner you meet a few friends, then you chatter a while and go home without any further intimacy. When you go for the first time to a tea-house in which you do not know any of the girls, they are introduced to you one by one and you give the name of the young beauty with whom you want to converse to the servant. The girls are always dressed in charming clothes which are usually made in Shanghai or Suchou. The girls are gay and friendly and they know very well how to turn away any blunt attempt to approach them. A really clever girl will manage to converse with several guests whom she has accommodated in different rooms at the same time. She talks to the first one a little, flits away almost unnoticed to converse with a second and so on and so forth. If a guest shows impatience at her absence, she is back on the instant with the most innocent expression and manages to convey the impression to every one that he is the only guest she cares for; she takes all his orders and accompanies him to the door when he goes. The conversation usually turns on the artistic and literary life of the day and politics are also discussed. Many a serious man feels the need for forgetting the worries of the day in harmless conversation with his little friend. The girls are on the whole most discreet. It is part of their education never to speak with a man about another guest.

In the course of time such a relationship may also become more intimate. But such intimacy is by no means the most important factor. Even then the mutual relation retains its delicacy and is far removed from the brutalities associated with prostitution in Europe. The man has always to continue to woo for the girl's favour and if she grants it to her lover, the fiction of a prolonged or short marriage is always maintained. It is for instance absolutely impossible that a guest in a tea-house carries on even a purely friendly relationship with two girls, as such a proceeding would be an offence against good taste.

In one respect a remnant of liberty is left to the poor little girls, in spite of the unhappy fate which falls to their lot. They are usually very young when they enter a tea-house and frequently spend many years which are devoted to the study of music and conversation with the guests. No young girl is compelled to sell her innocence. She gives herself to a man for the first time of her own free will. It has happened too that such delicate bands have proved themselves sufficiently strong to induce the lover to purchase the liberty of his beloved by payment of money and that he has made her his concubine or even his wife. Generally these girls are by no means the worst companions and they frequently make his life as peaceable and pleasant as possible owing to the gratitude and affection they feel for him as their deliverer. It can of course happen that one of these exquisite children develops into an intriguing female who is capable of bringing chaos into the whole family. There, as everywhere else, good and evil are found side by side.

Although these things are veiled by a certain poetry, which makes them appear to foreigners in a far more charming light than similar circumstances elsewhere, the lot of these tea-house girls is usually infinitely sad as the following story shows.

Little Siu Ying was the child of a simple merchant of Shanghai. She spent her innocent childhood in Honkew, the harbour quarter of the town. The hope of happiness and duty filled the child's dreams. A fortune-teller had once prophesied a fair future and said that her destiny would be no ordinary one. She would either be educated in a school or make a name for herself as an artist. Siu Ying was a shy, gentle child and played in the streets like other children. A small brother came into the world and she was entrusted with the care of this little squealing object. Life took a grave turn for her. The little brother was a tyrant and his sister had a hard time in looking after him and satisfying all his wants. The father died suddenly just as she was beginning to mature from being a child into womanhood. It appeared that the father not only failed to leave an inheritance, but that his business owed considerable debts. One day a lady friend came on a visit, she looked good-natured and kindly. She talked with the mother about little Siu Ying. Such girls had often made the fortune of the whole family. She promised to have the little girl educated as an artist and to take her with her to the capital. There she would earn a lot of money, so that she would be able to feed the whole family and in time she would no doubt be able to repay the debt of her dead father and thus cleanse his memory before the world. The kind lady was even prepared to pay a few hundred dollars at once.

Merely for the sake of form a contract was made: the girl was handed over to the kind lady as a pledge for the borrowed money which was to bear interest at four per cent. per month and the little girl was to be free as soon as capital and interest were repaid.

Siu Ying was in the seventh heaven when she heard of the

journey and all the golden things at the other end. Beautiful silk clothes were bought for her and she looked very pretty in them in the mirror. Before long, the journey started over the sea to Peking. Her mother gave her a ring of green chrysoprase when she said farewell. The girl took the little brother with her to relieve the mother of her anxiety for his education. Another aunt who had also lent a little money went with her. The first aunt had a small daughter and so there was quite a family, when, filled with high hope, she said good-bye to her mother.

She had said good-bye to youth and happiness. A small dark room was rented in Peking and a place was reserved for her in a first-class tea-house. The furnishing of the room cost another few hundred dollars. A teacher was engaged to teach the little Siu Ying the rudiments of singing. She had to learn a great number of songs by heart and to sing them mechanically to the accompaniment of the shrill tones of the violin of the teacher. Another master gave her and her brother lessons in reading and writing and all these tasks meant wearisome and hard labour. It was not singing like the free and happy song of the birds. It was a tortured imitation of notes played to her and her heart was not in her work. The writing too was very difficult for her little unpractised fingers.

The best of it was the clothes. They were made after the latest fashion and she was pleased to look pretty when she made up her little face in front of the mirror. She had to entertain the guests and that was terrible. On one or two occasions a few young men had chosen her for fun as hostess. They said such strange things and looked at her in so strange a way. It was awful even when they laughed. She did not know what they wanted. She became frightened and more shy than ever while at night she was home-sick and cried bitterly.

It was hard for her. Owing to her shyness she had to be content with low earnings. Out of these she was expected to support all those people who had attached themselves to her, and on top of that she was to pay the interest on the advances which had been paid. She could not make enough money, and her debts instead of being reduced continued to grow. For a little while there was a rift in the clouds of her life. One day a European came to the tea-house with some Chinese friends. He knew Chinese and spoke to her. At first she was terrified because she had heard that the foreigners eat children and she did not know what might befall her. The aunt however laughed at her: "The foreigners are human beings like ourselves, why should you be afraid of them?" Gradually she noticed that the stranger was kindly. He asked nothing evil of her. Sometimes he would bring little presents and he often told queer foreign fairy tales. He also used to make her tell stories and she told him all the fairy tales that she remembered from her childhood, and when she had come to the end of her fund of tales she used to ask the aunt to tell her more in order to repeat them in the evening to her friend. She also sang the songs she had learnt to him. He inquired about her reading and writing, and for his sake she learnt a poem by heart which she recited to him as a surprise when he returned. Gradually she got used to him as a good friend. To please him she also learnt to sew. There were such a lot of naked little beggar children in the streets in winter for whom her friend bought cloth and linings long beforehand and she sewed them during the day when she had time. When the winter came twelve suits were ready and she was pleased to think that the poor children in the streets would have some clothes from her. As she was now able to sew well, she made a pair of slippers for her friend with a proper embroidered pattern on them. She always returned what she received in the form of some little attention because she did not wish to be ungrateful. Her friend helped her sometimes in her need. When the lady of the house had a birthday or there was some other festive occasion on which the employees looked for tips, he would invite friends so that there would be a real feast in her room which made the other girls look up to her. It is very important that a girl has guests on such occasions, otherwise she is treated badly and put in charge of quite an insignificant little room.

Sometimes the heart-felt crying of a girl could be heard from outside the curtains because she was lonely and waited in vain for a visitor. If no one came, she would be beaten and scolded and everything was terrible for her. Little Siu Ying did not have a bad time of it as long as her friend visited her and she also paid him visits. She wanted to know what an European house looked like. The aunt came with her to protect her because she would not have dared to enter a strange house alone. She brought a few sweets as a present, and was rather frightened because everything was so large and beautiful and weird in such a foreign dwelling.

In the summer the friend departed. This was very sad because she soon got into money difficulties. Her debts continued to pile up and she often cried all night because she did not know how she could ever pay them. She had a chance of running away and going to an institution where such girls find protection and are liberated from the clutches of their torturers, but her courage failed her. Her aunt had always told her that everybody had to pay the debt they had contracted. If one did not do so, one would be born again as a cow or a dog and one would have to serve the re-incarnated creditor until the last farthing was paid. For these reasons she had refused her friend's offer to save her from the tea-house, although he had promised to get her into a girls' school so that she could be taught properly and could start a decent life. At first she was delighted because none of these girls would hesitate for a moment if a chance was afforded to them which leads up into the realm of real life. She had had a talk with her aunt who had thereupon terrified her so much about her debts that she did not dare to accept the offer.

Her fate was thus sealed. Her friend was away and could not help her. She had no one else in all the world. Then a student came from the Yang Tse district. He seemed to care for her and was wretched when she did not return his love immediately. He swore that he would persuade his mother to let him marry her. Every day the aunt persuaded her more and more. Eventually she gave in. Then followed a few brief weeks of sweet love during which the girl matured into her full beauty and profundity of spirit. The student returned home and promised to write immediately. He has never shown any signs of life.

Siu Ying awaited his return with anxiety. She felt something strange within her body. The aunt consoled her and said it was no doubt due to the spirits which sometimes torture girls. She told her that perhaps she would bring forth a mouse and that would not be terrible. At the same time she gave her all sorts of medicines, but she did not bring a mouse into the world. Wherever she went people began to whisper and to giggle. Several of her friends laughed spitefully at the misfortune that had befallen her; others were sorry for her, but no one could help her. She had to disappear out of the tea-house and hide somewhere. Whatever may have become of her?

In this way tragic events take place behind the bright exterior of the festive illuminations in the eight alleys in which night after night the motors throng and distinguished guests visit the little girls in the tea-houses.

Near these streets are the theatres where performances are given until far into the night. There are different categories of plays. There is the great historical drama. The historical drama announces itself already in the appearance of the actors. They wear gorgeous armour and carry pennons. If they carry a whip, it signifies that they are on horseback and their imaginary horses jump about wildly until, for instance, they dismount and forgather to hold counsel of war. The commander-in-chief seats himself upon a raised throne represented by a table. If a town is to be taken by storm, a blue cloth on which a city gate is painted is carried past. In the Chinese theatre there are no wings in our sense of the word and the imagination of the audience is only supported by general indications as in the Shakespearian stage. The battles of the heroes and their frequently amazing acrobatic feats, their songs and their majestic movements are accompanied by resounding music which is exciting chiefly by virtue of its rhythm. The masks are all symbolical. Courage and bravery are indicated by a gaily-coloured and terrible make up of the face. Faithful warriors generally have deep red faces, whereas false traitors reveal repulsive patches in a suspiciously pale face. The actors strut about in high buskins. Everything is highly stylized and designed to be seen from a distance, because the plays are normally performed before an audience numbering many thousands of spectators.

The bourgeois drama is much more subtle. This too consists of alternating speech and song, but the orchestra is far less noisy. The numerous percussion instruments and drums, which frequently make too great a demand on European ears, are to some extent supplanted by violins and flutes. In these dramas action and movement are also highly stylized. Every motion has its own well defined expression. A woman who is afraid, for instance, holds one arm in front of her face and the other behind her back. Extreme excitement is indicated by a trembling of the whole body and so on and so forth. These well-known symbolical forms of expression facilitate the comprehension of the entire action enormously, especially since the libretto which is sung in Chinese is no more comprehensible in China than Europe.

In the ordinary course of events it is very rare that an entire play is performed at a sitting in the larger theatres. Usually individual acts are given. The practice is to perform parts of five to seven different plays in the course of one evening. Since the action is familiar to the Chinese threatre-goer, he has no difficulty in following these fragments of plays.

There is a third category of plays, a kind of comedy in which the parts are only spoken and not sung. These plays are easily intelligible for Europeans by virtue of their drastic action, and in them the remarkable Chinese gift for humour is seen to its best advantage.

The European spectator is struck by the habit of the actor of announcing his name when he appears and also giving a short description of himself. This method is not really so different from the monologues which we find in our earlier dramatic literature.

Until recently there were only actors and no actresses in China. The women's parts used to be played by men, and there are a number of actors who play these parts admirably. Recently theatres have come to exist in which girls play, and in these cases the men's parts are played by girls. The actresses are usually quite young. They are at the height of their career when they are sixteen or seventeen years old. By the time they are twenty they have usually found a lover. The performances of these young ladies are frequently of such a kind that they have to be numbered among the greatest artists. A Pekingese actress, K'in Hsuo Fang, plays for instance the scene in which a woman goes into a convent. Her hair is cut off and when she holds her beautiful long hair in her hands, gradually realizing the terrible farewell she has taken of the world, she plays this part so magnificently that even in a Chinese audience there are tears in the eyes of the spectators, who grow quiet and attentive, which is all the more remarkable, because in the Chinese theatre, as in the theatres in southern Europe, the audience is by no means used to paying the close attention to which we are accustomed. They converse continually and smoke and drink tea. Salesmen wander about with refreshments; they provide hot damp cloths which are particularly agreeable in summer for purposes of wiping your face. This gay activity in the audience is silenced when really great art moves the hearts of men and then such moments are all the more impressive.

Until recently the life of the actors was somewhat despised. It is only recently since a number of educated people have joined the profession that they begin to be appreciated as artists. The most famous among them are at present drawing princely salaries. It is not uncommon that an actor receives ten thousand dollars for the performance of a single evening. Especially the actresses decorate the stage with their own curtains, cushions and tablecloths which have been presented to them by ardent admirers. Nevertheless, it is very rare for actors to amass considerable wealth. Their expenses are too great. They have to pay out of their own pocket for the precious silk embroidered dresses and they have to pay salaries to their servants and assistants, while the best known stars support a small orchestra of their own.

In earlier days the theatre was regarded as a means of popular entertainment but not as a serious matter. Even the entire dramatic literature which can point to very remarkable treasures was not appreciated. All that has changed today. The drama is now the subject of conversation among society people in the towns in China. The leading artists are listened to with extraordinary patience. Since the lesser actors appear first, it is rare that the real stars appear before midnight.

In Europe, people are familiar with Japanese actresses, but the Chinese art of the theatre is altogether unknown. Chinese drama, however, is passing through an evolution which gives rise to the hope that, in this domain also, European art will derive a valuable stimulus.

EAST AND WEST

T HE journey through China now is behind us. We have looked into the old times in so far as their effects reach into our century; we have seen the process of transition and obtained an insight into the forces which are expressing themselves there today. We now ask ourselves what are the profoundest, the ultimate forces upon which China and the East are based? What are the lessons which the East has to teach us? What light do they shed upon the West and its evolution? We also inquire what the changes are which are taking place in the old cultural body of China and what are the consequences and the alterations which may be predicted from present conditions? Is the West able to provide a directive and an explanation for these changes?

I

The East is not a uniform entity. There is indeed a kind of common element which characterizes every form of culture from Constantinople to Calcutta and Tokio if a comparison is sought with western Europe and America. This common element can be defined briefly as the eastern adhesion to a natural profundity of soul as opposed to the relentless mechanization and rationalization of life in the West. Within the boundaries of this sphere, we meet with a wealth of diversified forms of expression. For our purposes we may disregard the Turkish and Arabic East which is linked by cultural ties to the West and forms, at times, a somewhat isolated but nevertheless essential component of the cultural activity of Europe. The pendulum of cultural growth swings backwards as far as central Asia.

There is a substantial difference, moreover, between India and the Far East. In India, intellectual life is incorporeal. The contours of external existence again and again vanish there before the energy of mental penetration into the depths of the world: life resolves itself into indifferent or dangerous illusion. All that maters is the inwardly eternal. Thus Indian culture provides us with a contradiction of a tropical wealth of vital manifestations, all of which are none the less without any historical significance. Consequently, India has externally been the object again and again of the politics of transplanted peoples whereas her thinkers were swallowed up by their passion for destroying the illusion of existence.

China, on the other hand, possessing a cultural evolution which has indeed been fertilized from the outside through its development in essentials has been unerringly consequential, has never allowed its thought to be separated from the soil of its life. Its centre of gravity did indeed move within the boundaries of the Far Eastern continent—to put it more precisely, we may say that instead of a centre of gravity, we observe a number of foci—but it has always remained within its own confines and the rays of its life have lit up the neighbouring cultures: In the west and the north the Mongol, Turkestan and Thibetan culture, in the east and south those of Corea, Japan and the south of the Far East.

The old culture of China blossoms in a northern and a southern form which fertilize each other and thus create a unity of immense duration. The northern form of this culture groups itself about the bed of the Yellow River. The Yellow River is not navigable in its lower reaches; it becomes more difficult as it approaches the coast and this culture seems thus to be of a continental origin. The east and the sea are reached only at a late period. It was the work of the great Yu, one of the heroes of the culture of this region, to give the rivers access to the sea, and thus to secure the country against inundations and to make it habitable.

The old Chinese state is a religious formation reposing upon a cosmic foundation, which is conditioned astrologically. Heaven, Earth and Man are the three world forces and it is man's function to bring the other two into harmony: Heaven, the creative power of temporal events, and the Earth, the receptive power of expansion in space. Heaven reveals the images which the chosen realize; *The Book of Change* in which this phrase occurs, is based upon the recognition that quiescent conditions are not the ultimate reality, but the spiritual law from which events receive their significance and the impulse towards constant change. The man who wished to be effective must match the seeds and sow in the field of the future.

Of all the social forms, the patriarchal struck the firmest root. Round about the year 1000 B.C the Chou, who came from the West, ordained this patriarchal social form as their religion in its purity and they linked it up with their cosmic cult of the stars. During the great sacrifice, in the open, the ancestor of the race is joined with the Lord of Heaven. Five hundred years later this world reached its high-water mark in Confucius and Laotse.

Confucius erected an edifice of spiritual forces capable of supporting and embracing Chinese culture for centuries upon centuries. His profoundest thought is the ultimate harmony of polar forces. Harmony is something eternal and lasting only in the transcendental nature of the significance of the world. As soon as the eternal is realized there is motion, transition. If these changes, however, are guided in the right way, they form the harmony of transitional growth. It is possible to guide what is changing in the eternal sense by means of the magic of words. If the names are found which express the innermost nature of being, their application allows the world to be regulated. If, for instance, I so define the names "father" or "son" that they really express the essential quality upon which they are based, then they suffice to regulate the reality which is designated by them. Every father must simply be a father in the right way and every son a true son, and in that case, the relations between fathers and sons are in order. This is the reason why the fundamental effort of Confucius was the rectification of names. These names—not taken from accidental reality, but understood according to their significance—can serve as a criticism of reality and therefore as a means to rectify it. When all things in the world of men are called by their right name, they are "righted" or put in order by this process.

The criticism of society was, however, only one side of Confucius' activity. What he strove for on the other side was harmony between nature and culture. Culture was not to violate or distort the nature of men but to transfigure and purify it. He therefore defended the family as the foundation of society. Within the family live the natural feelings of inclination. Parents and children love each other from free instinct, likewise man and wife and brothers and sisters. The love of your neighbour is no oppresive compulsion, but a sheer matter of course, an impulse of nature. The point is merely to shape these impulses so that they interlock harmoniously and so that order and discipline are preserved in the face of all community of feeling. It is proper to the name "father" that he formulates his love for his son differently from the form adopted by the son towards the father. The true father has a tender care for his son, the true son has a reverent obedience towards his father. The real husband shows kindly consideration for his wife, the real wife knows how to comply with her husband graciously. The elder brother helps his younger brother and protects him, the younger brother subordinates himself and gives in to him. Thus the family forms itself into the harmony of its relationship and love is transcended by the gentle guidance of manners. In this way the transition from the cultivated nature of the family is not difficult to the natural culture of the state. The feeling of reverent love for the father, the friendly subordination to the elder brother become the duty of loyalty towards the prince and subordination to superiors and vice-versa. Thus duty becomes the expansion of love and the state forms an enlarged family. This formation sets no limit to contemplation. Just as the ever-present sky is spread in protection above the earth, so does humanity remain the ultimate entity of culture regulated harmoniously by the exercise of ultimate ideals.

These are the fundamental thoughts which Confucius has grafted irretrievably into Chinese culture. It follows from the law of change of all that is earthly that such a condition of peace possesses no continuity since Heaven and Earth are in contact, superiors and inferiors are united and since the noble rule while the common serve. "Never a plain which is not succeeded by a decline, never a journey which is not followed by a return: that is the boundary between Heaven and Earth." In this way times of order and peace are followed by periods of chaos and stagnation. Such conformity to the law brings its own consolation with it. No matter how often the Chinese world has been plunged into revolution and chaos, again and again men of law and order have been found, who have restored peace by the application of the eternal laws of harmony. China has often been compared with a dice secured within itself: it may fall over, but no matter to which side it falls, it always regains its stability and balance.

The southern direction, if one may use this term, of Chinese culture shows different traits. Whereas the north concentrated itself upon the organization of humanity, its "significance" being the attribute of the noble, the south sought to understand man in his general relation to nature. Laotse's "significance" is the meaning of Heaven. For him, man is merely a part of nature. Everything which violates and dominates nature is evil. The return to nature is the only salvation. Laotse prepared the way for the influences which later penetrated into China through Buddhism. This form of life is to be found in the river system of the Yangtse. It is a district which had always manifested a connection with Chinese culture, earlier than the regions round about its middle and upper reaches. It is no accident that the legends here always speak of the "Southern Sea" from which the gods and saints have come upstream. The island Putou, where the "saint of the Southern Sea, the great master" Kuanyin [1] is revered, is only one instance of this attitude. It is to this place that the myths belong which relate that secret revelations and plans for the

[1] Kuanyin is the translation of the Indian Avalokiteshvara who, originally male, gradually became in China, in connection with a local feminine deity, the mother of charity.

regulation of the world were brought up from the water by curious animals which resembled dragons.

These considerations must not, of course, be carried too far. Chinese culture, as such, is composed of both elements and the fact that any given influence is of northern or southern origin has ceased to be effective, except that life in Suchou or Hangchou appears, as it were, more fluid, more easy and more natural than the severe and drier variety in the north. The southern tendency of thought is not in opposition to that of the north. The latter envelops and embraces the views of the former. Myth has made Confucius into a kind of pupil of Laotse. There is a certain truth in that story, even if the two never saw each other. Taoism in China is, in spite of all its mystic profundities, more harmonious than the Indian forms of thought. It looks upon the life of nature, smiling kindly, and conceding its right to existence. It is supported and transfigured by its own significance. Its aim is not the supersession of nature and an antagonistic opposition to her but a kindly forbearance and union with the sky and the earth, an aspiration towards the sun and the moon, the effort to give eternity to the individual life through its unification with cosmic forces. It may be said that the inclination for nature, on the part of the mysticism of the south as much as the same inclination of the rationalism of the north, have brought it about that the Chinaman has never severed himself from his ancestral and earthly soil and that he has found a harmonious existence by virtue of a profound acceptance and affirmation of the world as his cosmos. The evident insufficiencies of reality provided no soil for pessimism; they were countenanced in the certain knowledge that in the long run, everything will be balanced in a harmonious equilibrium.

Such a philosophy knows neither the fundamental breach between man and the universe, nor the strife between the individual and society. The individual is safely imbedded in a firm and well-supported cohesion with the higher organism of the family, the nation and mankind and similarly mankind enjoys its own secure and harmonious position in the universe.

The order of Chinese society depends upon the fact that every one occupies the natural place that is due to him and from which he is at liberty to practise his activity to the full while to go beyond it is neither right nor desirable. In the Chinese view of the world there is no place for titanic pride, for since no one challenges man's place it is not heroic but criminal to attempt to go beyond your own position. For this reason, we meet in China men with the same unconditional stubbornness, in that fight for the situation which is their due, as we meet with a satisfied resignation in the face of the unattainable. There is no titanic revolt even against the heavenly powers: the Chinaman does not consider himself in the presence of a personal autocrat who directs the world at his whim and with injustice, but he considers the profoundest significance of the world to be above personality. There can be no revolt against this being because he is, after all, nothing strange but essentially one with the roots of man. Whatsoever is done wrong or badly by the lower grades of the government of the world should be corrected as far as possible by magical means, and when all else fails inclement necessity rules supreme and man must bow the knee. "Me Yo Fa Tse" (spoken with a shrug of the shoulders), means "there is nothing to be done," or "Pu Yao Kin," which means "it is no matter"—these are the answers given to men who will not give way.

Similarly there is no essential tragedy. There are sad things, terrible things, the consequence of things done badly, which reserve their effect and might have been avoided if the right course had been adopted. Such blows of destiny, of course, often also fall upon innocent men whose fate is connected with that of the criminal. There does not exist, however, that internal division of the world which in its heroes and opponents creates a necessary interchange of crime and punishment; and it does not exist because the graduated scale of duties is not built upon differing foundations but forms an unified cohesion. There is a clear sequence of duties which always permits of the right choice if there is sufficient good will.

"I like to eat fishes, I like to eat the paws of bears. If I cannot have them both, I renounce the fish and stick to the paws of bears. I love life, I love duty. If I cannot combine both, I renounce life and abide by my duty." In these words Mongtse has given the best definition of this fixed and therefore reassuring scale of values. The same positive relation to life which precludes tragedy manifests itself in the omnipotence of tradition. There is a right action for every situation. If one does not find the right one, it is merely a matter of ignorance, not a tragic necessity.

The external and the internal must be brought into harmony. An attitude or a good intention which does not manifest itself in the right way is not really good. Hence, too, the strict injunction to avoid causing the feeling of shame to another and that one should not "lose one's face" oneself. The "loss of one's face," that is to say to feel ashamed, is not something external from which one can dissociate oneself in inner freedom, but something essential which affects the whole man. It is significant in this connection that the same word signifies the body and personality.

If we sum up, we find that Chinese culture reveals an ideal essentially bent upon harmony and closely tied to reasonableness in the organization of the cosmos and society. For this reason, the lives of the least among them are relatively happy and contented, not made sickly by the pallor of thought.

It goes without saying that there are certain economic and even geographical conditions which constitute the basis upon which this culture is built. Culture has here taken the agrarian form and presupposes a wide area so that the right application of the existing productive forces provides the possibility of maintaining a sufficient existence. It presupposes further that within the social frame, the tension between the distinguished and the insignificant, the rich and the poor must not be excessive, so that they can be regulated by traditions and customs. The rich and the distinguished recognize social obligations and maintain contact with the masses of the people by family relationship and consideration. Hence the instinctive unification of all the sections of the people when it is a question of fighting against the violation practised by foreigners. The form in which the obligations of the distinguished families expresses itself could be seen in a beautiful instance on the occasion of the great Japanese earthquake. The distinguished families who had been brought up in the Chinese school of thought and the princes of the Imperial house opened their parks and palaces to the homeless refugees as a matter of course; the merchants and business people, with the European attitude, barricaded their doors and had them protected by the police.

Chinese culture already passed through a crisis about 2,200 years ago. It was then that its old culture entered upon its mechanical phase. All kinds of technical inventions were made and a kind of capitalism and industrialism came to exist. The old families disappeared and the new aristocracy of ownership and power was founded. Thought began to be atomized. The philosophy of Yang Chu revealed the glorification of the individual who would not renounce a single one of his hairs, nor a thread even if by so doing it could have profited the whole world, but on the other hand he would not have accepted even a mere thread that was not his due. Mo Ti appeared in opposition with the national belief in a personal god conceived anthropomorphically, whose will it was, that all men should love each other. He wanted to build up a Society upon this general love of mankind which he organized in a church and based upon a rational pragmatism and utilitarianism. In his view what was proved by history, what brings about practical benefit, what corresponds to man's healthy common sense, is true.

The horizon of science had taken a cosmic expansion. Astronomy recognized the infinity of space and time within which the world of man was only an insignificant particle. On the other hand, the rigid measures of right and wrong were submitted to an annihilating critical examination. Man, that is to say the individual, was set up as the measure of all things.

The social conditions of the family and the state were exposed to the danger of destruction. Such tendencies of the

age were indeed opposed by the representatives of Confucianism who desired the organic cohesion of society, but, on the
other hand, culture and its values were called in question.
The legal exponents, even so far as they represented Confucianism, departed more and more from the humanistic ideal and
adopted more and more the principle of state government by
the mechanization of laws and institutions.

This period, however, passed away without leaving any
traces. The world was ·not yet ripe for a real mechanical
age with its consequent manifestations of industrialism and
capitalism. Apart from this, all the points of support for a
mechanical order of society were destroyed again by terrible
wars in the course of which the entire culture of ancient China
was destroyed. Much as the Teutons began with a new form
of barbarism to build again upon the ruins of the Roman state,
so did conditions in China become primitive again, during the
Han Dynasty. The population was decimated and cultural
monuments were destroyed on a large scale. The law of patri-
mony was constituted once more upon an agrarian foundation
and in the process the old ideals returned. The doctrines of
Confucius were extricated from the dust and it was only then
that they gradually acquired their full power.

It would take us too far if we were to follow all the paths of
Chinese history. It is sufficient to note here that a progressive
stabilization, and consequently also an ossification, of the
Chinese forms of life took place which has continued into the
new era with occasional interruptions.

If we inquire what China, with the rich inheritance of the
past, has to offer us, it is hardly possible to suppress the view
that the maintenance of China into the modern era is of positively providential significance for the development of mankind. It is of course true that the Chinese spirit, in the form
in which it has been described, signifies from an evolutionary
point of view an "older" type of the genus man than the genus
which has been evolved in the West. There are certain points,
however, at which the concept of age and youth have no connection with our concepts of height and depth. In the same

way man represents in a certain sense an older type compared
to the monkey. The older element is, as it were, a conglomeration of sources of strength which can be directly assimilated
by the future into the stream of events. In this way Laotse,
for instance, is considerably closer to the fundamental principles of the matriarchal world than Confucius, who represents
in China the later development of the patriarchal system, and
yet it cannot be said that Confucius has outstripped Laotse;
on the contrary, he has derived many of his most valuable
instructions from Laotse and Taoism continually acts as a
regulator which preserves Confucianism from superficiality and
utilitarianism.

It is in this sense that Chinese wisdom is the cure and salvation of modern Europe. Curious as it may sound, the old
Chinese philosophy and wisdom possess the power of childish-
ness. Old as the Chinese people is, there is nothing servile
about it, but it lives in that spirit of innocence peculiar to
children. The innocence is far removed from ignorance or
primitiveness. It is the innocence of the man who is anchored
in the deepest depths of being, there where the springs of life
well up. For this reason, the Chinaman attaches in the first
instance no importance whatever to what he does externally
but merely to what he is as a potential being. This form of life
is not an inanimate existence, but a peaceful and concrete
reality from which influences emanate which are all the more
powerful because they are not arrived at consciously, and
because they express something which is a matter of course
and involuntary great calm and self-possession are thus
formed. Man's vision is not caught by the diminutive ego of
an accidental personality, but penetrates to the wider horizon
of humanity. Chinamen live, as it were, with the rhythm of
destiny and for this reason they ride like sovereigns upon the
surface waves of life. A Chinese proverb says: "A great man
has the power to change great difficulties into small ones and
to dissolve little difficulties before he does anything at all."
Leading personalities have, in addition, the patience not to
desire to act directly and to seek external success, but to influ-

ence the seeds of evolution and to practise the magic of creative construction at a long range of time.

That is what we need and what old China can give us. Mere imitation cannot help us, nor external fashion, nor the artificial approach to an appreciation of things which are alien to us, but we must find ourselves. We must find our own depth and proceed to the sources from which our life springs. In so far as we see that this peace is possible, that the approach to the furthermost regions of true magic is open to us, it gives us the courage to turn away from what is external, to renounce that paltry activity which takes place upon the external shell of existence. We will learn to become children and to find the mother who feeds her children and calms them and gives them the power to influence events from within instead of losing themselves in the chase for success in the world, which one fancies to control at the moment in which the re-action to the desired effect sets in already in accordance with the firm and immobile laws of the change of all earthly things.

II

While we let the old wisdom of China exercise its effect upon us and seek the sources from which we draw what we need, we certainly notice that China, in fact the whole of the East, is undergoing a rapid change. The West has in the course of the last century created a mechanical civilization excelling everything which has happened upon earth since the memory of man. It is not merely a single culture but the whole of humanity which has entered upon this period. For the first time engines play their part which are no longer limited to human or animal powers, but which have subjugated the whole domain of mechanics in their service. The only event of comparable significance in the evolution of humanity was the day on which man brought the forces of animals into his service. This is perhaps the change which established the patriarchal in the place of a matriarchal system, because greater strength than women, who had hitherto tilled the soil, possessed was necessary to plough with oxen. Today the reverse has occurred.

While draft animals brought the stronger sex to power, machinery tends to level the sexes. It saves strength, women and children are able to use and control machinery almost as well as men, hence machinery turns those who run it into a proletariat. In consequence, patriarchal marriage does not merely cease to exist, but an end is set to the heroic patriarchal state and the masses conquer.

This peculiarity of the civilization of machinery also explains why every corner of the earth has opened its doors to it. Wherever it appears, all autochthonous cultures disappear. It annihilates all other forms of human existence just as the presence of the wandering rat puts an end to the house rat. The proud red Indian chieftain in his feathered head-dress and his eagle eye trained for the chase, the splendid Maori in his attire decorated with sea shells and crowned with crinkly hair, the negro in his war paint—all sink to the level of modest proletarians when they assume the unimaginative clothing of Europe and they thus exchange all their individuality for an awkwardness of demeanour. The culture of machinery destroys everything else because it is too simple. Whenever man is offered the choice of making fire by the friction of carefully chosen wood or by the use of matches, the matches will win the day with absolute certainty, because it has in its favour the logic of the law of the line of least resistance. And this is eventually the history of everything mechanical because it requires neither wisdom nor strength, but merely skill and practice.

China too has accordingly been overrun by the Western mechanical culture of life. No resistance was of avail. The West, however, came to China in a particularly unsympathetic form, which was bound to cause revolt: it came with mere violence and a desire for exploitation without any moral superiority or beauty. What the West brought was practical and simple and was bound to establish itself. In the long run it is impossible to fight against the steam plant of a spinning mill with the weapon of spinning by hand. Such a struggle can be successful for a time when supported by inner enthusiasm, but it is eventually doomed to failure. China is, of course, an immense agrarian country and it will take a long time before it becomes entirely industrialized, but the essential factor is controlled by events in the leading cities since the decisive elements in the cultural formation is not the open country, but the small circle of the élite of the intellectuals who draw in the culture of the West with a deep breath.

The process resulted, as we have seen, in important changes in the entire intellectual life. In the throb of machinery other relationships apply than in the natural inter-dependence of a culture based upon manual labour and the tilling of the soil. The consequences for China did not fail to manifest themselves, at first slowly and with opposition and subsequently at an ever-increasing rate. One little piece after another fell from the imposing structure which the ancient skill of China had erected. The younger generation threw itself with an almost anguished hunger upon all that came from the West. They began to be ashamed of all things ancient and Chinese. In the matter of clothes no less than in philosophy, they regarded what was Western as desirable. The fundamental principles of Chinese philosophy were discarded just as much as the pigtail and indigenous clothing. They went about in European garments, gave up customs and traditions of their daily life and adapted to their domestic use the pragmatic and utilitarian philosophy of America. It appeared as if everything implied greater simplicity and new facilities. While hitherto the Chinaman had been prepared to devote ten years of strenuous labour to the mastery of Chinese writing, they could now learn the European alphabet comfortably in a fortnight. Much the same thing happened in the case of many reforms. The old copper coins which had a square hole in the middle to allow them to be threaded on a string were sound money of the full value of their denomination, but it was not modern to have a coin which was threaded on strings and whose denomination was so small into the bargain. This money was melted down and every five of them were converted into modern coins, without a hole, of the nominal value of ten of the former pieces. People became rich as in a fairy tale. The consequences were, of course, that gradually all prices increased accordingly, by means of which the standard of living was lowered proportionately among the people. This procedure is only one typical example of what China experienced in the course of the mechanization of its life. People ceased to maintain their Chinese culture on its old level and they were threatened with becoming Europeans of secondary rank. On the one hand, that side of European culture which could be applied to the short-cut process of a high-speed printing press was, after all, only one of its most superficial aspects. On the other hand, the fact had been overlooked, that while a large number of enthusiastic eulogists extolled European culture and many of its agents were active in China, the old European states were not prepared by any means to accept the new China as a member with equal rights into the cultural comity of the West. There were a number of individuals and even individual states too polite to say so bluntly, but the fact remained that, for instance, in the domain of politics no one drew from the reform of China the conclusion that she should be allowed her own legal authority or that she should be granted the autonomy of her own excise and customs. A frivolous game of promises was indeed played with China which was treated, however, none the less like a negro state of secondary importance, for it is part and parcel of the structure of European psychology to rouse the demand for European culture by every conceivable means in countries outside Europe, but merely for purposes of obtaining a larger market. It was therefore entirely desirable that negro chieftains should wear top hats or Chinamen sporting caps because it produced an increased sale for the corresponding goods, but the negro in a top hat or the Chinaman in a sporting cap was not, for that reason, regarded as an equal. The explanation was to be found in the imperialistic principle of power by means of which Europe forced its rule upon the whole world and also the primitive instinct manifested by every cultural group which despises and stigmatizes as barbarian everything which differs from its own practice. The ancient Greeks acted thus no less than Chinamen while they were still deeply rooted in their old culture.

For these very reasons, a profound disappointment took possession of the new China and especially of its most distinguished brains. Japan had been faced with the same problems some time ago. There, they had set their teeth and borne the shame, but they had quietly worked with tenacity at the construction of a powerful naval and military force by means of which they compelled at any rate external respect in the course of a few powerful attacks and were allowed, as far as the Asiatic states were concerned, to ride the high horse. The mentality of Japan, however, developed cramp-like symptoms and it suffered in the process an injury which gnaws at its vitals.

China was spared such a fate. At the eleventh hour, just as it was to be her last and fearful fate to sell herself body and soul to mechanical civilization, the terrible spectacle of the collapse of this civilization occurred. European culture did not collapse as earlier cultures had decayed in the course of gradual coarsening and ossification; quite on the contrary, the mechanical element developed into even more subtle delicacy and refined efficiency. Never have such subtly conceived engines of destruction been invented as those with which Europe tore its own flesh to pieces during the war. What collapsed was what we may call the supporting moral substratum. In Europe, men had lost control over the machine and had fallen a prey to it. Mechanical science had excelled itself. Men grew poor because of the primitive attitude of mind and soul into which they were driven by senseless hate. Thus the means of culture remained—technology is at its full height even today—whereas the soul of that culture received a mortal wound.

Nothing contributed so much to make China come consciously to its senses while travelling the road to ruin as the Great War. Where was now this much vaunted power? What was the use of the wealth and perfection of technical science? And above all, what had become of Christianity which the missionaries had always praised as the soul of this culture?

About the same time as this awakening which was made particularly rude by the manner in which China was defrauded in Versailles of the reward of its alliance, the effects of the Bolshevik revolution began to be felt. This showed with particular clarity how corrupt the moral tissue of European middle-class culture had been towards the end, since it collapsed completely in the face of the terror of a comparatively small number of determined men. These considerations gave food for thought.

Russia announced with a somewhat loud flourish of trumpets, that it was prepared to recognize China as a power with equal rights. Germany had offered this recognition already. As far as Russian politics are concerned, they displayed Soviet principles towards China, that is to say, they recognized her right to deal with her own problems and supported her morally in her fight against the brutality and Imperialism of the West. China accepted the hand which was proffered without much enthusiasm. The impatient manner with which Russia, sword in hand, offered its amenities delayed rather than accelerated the negotiations.

As far as the relation of China to the West is concerned, she has travelled along the road of accepting the mechanical culture of Europe too far to leave room for any possibility of retracing her steps. They desire the advantages of industry which means that they must also accept capitalism, the development of the proletariat and the deracination of a manufacturing population. What is more, the growing traffic, the exploitation of the mineral wealth, the industrialization of wide districts, will not allow the consequences for the structure of Chinese society to be avoided. The organism of the Confucian family state is being dissolved of necessity. Society is bound to become atomized.

China is not prepared to pass through all the phases of capitalistic industrialism, which has caused so much misery in Europe in the same manner as Europe had to do. They enjoy the advantages of the present situation. So ghastly a dehuman-

ization of the proletariat, if the phrase may be permitted, as
Europe witnessed in the nineteenth century is morally no
longer possible. The workman in China, moreover, is not so
liable to be exploited by enterprise as he was in Europe when
the unforeseen invasion of machinery with all its consequences
occurred in the West. China has inherited the faculty of or-
ganizing itself from its own past. The guilds of merchants
and craftsmen in the towns still possess real vitality. These organizations are the fruit of a system of village administration
based upon the cohesion of family organization. They form
the seed for the organization of the workers by trades. In
addition, the workman in China is not compelled to fight un-
armed and deserted in the quagmire of misery. They are finding leadership, support and moral encouragement among the
students whose feeling of solidarity with the struggling proletariat is so strong that they stand shoulder to shoulder.

The spirit of the old Chinese tradition provides solutions
for all these problems. The more sceptical Chinamen have
become of the European gospel, which claims to be the only
means of salvation, the more do they remember the virtues
which their own past has produced and they revert to them.
The representatives of young China have accepted the immense task of examining and testing objectively all that is good
and useful in their own and in the foreign elements and what
can be fused in the synthesis of a new culture.

Let us now ask what Europe has to offer them in their
present position. We need not speak of the technical question
which has ceased to be a problem today and is, after all, no
longer the peculiar property of Europe. The revolution which
is in progress today from Tokio to Fez against the supremacy
of Europe is entirely based upon European technology. This
technology would probably—if not today, certainly in twenty
years—remain the possession of humanity, even if Europeans
were to cease from contributing to the cultural labour of humanity. The question which we have raised touches something
more profound. We are convinced that Europe will be bound
to accept the other intelligent races as members of the comity

of nations with absolutely equal rights, that is to say, that
Europe will lose in practice its solitary supremacy. What we
are concerned with is the question: Does Europe possess in
its culture mental forces peculiar to it, which can be, in the
course of the future development of humanity, of similar value
for other races, as the profoundest content of Chinese wisdom
is for us?

If we examine the development of the European mind, in
relation to the foreseeable evolution of human culture, we
do in fact perceive certain manifestations to which we may
ascribe such significance without self-exaltation. As to the road
along which humanity travels at present, we shall recognize
without hesitation that it is travelling towards a period in
which specialized cultures and geographically limited cultures
are approaching their end. These cultures succeeded each
other in the past; they passed through the stages of childhood, maturity and senility in order to leave on their death-
bed a heritage of cultural seeds destined to blossom afresh
in a new form. In this direction the possibilities are exhausted.
The fundamental structure of the various ancient tendencies
is altogether worn out. Its ruins lie about us. The triumphal
progress of the technology of machinery provides, however,
a universal basis for every form of culture which is possible
in the future. The new culture will, so to speak, become a
culture of a secondary type whose elements are no longer
natural but cultural products: a superstructure above all
previous cultures.

In this connection the individual is becoming more and
more autonomous. The natural ties of the individual with
the spontaneously evolved groups recede more and more into
the background. The organization of society becomes more
and more conscious, rationalized and free. The cultural fabric
will in future no longer be borne by the group, but by the
individual. This development is perfectly consistent with the
increasing strength of a conscious nationalism as manifested
today alike in the Soviet concept and in Fascism.

Herein lies a great danger. A materialistic destruction of indigenous and super-individual cultures would reduce humanity to atoms in the process of which humanity might at best turn into a machine. We would thus really come within dangerous proximity, not merely of the decline and fall of the West, but of the whole of humanity.

At this juncture, we perceive the providential factor in the evolution of the West. When Greece severed herself from the Persian East by means of her superior weapons, Europe began to travel along its own path, which departed more and more from the Oriental mode of life, by the development and manifestation of power. In Greek philosophy, man opposed the superior powers of nature with the free spirit of the Titans and wrung from her—even though he might have been crushed in the process—one secret after another. This attitude gave him his independence, as opposed to nature, to a degree in which humanity had nowhere possessed it. The process did, indeed, cause the fateful breach between mind and nature in the human breast, but it gave man simultaneously the liberty of his soul in the face of the entire world.

In the sphere of religion, Jesus of Nazareth expressed this new position of man, in the words: "What shall it profit a man if he gain the whole world and take harm in his soul? Or what shall a man give to regain his soul?" Jesus destroyed the entire cohesion of earthly and temporal manifestations of culture. He robbed the family of its essential significance: "Whoso loves his father and mother more than Me is not worthy of Me." As to the highest problems, He pushed the state aside as being insignificant; "Render unto Caesar the things that are Caesar's (that is to say the worthless Mammon by which he attempts to bind men to his image) and render unto God the things that are God's." He released man from all the cultural connections of possession, power, art and whatever the cultural values may be called. The complete extent to which He was revolutionary in the domain of religion, not merely putting an end with angry scorn to the church, but also removing, in childlike simplicity, the judging God of justice from his throne, situated somewhere outside in the universe, was shown most clearly by the fact that He was condemned, for this very reason, by the unanimous co-operation of those who defended the altar and the throne.

He did indeed proclaim the Kingdom of God, but this kingdom, for Him, is not of "this" world. Nor is it a thing of the world beyond but: "behold, the Kingdom of God is within you." In liberating man from all the individual manifestations of life, Jesus, while accepting and affirming life, has created in man that inner attitude which alone is capable of giving him the ability to assume a sovereign position over the whole of external nature and culture, as the man of the future will need to do, the universal man, who at bottom is profoundly lonely. It is the only means to enable man not to be crushed

Let us summarize! In the process of severing itself from the ties of time and space, humanity needs two things: the profound penetration into its own subconsciousness until from those depths upwards, the road to all that is vital, which is experienced intuitively in a mystic and unified vision, has become liberated. This is the possession of the East. On the other hand, it needs the ultimate intensification of the autonomous individual until it has acquired the power to match the whole pressure of the external world. This is the possession of the West. Upon this ground, East and West meet as mutually indispensable brothers.

INDEX